BASICS FOR COMMUNICATION IN THE CHURCH

Part I
Teachers in Process of Becoming
BY IRENE S. CALDWELL

Part II
Communication, the Teacher's Tool
BY RICHARD A. HATCH

Part III
The Journey of Communicating and Learning
BY BEVERLY WELTON

HURST MEMORIAL LIBRARY
Pacific Christian College
2500 E. Nutwood
Fullerton, CA 92631

WARNER PRESS, INC.   Anderson, Indiana

Copyright ©, MCMLXXI, by T. Franklin Miller
Library of Congress Catalog Card Number 78-150370
International Standard Book Number 0 87162 121 5
All Rights Reserved
Printed in the United States of America

Scripture quotations, except where otherwise noted, are from the Revised Standard Version of the Holy Bible (copyright, 1946 and 1952, by Division of Christian Education, NCCCUSA) and used by permission.

Contents

PART I
Teachers in Process of Becoming

Chapter	Page	Chapter	Page
1. The Teacher in the Midst	5	5. Explorations in Creativity	39
2. Focus on Identity	14	6. Re-Creation of Values	47
3. Humanness Too!	22	7. Experiencing the Message	54
4. The Source of "Aliveness"	31	8. Being—Behaving—Becoming	60

PART II
Communication, the Teacher's Tool

9. How Communication Works	65	12. . . . To Make Available Materials in Some Form . . .	95
10. Someone Perceives an Event . . .	74	13. . . . Conveying Content	106
11. . . . And Reacts in a Situation . . .	83	14. . . . Of Some Consequence	117

PART III
The Journey of Communicating and Learning

15. A Starting Place for the Journey	125	21. Media Resources for the Journey	179
16. Reach Out for Someone	135	22. Awareness of Fellow Travelers	187
17. New World, New Wineskins	144	23. Interaction with Fellow Travelers	193
18. A Vision of Tomorrow	154	24. Gifts Along the Way	201
19. Bridges to Tomorrow	163	25. "I Am the Way"	211
20. Inner Resources for the Journey	169	26. Bridges to Other Persons	218

Introduction

What good does it do to teach if no one learns? What good does it do to lead if no one follows? Many people who teach and lead in the name of the church grow increasingly frustrated when they do not seem to be communicating, when the gospel is apparently not heard and acted upon. This textbook—and the course it undergirds—is designed to help those we shall call "teachers" in the church to deepen their understanding of how communication takes place and to sharpen their skills at two-way communication. By "teachers" we are thinking of a wide range of people who seek to communicate the gospel—youth leaders, parents, teachers in the church school, ministers, lay leaders in various aspects of the church's life and ministry.

The textbook and the course focus first on who the teacher is, then on how communication takes place, and finally on teaching-learning activities that foster communication in the church. The three parts of the text reflect this structure for the course.

The teacher here is seen as a servant in the midst of life, seeking to know himself as a child of God, to experience the message from God, to demonstrate it creatively in the spirit of Christ. Communication becomes the teacher's basic tool, and in Part II we seek to learn how communication works, how we can make full use of it, how it involves differing individual perceptions and develops as feedback enters the picture. In Part III we embark on a journey of communicating and learning. In this process we explore communication in such areas as group development, setting goals, planning, individual study, and the use of media. Interaction with others and growing sensitivity are part of this area.

Those engaged in structured individual and group study should early browse through the text and with other fellow students determine the focus of the course for their particular situation. What parts seem most relevant? What aims need adjustment to fit the situation? How will time for the course work out? Where do the students wish to modify, contract, expand, or adjust the course material?

The book is designed to help you carry on this study in a meaningful way. The main text matter is divided into chapters which can form the basis for twenty-six sessions. If held weekly, they would run about six months. Or, longer sessions offered more frequently would allow this study to be completed in much less time. The three parts of the text allow the study to be carried out in shorter segments and in differing styles. A large class could study the first unit together. The second part could be a period of individual study, with the third part being carried out in small, informal clusters.

The notes in the wide margins are designed to interrupt your individual reading and lead you to your own lines of thought about the course. You can also use the margins for your own study notes. At the bottoms of many pages come study directions, largely for organized classes. This is published in the text for all to read, since everyone concerned in this course is also interested in classroom procedures and the mechanics of group study.

PART I

Teachers in Process of Becoming

By Irene S. Caldwell

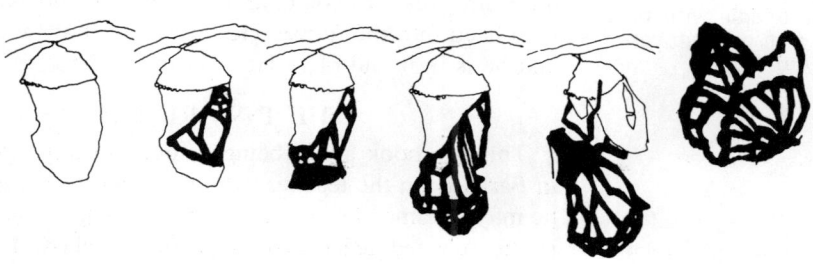

"A teacher affects eternity, he can never tell where his influence stops."

—Henry Brooks Adams

"As for us, we have this large crowd of witnesses around us. Let us rid ourselves of everything that gets in the way."

—Hebrews 12:1a, TEV*

The inward journey of the Christian teacher is long and expansive. It is placed in a revolutionary point of history. It turns backward, not only to Jesus, the master teacher, but even to Abraham, Moses, and the prophets. The Christian teacher can feel a part of that mighty force of witnesses who have found themselves in

*Wherever TEV appears the passage is taken from Today's English Version of the New Testament. Copyright © American Bible Society, 1966.

CHAPTER 1

The Teacher in the Midst

An Introduction to the Study of Part I

To write a book is to place your heart in other people's hands—especially if the book deals with the journey of the self. In writing the section "Teachers in Process of Becoming" I am placing my heart in your hands, for I have been taking the journey with you. All of the stories are true and most of them are experiences of teachers I know and love.

The book is addressed to teachers; that is, to all those Christians who are investing themselves in others through the educational work of the church. It could be for parents and for all others who search for genuineness in their relationships.

The purpose is that those who read and study Part I may take a long, deep look inward and find understanding and grace to become authentic persons and good teachers.

The plan is such that the reader may join with a group or he may make the explorations alone. The marginal notes will help guide individual study.

I am convinced, however, that the greatest progress can be made through sharing with a group. The subject requires a special kind of group if it is truly to be an experience in the process of becoming.

The group will need a leader who will be "in the process" too. The leader will have responsibility for initiating experiences of exploration and sharing. Each member will study the chapter and do personal searching as he opens his "self" before God. Then the group will clarify ideas, share feelings and explore meanings together. Such a group will need to be built on the trust and integrity of every member. It will be informal but serious and there will be great dependence on the guidance of the Holy Spirit.

Teaching may be thought of as providing clusters of experiences which are planned to open people to the discovery of new insights. This

> Think of the teacher which had the greatest influence on your life. What were the qualities that made the difference?
>
> Do you feel in harmony with the spirit of Christian teachers of the past? Do you have fellowship with other teachers today? Can you even feel you are in the middle with responsibility to see the message carried on to the future?

nurturing children, in inspiring youth, and in challenging adults. He can experience himself as alive and making a difference at present, and he can feel something of the past and future in the reach of the teaching fellowship.

The teacher need never feel alone if he but makes two turns of the head. One turn can be a look back to the great host of teachers throughout the ages. Seeing their courage and influence renews the spirit. The other turn views the long procession who will be teaching in the years to come, and the teacher knows the only direction is to head into the future. He understands anew that all life is one, and he is in it and of it. He is in the midst.

THE INWARD JOURNEY

This is a book about being a communicating teacher. The focus in Part I is on the teacher, who he is, why he is teaching, and what he may become. The teacher is not thought of narrowly as one who is the selected teacher of a particular class. Rather this inward journey is for all persons involved in the educational work of the church. In a sense all are teachers and all Christians could grow by a serious exploration into self-understanding in relation to God, to the world, and to others.

Elizabeth O'Conner has written a book entitled, *Journey Inward, Journey Outward*.[1] She points up the important truth that within each person there is a self to be known and cherished. She says that there must be the inward journey before the outward journey can be valid. There are three engagements in this inward journey.

THE FIRST ENGAGEMENT IS TOWARD SELF-KNOWLEDGE

Those on the inward journey are committed to becoming people who are in touch with their real selves, and who understand the deep roots of their own motives and emotions.

---

[1] Elizabeth O'Connor, *Journey Inward, Journey Outward* (New York: Harper and Row, 1968).

---

comes into special focus in this study, which is intended to probe into the feelings, motives and goals of the learners. The clusters of experiences should center around the aim for the session. The experiences should progress; that is one should be built upon the foundation laid by the previous one and provide opportunity for decision. You may need to select from the suggested experiences or spend more than one session on some chapters. Since the chapters in Part I are built one upon the other, each is necessary for a well-rounded study. Suggestions for clusters of learning experiences for each session are given in the guidance materials. I earnestly covet for all who study the book a true experience of self-discovery and fulfillment in Christian service.

Guidance for Session 1
THE TEACHER IN THE MIDST

Aims for the Session

To introduce the course with its concern that teachers become effective communicators of the gospel. To identify with the long line of Christian teachers of the past, present, and future who have sought to communicate well. To experience strength and renewal through feeling a part of this great company. To realize anew one's own potential in order that he may become more secure in his relationships with the learners.

An Introduction to the Unit

Spend some time looking through the text with the study group and at the three units which make up this course. Consider together some of the chapter (session) titles. Examine some of the statements of aims. Look at some of the marginal notes. Ask the students to state what some of the learnings and experiences are that they hope to have in this course. You may want to work as a

THE SECOND ENGAGEMENT IS WITH GOD

People on this inward-outward journey will never really know themselves unless they take the study off self and meditate on the majesty and greatness of God.

THE THIRD ENGAGEMENT IS WITH OTHERS

This engagement in depth is to be with others of the Christian community, the church. Before the person is able to make the outward journey, he needs the support of these three engagements. It is not that the inward journey is to be completed before the outward journey is begun. Rather the inner and the outer become related in such a way that each brings meaning and richness to the other. This is the journey magnificent open to you!

The teacher today stands in the midst of a revolutionary but exciting time. It is a time of great agony. There are deep cleavages between men. Human dignity that has been violated is asserting itself. Man is frightened, for never before has he had the power to destroy himself and all mankind. He knows that time, a place on earth, and food are running out. Yet he has ingenuity enough to travel into outer space and explore the moon and the planets. What does it all mean? Man is in a desperate search for meaning.

The teacher stands in the midst of all this, not as a spectator but as a participant. He is there as a reconciler, a transforming agent, and an interpreter. He has a vital aliveness and involvement with all that is happening and accepts all life as worthwhile. He may not understand all that is going on. He does not have all the answers, and sometimes not many of them, but he has a feeling of "enoughness" that gives him energy to search for answers and to learn from anyone who has anything important to teach. He has developed a courageous attitude toward this changing, frightening, emerging, but challenging world. He approaches all experience from a Christian perspective.

To what degree must a person have the "three engagements" if he is to be a teacher?

What do you see as your role in the present social crises, in relation to the deep cleavages between people?

What are the sources of a vital aliveness? A feeling of "enoughness"? An acceptance of all life as worthwhile?

---

planning committee to outline the course in terms of meeting the greatest concerns and felt needs of the group. Under any circumstances, try to get a general overview of the course as you begin.

Clusters of Learning Experiences

I. Look at the picture on page 5 and after several minutes of meditation share what it says to you about the teacher. Where in this process do you see yourself as a teacher?

II. Turn and look backward and think as far back as you can of teachers who have influenced your life. Think not only of direct influence but of those who influenced your parents and grandparents. Think of those who influenced you through books, music, art. Share how you feel about their influence.

III. Now look forward into the future. Who will be the teachers? Will there always be teachers? Might they be people whom you influence? How do you feel about standing in the middle?

IV. Divide into groups of eight or ten and have someone read the true story of Jerry. Write down what you believe made the difference. Now read the story of Mr. Z and see if the reasons for the difference are the same. As you join groups discuss ideas and questions concerning these two experiences. Have the total group make a list of the marks of greatness expressed in the life and relationships of Jesus.

V. Share Jesus' teaching about greatness (Matt. 18:2-4, 23:11, Mark 10:43, Luke 22:24-31, and others).

VI. Analyze Fred. What was the source of his power? Where did he get his ideas? Why did youth respond?

VII. Think of the leader who went to Japan. Could she have succeeded if she did not have wide experience and preparation in teaching? What are the ingredients of her good experience?

The Teacher in the Midst / 7

LOVE CAN MAKE A DIFFERENCE

The two following stories are about love and what love can do. They are both true stories as told by those who were present. We have no way of knowing what all happened in the background. Barriers do not often melt as magically as they seem to in these stories. Yet genuine love warmly expressed and deeply felt can restructure the pattern of relationships.

JERRY

Do you really believe that your teaching makes an eternal difference for some?

Jerry was a ragamuffin four-year-old that first day he showed up at the nursery school. His clothes were clean but carelessly put together. He had a noticeable speech defect. He was thin and pale. He clutched a dirty, worn-out teddy bear every minute of the day, even while he gulped his orange juice.

The teacher tried to interest Jerry in the games of the day but could not get through to him. Day after day he became more withdrawn. He slumped in the corner. He almost cried some days, but always he clutched his teddy bear.

Do you know your students well enough to feel for them as the teacher came to feel for Jerry?

On investigation, the teacher learned that his home had been broken and he had been passed from one relative to another, and had even been in several foster homes. He had no place, and nobody seemed to want him. He had taken the teddy bear from one place to another. It seemed to be his only link with anything permanent—and it was becoming a mere rag.

The teacher wanted to love Jerry. She tried to show him love. She prayed. She tried every way she knew to break through to him. She felt helpless and frightened. One day she was thinking about Jerrry and praying when the scripture flashed into her mind, "There is no fear in love, but perfect love casts out fear" (1 John 4:18). A feeling of warm love toward Jerry seemed to come over her. She went over to Jerry and took him in her arms. He responded with warmth and even cuddled to her. They sat for a long while.

Browse through the Gospel of John and try to identify qualities of Jesus in his relationships with people.

The next day Jerry walked a bit faster and stood a bit taller as he came toward the school. He still held his teddy bear, but as he edged up to the teacher, he lisped, "Let's throw teddy in the wastebasket. I don't need him anymore."

MR. Z

Read scriptures in which Jesus defined greatness: Matthew 18:2-4, Mark 10:43, John 14:15, 16. Try to find others where he talked about greatness. How do these relate to teaching?

Mr. Z was a stingy, bitter man. He had alienated both family and friends because he was so self-centered. The more he felt isolated, the more he withdrew into himself and was hostile toward others. He even seemed to shrivel up physically, he was so tightly bound up in himself. As material things became his only security, he got more and more houses and land. He even began to cheat in his business to gain more money. He became rich but was a lonely and hated neighbor. Nobody ever went to his house.

But there was a teacher who saw beneath all this mad search for meaning. He knew the man must be terribly lonely and afraid. So

8 / Basics for Communication in the Church

the teacher went to visit the man in his home. When the neighbors saw that the teacher was going home with the stingy, cheating rich man they began to criticize the teacher and to grumble. "Look," they said, "this man has gone as a guest to the home of a sinner." Then Mr. Z stood up tall and said, "Listen, sir! I will give half my belongings to the poor; and if I have cheated anyone, I will pay him back four times as much" (Luke 19:1-8, TEV).

IN THE SPIRIT OF THE MASTER TEACHER

The Master Teacher always made a difference. As a teacher today you will find meaning in thinking much about Jesus and his relationships with all kinds of people. Try to understand his faith in the power of the humble disciples to carry on the work for which he was giving his life. Get beneath his long-suffering patience with the blundering Peter. Think how his heart must have been torn when the rich, young man with so much potential turned down his challenge. How do you think he must have felt when those whom he had tutored for three years were quarreling about who would be the greatest on the very night that he was to be taken for trial? Then they even went to sleep while he was agonizing in prayer at Gethsemane. Yet he never lost faith in them.

As you saturate yourself with his spirit think how he looked behind an act to try to find the feelings of persons and judged them by their motives rather than by their deeds. Why did he commend the widow's offering (Luke 21)? Why did he spend so much time with the woman of Samaria (John 4)? Why did he not condemn the adulterous woman (John 8:1-11)? Try to feel how real he was. He joined in the wedding festivities. He cried with Mary and Martha over the death of their brother. He drove the money changers out of the temple. He took little children in his arms and loved them. He was able to feel deeply with people in all kinds of circumstances. He touched their deepest need and brought them forth as persons.

TEACHING AS SERVANTHOOD

Jesus struggled to make clear to his followers the true meaning of greatness. When they asked him to define greatness, he called a child and had him stand up and said: "Remember this! Unless you change and become like children, you will never enter the Kingdom of heaven. The greatest in the Kingdom of heaven is the one who humbles himself and becomes like this child" (Matt. 18:2-4, TEV).

The key quote from Jesus on greatness was given in a very human situation. James and John had come to Jesus to ask to be favored. They wanted him to promise that when he sat on his glorious throne, they could sit with him, one on each side. When the other ten disciples heard about this request they were naturally angry. So Jesus called them all together and tried again to help them understand the nature of true greatness. He said, "This, however, is not the way it is among you. If one of you wants to be great, he must be the servant of the rest" (Mark 10:43, TEV).

The style of teaching, seen in light of servanthood then, would seem to be not that of a dominating leader who pours out his "gems" of wisdom upon the lowly students who sit at his feet. The teacher is there to help, not to have his own ego built up. The teacher is there to share humbly, not to dictate or to demonstrate his own superior knowledge, skill, and authority.

Jesus not only showed greatness in his every relationship, and taught the spiritual laws of servanthood, but he made greatness available to all persons, even today. In his last days on earth he said, "I tell you the truth: whoever believes in me will do the works I do—yes, he will do even greater ones, for I am going to the Father" (John 14:12, TEV). Then he gave the promise of the Holy Spirit. He said, "If you love me, obey my commandments. I will ask the Father, and he will give you another Helper, the Spirit of truth, to stay with you forever" (John 14:15, TEV).

Through his sacrificial death and his making the Holy Spirit available, Jesus made greatness possible for every one of his followers. The sensitive Christian does not cherish a worldly sort of greatness but that kind of greatness which comes through following the spiritual laws of servanthood.

VIGNETTES FROM LIFE

HE FELT LIKE A "STAND IN"

Fred and Loren had been good friends in college. They were both preparing for the Christian ministry and often had studied together. In graduate school they struggled through the agony of developing a firm faith and of finding their place of service. By graduation time they had their directions and each was starting toward his lifework. Fred got on the bus to go to his first pastorate. Loren, with his bride, got into his battered old car to go East for further preparation, with an assignment from his mission board to go to India. But that very night an accident on the turnpike brought instant death to Loren.

Fred had deep and long battles to fight. He never questioned or blamed God, but he found no answer to his "why?" He found some consolation in the rededication of his own life to do his work and Loren's, too. Invited to speak at a youth convention, Fred felt that God wanted him to challenge youth to greater dedication and service. He prepared well and opened himself to God. After he spoke several hundred youth had dedicated themselves to some kind of Christian ministry.

Fred felt that there needed to be a plan for these youth to carry out their dedications. He helped them organize prayer fellowship groups wherever they lived. He sent them the following covenant and encouraged them to sign it prayerfully if it expressed their life intention.

What relationship do you see between Fred's deep struggles, and the result of his sermon? Is suffering and struggle necessary for growth?

"I will live my life under God for others rather than for myself.

"I will not drift into my lifework, but will do my utmost to discover that form and place of lifework in which I can become of the largest use to the kingdom of God.

"As I find it I will follow it under the leadership of Jesus Christ, wherever it takes me. Cost what it may."

Out of the group meetings there developed a volunteer service program that summer. More than one hundred youth gave of themselves working in vacation church schools, youth camps, and work camps. Fred no longer has the names, but he knows a great number of these youth who are serving in sacrificial ways throughout the world.

Fred says that he doesn't know where the words came from for that message. He can't even remember what he said. He doesn't know the source of the follow-up ideas, but he says, "I felt like I was a "stand-in" for Loren and even for Jesus."

> To what extent is a sense of inadequacy a necessary part of becoming a channel for the Holy Spirit?

SHE BECAME A CHANNEL FOR THE HOLY SPIRIT

A Christian leader had been asked to do a new and challenging task. She had been invited by the Board of Christian Education of Japan to come there and demonstrate good teaching in the church school. When they sent the invitation they said, "Now, we don't want lectures or discussions of theory. We are an educated people, and we have plenty of theory. We want you to *show* us how to teach."

So the teacher was frightened. How could she demonstrate teaching when she didn't even speak the language? And she didn't know either the people or their culture. She had been told that they would certainly not take public criticism, especially from a woman and a foreigner. It seemed an impossible request. Yet as she searched her motives and prayed, she felt she must try.

One day as she was praying, she thought of Jesus and how he came to be a demonstration of God's love. In the depths of her prayer and her struggle with decision, an inner voice seemed to say, "All I ask you to do is just go and show my love." She arose from prayer with assurance and confidence. New and creative ways of demonstration came to her mind. She developed a great admiration and deep love for Japanese youth. Japanese leaders testify that her work brought a permanent change to church school teaching in Japan. She says, "I felt that I was merely a channel for the Holy Spirit."

HE DIDN'T KNOW HE WAS GREAT

Bill Richards was counselor for a group of ten junior high boys at Camp Warner. He spent most of the day with the boys. One day they went on a long hike up the mountain. Another time they cooked a hobo dinner over an open fire. Once they went fishing, and most days they went swimming together. Every day they met

The Teacher in the Midst / 11

with other groups to discuss "The Christian Trail." Bill was the leader of this discussion based on the scripture, "The gate that leads to life is small and the road is narrow, and those who find it are few" (Matt. 7:14, NEB). Along with this scripture he used the well-known John Oxenham poem,

> To every man there openeth
> A High Way, and a Low.
> And every man decideth
> The way his soul shall go.[2]

The boys made a rustic motto with the words "We choose the High Way" and put it on the front of their cabin. They discussed everyday decisions which they faced, and Bill's challenge was to pray and think through to the high way, then to choose that way even though it might be the harder way. Bill came home from camp refreshed. He had a close relationship with the boys and they had fun together. It was a good camp and he planned other meetings with the boys.

Twelve years later at Christmastime he got a letter from one of the boys, now pastor of a large church and an outstanding preacher. It said: "Perhaps you don't remember that I was one of the boys in your group at Camp Warner so long ago. I do want you to know, however, that I remember the sessions vividly and I do attribute many of my basic Christian concepts and convictions to time I spent in your classes. One thing that has stuck with me through the years is this: One time you said that if a person was faced with two choices and they were both Christian but one was a little more noble than the other, it was the duty of the Christian to do the most noble. This has been a guiding principle when I have been faced with a situation of that type.

"I know it is rather late, but I do want to thank you most sincerely for the influence you had upon my life during its very impressionable years. Probably one of the reasons that I am so very happy today as a result of working in the ministry can be attributed to you and your influence those years ago."

Bill didn't even know he was making much of a difference.

CALLED TO TEACH

What then are the marks of the kind of lives to which teachers are called in the midst of this exciting, changing, suffering age?

---

[2] John Oxenham, *Gentlemen—the King* (Boston: The Pilgrim Press, 1928), p. 72.

How do you account for the influence of Bill Richards on this one youth? What of the other nine? They didn't write. Some probably do not even remember the experience. What made the difference?

VIII. Take Bill Richards—from this brief description can you find reasons for his influence? How many camps might he have led, and how many classes taught before he got this one letter? What does this say about teaching?

IX. Look at the marks listed under "Called to Teach." From your sharing, your list on the chart of the teachings of Jesus, and your analysis of the three experiences, add any marks which are not there.

X. Use these marks as a prayer guide during the coming week, remembering Jesus' promise (John 14:16, Acts 1:8).

TO TEACH IS TO LIVE DEEPLY IN THE LIVES OF OTHERS

The teacher is aware of each member as a struggling person trying to make his way in a sometimes difficult world. He teaches with feeling for and with others, for deep within his own emotional life are forces that powerfully affect the development of those he hopes to teach. This kind of teaching takes a person out of a deep sense of love, concern, and identification, deeply into the lives of those he teaches. The teacher in Japan became a channel for God's love because she loved deeply. Reuel Howe in the foreword to his book *Herein Is Love* says, "As the love of God required incarnation in Jesus of Nazareth in order that it might be received by us, so the Word of God's love in our day calls for persons in whom it may be embodied."[3]

What is the meaning "the Word of God's love calls for persons in whom it may be embodied"?

TO TEACH IS TO SEE THE POTENTIAL IN OTHERS

It is not enough to judge the outcome by the present level of development. Faith in persons keeps on when it seems that they will never learn. Faith sees behind the sometimes disturbing actions and tries to understand the feelings behind the action. The sensitive teacher knows that there is no such thing as a type of person, but that each person is unique and will respond in his own unique way. He will know also that some may refuse to accept the challenge to become what they could be. He will be torn by those who seem not to be willing to learn. Some of his greatest suffering will come from youth's refusal to become what they could be. While he knows that each person has to be free to say no as well as yes, he never loses faith in them as persons striving to find meaning in life.

How can a busy teacher live deeply in the lives of his students?

If the student says no to a challenge or does not accept Christ and the Christian way, does this mean the teacher has failed?

TO TEACH IS TO BE A FULL MEMBER OF THE LEARNING GROUP

The teacher can gain a great deal as he identifies with class members in the discovery of truth. His may be at a different level of understanding, but it is just as real as for any member of the class. No teacher has solved all his problems or learned all there is to know about any subject, most especially about the Christian life. If he will get down off his teacher pedestal and become a full member of the group, true learning may take place for all.

Can a person be a teacher and at the same time a full member of the learning group? What do you see as his stance: equal, above, a pal? Do you see a problem here?

TO TEACH IS TO BELIEVE THAT TEACHING WILL MAKE A DIFFERENCE

Such belief transcends the present circumstance and sees beyond it. The teacher has the conviction that what he is teaching makes a life-and-death difference in the life of the learners. He is not nearly so much interested in the learner's remembering everything that he says as he is interested in providing an experience that will bring about deep change in the life of the students. He and

When has a person really learned in the Christian sense?

---

[3] Reuel L. Howe, *Herein Is Love* (Philadelphia: The Judson Press, 1961).

What is the meaning of an "unconditional affirmation of life"? Is this the same as commitment to God? If he once makes such a commitment, will he ever need to reaffirm the commitment?

the learners are caught up together in the seriousness of life and he feels that his being in there with them does make a difference.

The authentic Christian is so taken up with the adventure of sharing life as pupils and teacher live and learn together, that he never thinks about his own success. Bill Richards' experience is a good example of this. He lived with the boys and they had fun together. He shared with them his own feelings and practices of life. He felt it was good experience, but he didn't know until twelve years later what the experience meant to one of the boys, and even to this day he doesn't know about the other nine.

TO TEACH IS TO MAKE AN UNCONDITIONAL AFFIRMATION OF LIFE AND COMMITMENT TO GOD

A teacher is wise to take a direction and make it a positive one. He will forever have conflict if he dallies between saving himself and investing himself. When he is fearful that he might give too much, his noncommitment is showing. The committed life has to be daring, and it has to take a direction. It has to come out somewhere. The committed person has his loyalties clear. He knows what comes first in his life.

A man said to Jesus, " 'I will follow you, Lord; but first let me say farewell to those at my home.' Jesus said to him. 'No one who puts his hand to plow and looks back is fit for the kingdom of God' " (Luke 9:62). Once the teacher says an irrevocable yes to God and to life, he is ready to enter the gate of that kind of living which comes through servanthood.

As you think of the teachings of Jesus on greatness, and study this chapter, why not make a balance sheet of your own strengths and weaknesses and bring them before God in regular periods of prayer and searching as you study the book.

CHAPTER 2

Focus On Identity

To be your real self in a world which is doing its best to make you like everybody else—means to fight the hardest battle which any human being can fight, and to never stop fighting.

"What will a man gain by winning the whole world, at the cost of his true self."

—Matthew 16:26, NEB

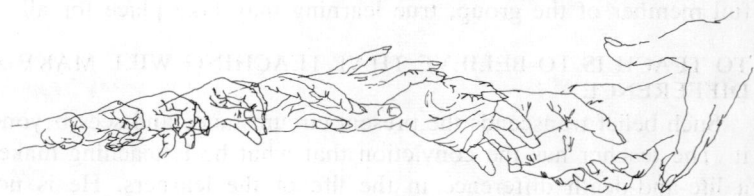

The Christian teacher is called to stand alone before God, to know who he is and what he has been called to be. Such an affirmation requires an honest effort to understand himself as a unique person empowered by his Creator. He is called to live in such a

14 / Basics for Communication in the Church

way as to develop respect for his own integrity and style of life. He needs to feel that he is becoming what he was intended to be. "Think what sort of people you are, whom God has called" (1 Cor. 1:26, NEB). These words of Paul addressed to the Corinthian church hold a message of hope. Then he goes on to say, "Few of you were wise, or powerful, or of high social status, from the human point of view. . . . But God has brought you into union with Christ Jesus, . . . by him we are put right with God, we become God's own people, and are set free" (1 Cor. 1:26ff., TEV).

God has built into all persons resources and qualities which most never realize. He has given to all the stuff of great living if only they dare to be authentic.

"Rubbish," is the name a modern artist, Hoffman, has given to his painting of a dejected, discouraged man of middle age. It pictures him dressed in a business suit, as he slumps on an old box. Beside him is an unfolded newspaper and two garbage cans. Dimly in the background, one can discern the towers of the city—symbols of wealth, competition, and technology. Yesterday he stood up and said, "I am a person. I will make a difference in my world." But today, hope, the sense of self-worth and the feeling of destiny is gone. It may never come back. He may settle for conformity, the routine, and the defeated. He has lost his identity.

THE MEANING OF IDENTITY

In identity the focus is on *being* rather than on *having* or even on *doing*. Identity is the concept that allows a person to say "I am." "I am the active, organizing center of my life." Ross Snyder in *On Becoming Human* says, "You were meant to be. It is right for you to be fully alive."[1] He goes on to say that each person is born to become a unique, particular expression of human being, and that each person is responsible to remain in charge of his decisions and to determine what the experiences of life may mean and do to him.

There is an interesting opposite to identity recorded in Job 18:17. Here Bildad, in recounting the calamities of the wicked,

[1] Ross Snyder, *On Becoming Human*, (Nashville: Abingdon Press, 1967).

"Conformity blocks creativity. Freedom and spontaneity foster growth." Which is your characteristic response? Which do you foster in those you teach?

"We wait for God to make us his sons and set our whole being free" (Romans 8:23b, TEV). In what sense is the Christian free?

"To risk causes anxiety—but not to risk is to become a nobody." How does this quote relate to the Hoffman picture? How does it relate to Matthew 16:26?

"But when he came to himself" (Luke 15:17). What is the meaning of the lost son and the forgiving father story in relation to selfhood or identity (Luke 15:17, 32)?

"Failure to do with one's life what one knows one could do is a great sin." Do you agree? Why do people fail to be what they could be? Read Luke 19:11-26.

Guidance for Session 2
FOCUS ON IDENTITY

Aims for the Session

To grow in understanding of oneself and come to respect oneself as a unique person. To recognize some of the dimensions of the process of becoming an open, honest self. To develop integrity and openness as a Christian teacher.

Clusters of Learning Experiences

I. Consider the quote at the beginning of the chapter. What are some of the ways the world is trying to make us like everybody else? In this light what is the meaning of the scripture Matthew 16:26?

II. Describe the picture named "Rubbish." What is the artist trying to say? What are the effects of conformity on the personality?

III. Divide into twos. Try to answer the question, "who am I?" without referring to your material possessions, or the work you do. What problems do you have? Talk together about your feelings.

IV. Discuss the meaning of identity referring to the scriptures about Moses, Jesus, and Job. Why is a person's name or his picture so important to him?

says, "His memory perishes from the earth, and he has no name in the street." The opposite to becoming an "I am" is to become a nobody, a nameless one.

Even children react to being thought of in groups and to being treated as collections of things. The pastor was sharply awakened one day as he walked through the playground of the church nursery school. One cheerful, friendly child called out, "Hello, Pastor Thomas." When the pastor just as cheerfully answered, "Hello, boys and girls," an insightful child said, "We've got names too." What she was trying to express was, "We are persons too; we have an identity." From childhood, one deserves to feel that he is respected as a person and that his individuality is treasured.

Often, a person comes to think of himself in terms of what he can do, what he has, or what he represents rather than who he is. Once I tried to write out "who I am." I put down my name. I wrote, "A child of God." I wrote, "A woman and wife." Then I wrote, "A church college teacher." Already, I was off on what I do and what I represent.

True identity and the actualization of one's potential come in a setting where one is treated as sheer personal being, a unique self to be known and cherished.

Children and youth are quick to identify the person who is not real. They say, "He is a phony," and they hold little respect even though he may be a person of status and position. Perhaps this is the origin of the barbed epithet, "Way down deep, he's shallow."

Who does not know people who never seem real? With them, you never feel up against consistency or substance. They seem to be a pretense, trying to live by what they think others expect of them. They wear a mask because they feel that if people really saw them as they are, they would not trust them. They do not have a true sense of their own worth, and so they cannot believe that others would find them of worth if they should really know them.

It is possible for every person to develop the capacity to have faith in himself as a worthy and unique being, created in the image

---

V. Why do people play roles, put on pretense, play games, build fences that hide them from other people? Is this harmful? If so, why?

VI. Put the term "search for self" in everyday words. Why is it necessary that each person come to understand who he is and what his purpose in life should be?

VII. Read the story of Henry and analyze his actions. How did he find help? How does one get his self-image, the feeling he has about himself?

VIII. Manipulation is a word that describes the experience of one person being used to satisfy the needs of another. An example would be a teacher who fixes up all the children's artwork so that people will think she's a great teacher. Another is the mother who wants children for the security they will give her. Can you remember times when you have been manipulated? What did the experience do to you? How did you feel? Or are you willing to confess times when you have manipulated others? How do you feel about doing that?

IX. Study the drawing at the beginning of the chapter. What meanings do you get for your own self-understanding?

X. Can you give examples of other "eternal truths" which might vary in interpretation and application under different circumstances.

XI. Go through the Dimensions of Selfhood. Try to come to the meaning of each one. Is there agreement that these should be included? See if the group would like to add others.

XII. The Keys to Healthy Selfhood are for personal examination and

of God, and also to have faith in and meaningful communication with other selves.

THE SEARCH FOR SELF

The *self* is the inner core of personality that integrates and orients one's experiences. Salient features of *selfhood* are self-awareness, self-fulfillment, and self-direction, as expressed in such common verbalisms as "I am," "I see," "I do," "I feel," "I think," "I choose," "I believe." Central to the functioning of the self is the person's striving to find the meaning, value, and purpose of his life. This search for his own destiny, the unique meaning and purpose of his life, is what is meant by the search for *self*.

Part of the search for self will be in honest self-examination. One may put questions to himself and trust the answers that come from within. These answers may be sharp and thorny requiring severe pruning. He may examine his childhood experiences in order to understand who he is and why he feels as he does about himself.

Who am I? Who are you? This twofold question is being asked throughout life. One cannot be answered without the other. As the baby begins to feel himself a separate individual, his self-image takes shape as a reflection of the image he feels others have of him. If the significant beings in his life respect him and feel deeply that he is a person of worth, he will internalize this image of himself. But if when he reaches out for trust and love, he is rejected, how can he feel he is worthy?

Such had been the experience of Henry, an unwanted child. He grew up living with his grandparents, who had cared for him out of a sense of duty, and in order to shield themselves and their daughter from the community hostility toward unwed motherhood. The grandparents provided him with an excess of material things, as if to compensate for their real rejection. Since he had a weak sense of self and felt so worthless, he began to react to life in two ways. He developed a biting sarcasm that cut others, even his

"The real self is not a secret to be hidden but a gift to be used."

---

growth. They will probably be used best during the week as a guide to meditation and prayer. It seems essential that each member seriously make this self-examination. The leader will need to provide copies of the "keys" for personal use.

XIII. What is the source of becoming an inner-directed person? How is one able to transcend the ethic of his society?

XIV. How is God related to the teacher in the process of becoming? How does the Holy Spirit become operative in the process?

XV. Build a short worship around the scriptures Matthew 16:26 and Romans 8:19-25.

Keys to Healthy Selfhood

INSTRUCTIONS: In serious honesty rate yourself in the following dimensions. 1 is high, 2 is above average, 3 is average, 4 is low. Check the space which seems most appropriate. In prayer and meditation determine how to handle the average or low.

1. Self-concept 1.___ 2.___ 3.___ 4.___ You usually feel good about the things you do and say.
2. Flexibility 1.___ 2.___ 3.___ 4.___ You can change your routines and your ideas without too much resistance.
3. Trust 1.___ 2.___ 3.___ 4.___ You like and trust your work associates, friends, and family. You feel optimistic about people and their motives. You confide in someone.
4. Freedom 1.___ 2.___ 3.___ 4.___ You feel that your attitudes and

Focus on Identity / 17

friends and teachers, to the core. He delighted in holding up their weaknesses to public ridicule. Other students became afraid to speak in his presence, for fear of his making them appear ridiculous. He tore the church and the Bible to shreds with his brilliant cynicism.

The other cover of self was to develop a sharp wit. When he couldn't handle an argument or a situation, he turned it into a joke.

One day a teacher learned of this unfortunate childhood. He began to see behind the acting out, a struggling self, trying to handle his problems. He saw Henry as a naked self, fighting for all he was worth to keep from being entirely lost. In their counseling sessions, one day Henry said, "People think I'm the neighborhood clown, but I only tell jokes and use sarcasm to keep people from seeing that I'm crying inside."

A person forms his self-concept or image of himself as he perceives it reflected in the attitudes and feelings taken toward him by parents, teachers, friends, and all the "significant others" of his social environment. A positive self-concept—one which is based on acceptance, belonging, personal worth, and adequacy—is essential to wholesome growth and creativity. A negative self-concept—one full of fear, guilt, grievance, and hostility toward self and others—stifles growth and hinders relatedness.

Faithfulness to the *self* is the main source of strength in the individual. If the person feels deep down inside himself that he ought to decide in a certain way and yet because of the risk he fails to do so, he is being untrue to his real self. Then something within him dies.

Or if the pressures of the situation are such that the individual submits, while the very core of his being cries out against submission, the selfhood is threatened and the person may be unable to think, decide, or act. He may become the expectation, convic-

---

"More will be given to the man who has something already, but the man who has nothing will lose even what he thinks he has" (Luke 8:18, Phillips). What do these words of Jesus say to you about integrity, adequacy, and identity?

"Get rid of the role and be a person." There is a need for complete sincerity. Read Luke 11:37. What does Jesus teach about pretense, phoniness, and show?

"The test of inner integrity is a test no teacher can grade, for life gives the grade."

---

beliefs are your own. You make your own choices and do not act primarily on the basis of what others expect. You are not afraid to express your opinions and carry out your ideas.

5. Courage 1.___ 2.___ 3.___ 4.___ When you face a decision, you have courage to choose that which appears to be the highest choice even though it involves risk and may cost deeply. You consider the counsel of others, you prayerfully study the Bible, you know the alternatives; but the final choice is determined by your inner convictions. When the decision is made you act, and then take the responsibility for the choice.

6. Openness 1.___ 2.___ 3.___ 4.___ You can honestly consider any new idea or plan that may be presented. You can recognize yourself in the process of growth. You can listen to an opposite view and really hear the viewpoint. Your attitude toward truth is one of search and growing understanding.

7. Confirmation of others 1.___ 2.___ 3.___ 4.___ Do others appreciate you and believe in you? Are you secure enough that you do not seek evidences of others liking you? Can you function well without praise and special recognition?

8. Relationship with others 1.___ 2.___ 3.___ 4.___ Do you have close, trusting relationships with your family and with a few friends? Do you feel that you can confide your deepest problems to them and that they will stand by you? Can you give unconditional love to others?

9. A future thrust 1.___ 2.___ 3.___ 4.___ You understand your past and accept it as a part of yourself. You enjoy the present and look on crises and trouble as a challenge to growth. You do not fear the future but anticipate it. You feel an inner strength, that by God's grace and the empowering of his Holy Spirit you can meet whatever may come with dignity and victory.

18 / **Basics for Communication in the Church**

tions, values, and even the life-style of others, but he has no heart for it.

Manipulative methods of ruling another are prevalent in all circles today. Often persons are aware of the manipulation, but they do not have the courage or the strength to stand up for their inner convictions. Society has developed skills in psychological manipulation, so that while the individual is resentful and restless, he may not even understand what is being done to him. Such devastating experiences can cut the very heart out of life's meaning and leave the person with no sense of joy or aliveness.

DIMENSIONS OF SELFHOOD

In reality, the ultimate meanings in a person's life depend on the choices he has made and the values and convictions he had developed. Therefore, only the person himself can make this effort to understand whether he is being true to his own values or is substituting the standards and expectations of others for his own. Only he can know whether he is a deciding, choosing person, or whether he is allowing himself to fit into another person's plans and to act in a way which has no meaning or value for him. What then are the dimensions of selfhood?

GROWTH IN FREEDOM

To grow in freedom may be the adult's most difficult task. While the urge toward freedom is a positive force within the person, he has been schooled in conformity. The authentic person struggles to remain a free, deciding individual. He refuses to let the experiences of his childhood or the demands of life decide his destiny. He will not allow external pressures or the criticism of others to determine his actions or goals. While he learns to accept his limitations and to admit the circumstances, he also determines to find and fulfill the purposes for which he was created.

COURAGE TO CHOOSE

There are many crisis times in every life when a man has to make decisions. There comes a time, however, when he has to decide whether he is going to be a slave to the ideas of others and the traditions of society or whether he is going to think for himself, decide his own course of action and pursue it whatever the cost may be. In other words, he decides on a life-style of conformity or one of creativity. The courage to choose to think for himself and to act according to the dictates of his inner convictions will determine whether his life will be a running stream or a stagnant pool. He may well choose to follow the patterns of society much of the time, but it has been an open-eyed, thoughtful choice.

RESPONSIBILITY FOR THE CHOICE

Freedom to become and the courage to choose do not free one from responsibility. Rather, they make one responsible for

"One must transfer his base of security from external circumstances to confidence in one's self. Dependence on external circumstances is a form of slavery to things, a sense of inner adequacy brings freedom." How do you feel about yourself? Can you understand something of the sources of your feelings? Can you identify sources of your reaction to certain persons or situations?

"To settle for certainty is to die to the adventure and to life." Courage is the power to let go of the familiar in order to grow and to serve. Will you settle for certainty or for search?

"God created something entirely new —man—and took his greatest risk. We are created in his image, made to create, to risk, to adventure."

the outcome of his choices. Since he is no longer bound to his past, having declared himself free to use its meanings, he can no longer blame his childhood experiences for his choices nor for his behavior. Nor is he stifled by the present situation for he has decided to transcend the present and use present circumstances as a means to growth.

The consequential outcome is responsibility, with a realization of the need for disciplined, unified, and consistent behavior.

Freedom in this context does not mean the wild, confused, or fragmentary "acting out" sometimes thought of as self-expression. Rather, it is a freedom grown out of fidelity to the destiny of the self and willingness to take responsibility for whatever the outcome may be. Viktor Frankl, the European psychologist, has pointed up the need for responsibility by saying that the people of the United States need a Statue of Responsibility on their West Coast to balance the Statue of Liberty on the East Coast.

OPENNESS TOWARD LIFE

Persons in the "process of becoming" will have to learn to live with an attitude of "tentativeness" toward ideas and goals. They must somehow find a balance between certainty and search. That is, they believe what they believe with enough vigor and confidence to give their utmost to their faith, yet they are open to the exploration of other possibilities. They are willing to make an honest search into these sometimes opposing views. The open person does not give up his ideas or plans too easily, but neither is he so rigid that he sees no possibility that he could be wrong.

The Christian religion offers certain "eternal truth" basic to being human and to man's relation to man and to his Creator. This eternal truth does not vary with the change of place or space. It has been true in every generation and is true in every culture. But the way this becomes operative may vary with the generations and the culture. The danger is that the closed person may not be able to distinguish the truth from the way the truth is expressed.

Respect for the personhood of another human being is a basic right and eternal truth. The means of showing respect may be very different in another culture. It is always wrong to treat a person as a "thing" and to use him for advantage. The treatment, however, may take a different form in a new age.

Search also provides the opportunity for a growing interpretation of eternal truth. It is not that the truth will change, but that as one has widened experience his understanding of the truth may become so enriched that he sometimes almost feels that the truth has changed. Then, there is always the possibility that what he once thought to be eternal truth was not that at all, but a mistaken concept of truth.

Sidebar quotes:

"Humanity has tremendous and fearful potential!" However, man's ultimate confidence cannot and must not lie in himself. Only in relationship with his Creator can man find his human possibilities realized in faith and love. What is the balance between self-fulfillment and trust in God?

"To shape and sharpen the human self is a lifelong process. But the pathway is as important as the process. The direction which self-awareness takes as it moves from the inner self, to outer self, to other-selves, is of equal import." Do you agree that the development and direction of the "real" self is the great enterprise of human life? Is this what it means to be a Christian?

"The self needs others in order to live, and without others it soon perishes."

"It is within the choices and commitments of community that the real self comes to be discovered. The community of faith confirms the self." What do you see as the place of group worship in self-awareness? What is the place of the church?

If life is to be dynamic, and we are to think of selfhood as a process of becoming rather than a state of being, then a spirit of openness is essential.

CONFIRMATION OF OTHERS

The confirmation of others has a significant impact on the growing self. From the beginning of life this has been recognized as the way the self-concept is formed. This affirmation of the person as one who is trusted is necessary throughout life. This does not mean that the mature Christian will abdicate his values for the approval of others. Basically, it means that others whom he respects do believe in him, esteem him as a unique human being, and grant him the right to follow his own pattern of expression. In turn, he needs to confirm the being of others. In order to do this he becomes available to them, alert, open, receptive, and honest. Thus mutual growth takes place, even if one is the teacher and the other is the pupil.

RELATIONSHIPS WITH OTHERS

Another dimension of selfhood is deep and profound interpersonal relations with at least a few persons. The growing person is capable of deep caring and great giving of the self to another. This is what Ross Snyder calls "being *with* and *for* people."[2] He points out that being *with* and *for* persons does not mean agreeing with their ideas and actions. Neither does it mean losing your own individuality in the other. Actually a friendship is valuable only when each maintains his own integrity with strength to bring to the friendship. The foundation of a true relationship is basic trust. It requires that you are aware of the other as a struggling person trying to find meaning for his life. You are *for* him and he *for* you in your common struggle.

A THRUST INTO THE FUTURE

The growing self has made terms with the past. He knows that all the significant experiences of his past are embedded in what he has become. He is fully alive in the present. He treasures every experience, both the joyful and the bitter, for of the present he intends to hammer out what he is becoming. But he has a thrust into the future. He anticipates the future as good. His life has movement, direction, and goal. Hope springs eternal in his breast, and he knows he is not yet what he is to become.

THE PROCESS TOWARD WHOLENESS

Depth and direction are crucial to the growing self. Seldom will one come to a clear self-identity without great struggle. Sometimes conflict and suffering are a part of the experience; but the joys and satisfactions of life are a part of the living also.

"A man needs to find big enough goals that they never are finished; goals big enough that whatever happens he can land on his feet." What are some of the long-term goals a Christian should seek?

[2]*Ibid.*, p. 50.

One becomes willing to think of his life as a process of becoming, rather than as a fixed product. Yet the process is toward self-consistency and wholeness. The meaning of a person's life depends on the values and convictions he has developed, and the ultimate goal toward which he is directing his total energy. Values, convictions, and goals integrate the personality into strength and unity. Only as the person identifies and chooses values, convictions, and goals from his inner self does he come to know who he is and what his destiny should be. He is no longer pushed around by the demands of his childhood or by the society in which he lives.

Adjustment is not his goal, for he knows that to adjust to a materialistic society is a weakness. "Adjusted to whom and to what?" is his question. Perhaps to protest against being manipulated, against domination, or against being trampled on is a sign of strength. He most certainly will protest when he sees others being crippled by prejudice, discrimination, and greed. There comes a time when not to protest is a sickness!

Do you agree that "there comes a time when not to protest is a sickness"? Can you give examples?

He has become an inner-directed person, able to transcend the ethic of the age and to live by an eternal ethic. He feels himself in harmony with the God who created him in his uniqueness. This is true freedom! This is the real meaning of being a person.

Do you think it is possible to find a true sense of selfhood without a relationship with God?

The qualities of freedom within the self and openness to others is necessary if one is to become a channel of the Holy Spirit. When a man refuses to be open he closes off the Spirit to his own life and also to others. This is why it is so essential that the Christian teacher focuses on his own identity, realizing that until he affirms himself he cannot in truth, give of himself to others.

How is the Holy Spirit operative in the process of man's search for meaning?

CHAPTER 3

Humanness Too!

*The whole creation
is on tiptoe
To see the wonderful sight
of the sons of God
coming into their own.*
—Romans 8:19 (Phillips)

*In the longing for
sonship lies our hope,
and that longing is in
every one of us.*

*True personality maturity
resides in a feeling tone of
adequacy—a competency to deal
with whatever comes in a way
that one can prize.*

*"You must love
your neighbor
as yourself."*
—Matthew 22:39, TEV

The idea expressed in the words of Jesus, "Love your neighbor as yourself" (Matt. 22:39, TEV), implies that respect for one's own integrity and dignity cannot be separated from love and respect for another person. Love for one's own self and love for another self are interdependent. The scripture has been paraphrased to say, "Love yourself properly, and then you will love your neighbor."

If the Christian is to love and respect all human beings in such a way that he will aid them in their fulfillment, then he must accept and respect himself as a son of God also. Love of others and love of self are not alternatives, but rather an attitude of realistic self-respect will be found in all those who are really capable of loving others.

Selfishness and self-love are not synonyms. The selfish person is interested only in getting for himself. Every person and situation is looked on from the viewpoint, "What is there in it for me?" He shows interest in others only if he sees how he can use them. His attitude is the source of the quip, "Why, I have friends I haven't even used yet." Usually, the selfish effort to get things for himself is an indication of self-hate. Since he feels an emptiness and anxiety

Do you believe that it is essential to love yourself properly if you are to love others?

Guidance for Session 3
HUMANNESS TOO!

Aims for the Session

To realize that we are persons in process. To accept ourselves as human. To handle such realistic situations as failure, mistakes, and criticism; yet to create hope and a desire for growth.

Clusters of Learning Experiences

I. If you are daring you might start the session by role-playing a teacher coming into the classroom with the rigid characteristics described by "growing teacherishness." The scene would be several students sitting in rows, rather noisily talking and laughing. They hear the teacher coming down the hall, and immediately sit up straight. She comes in straight and stiff, with her pasty smile and says, "Good morning, boys and girls. Today. . . ." Now take it from there for about three to five minutes.

Have the group discuss such questions as:

How did the teacher feel playing the role? How did the pupils feel? Why did the teacher act this way? What do pupils learn in this kind of setting? What room is there for individual growth and creativity? Is the description of "growing teacherishness" applicable to teachers in the church?

II. If you wish you might have the role play again, using the same person, but this time the teacher is human.

The students would be busily helping the teacher get the room ready. Some might be arranging pictures on the display board. Others might be planning worship. Some could be working on an interest center. The teacher admits she forgot her Bible, borrows one, and they begin their study.

Humanness Too! / 23

Feelings determine the quality of an experience.

Think of the most selfish person you know. Why must he try to get the best for himself? How does he feel about life?

Under what conditions might it be harmful to give up things you want or need so that others may have them? What other illustrations of neurotic "unselfishness" can you think of?

about his own meaning, he is driven to snatch from life whatever satisfactions he can get.

One of the chief tasks of the young adult is to change the balance in receiving and giving. From the time he was born he has been making the change. The baby is entirely dependent both physically and emotionally. Gradually he works his way toward independence. Society provides a long period during which he is allowed to be on the receiving end, but by the time he is in his twenties, society expects that he is giving out more than he is receiving into himself. Some persons never mature beyond the receiving stage and are perpetual adolescents.

In some persons such emptiness and self-hate take the form of selfishness as just described. Such a person must have the largest piece of meat and the best of everything. He is never satisfied until he has the top position, regardless of how many people he steps on to get there. He must be the center of attention in every situation. His ideas must be accepted or he won't play. Such action is defeating, for he cuts off the very love he is striving so hard to win.

Strange as it may seem other persons try to fill the emptiness and lack of self-respect through being overly unselfish. To extol such as a Christian grace is to fail to understand the dynamics of the inner self. Feeling a weakness within himself, he strives to make it up by oversolicitous concern for others. Such a person will try to buy the love of others by doing everything for them. The mother will do without things she needs in order to give her daughter everything. The youth leader will give up his beliefs or principles to try to win the favor of youth. The teacher may use candy or cookies to try to tie the children to herself.

Such a person claims "not to want anything for himself." He lives entirely for others and is proud that he does not consider himself important. In reality, he is using a subtle technique to try

You might ask the same questions as above. Others might be:

Is the situation too ideal? What if some just have to be told what to do? What if they get too noisy, and the parents criticize?

The discussion leader will need to watch the aim of this discussion. This is not a session on student characteristics; it is the teacher and his willingness to take the risks of failure and criticism.

III. Discuss the meaning of Romans 8:19 as given in the Phillips' translation, and quoted at the beginning of the chapter.

IV. Discuss what it means to love yourself properly. Do you agree that Christians more often err on the side of underconfidence than of overconfidence? Share some feelings about their personal performances.

V. Ask the class to distinguish between selfishness and self-love. Perhaps they can give examples of each. Do they agree that "over-solicitous concerns" may be an indication that the person is really selfish?

VI. What does it mean to be a "person in process?" What are the dangers of trying to be perfect?

VII. Make a study of the drawings in the margins and discuss the questions listed there.

VIII. Discuss what dangers the class may see in setting some teachers up as examples or model teachers. How do the use of teacher standards, evaluative scales, merit awards, and "teacher of the year" citations relate to the teacher's self-image?

IX. What implications for self-understanding do you find in the statement, "Jesus was a living presence to them to help them become themselves"? What is the meaning "comparing himself with himself" (Gal. 6:3-4, NEB)? Give examples of ways one might compare himself with himself.

X. If the earlier role play was not used, perhaps you could have an interview now. One can be the department or church school administrator. Mrs. Martin comes to resign her class because she feels she is a failure. Have the interview begin just

to get that for himself which he needs most. He is trying to buy self-respect. This form of selfishness is difficult to handle. Often the person has deep disappointment, for his actions result in resentment from others which he cannot understand. "Look how they treat me after all I have done for them" is the cry of the neurotically unselfish.

How does the scripture "Not to think of himself more highly than he ought to think" (Romans 12:3) imply that one is not to underestimate himself also? Read the scripture in various translations.

YOU TOO ARE HUMAN

The truth is that self-love takes in the acceptance of limitations. The sound person is on good enough terms with himself that he can afford to recognize both his strengths and his limitations and to set about making a life out of what he has to work with. He is neither too secure nor too apologetic. It is probably true that more persons err on the side of underconfidence than of overconfidence.

Many teachers harbor an image of themselves that has been imposed on them by an ideal of perfectionism. When they are unable to live up to this image, they feel defeated and guilty. Often they are tempted to quit. Yet quitting is not within their self-image either, and so they battle along, worn out with struggling to be what they cannot be. When the false image is discarded and they are able to accept themselves even with faults, the sense of failure goes out with it. Then they develop the ability to be productive. Man lives on the razor's edge of what he is and what he can be. He is called to learn how to live with this tension and use both for his growth.

How realistic is your image of yourself? How did you get this self-image? How may it be changed?

FLAG: Drawing 3. (Mirror back perfection)............

REFUSING THE TEACHER ROLE

There is no greater threat to the real self of the teacher than the gradual substitution of the "teacher role" for the real self. The society and the situation set up the goals and communicate expectations so that what the teacher becomes may be the image of their idea of a teacher. Add to this the Christian image, and the leader in the church situation may have a real conflict to handle.

---

after Mrs. Martin describes the experience.

Mrs. Martin says, "I feel I must resign the class, because I know I have lost the respect of the class. I lost control and yelled at them. I accused Jimmy. I used reading the Bible as punishment. I even tried to make them feel guilty by saying they didn't want to learn about Jesus."

Try out various ways of answering and see what the reaction would be. Have the class discuss each answer.

Answer 1. "Well, that wasn't so bad. We all have off days. They'll probably be little angels next Sunday. Besides I don't know anyone else who would do better than you are doing."

Answer 2. "Well, I'm sure it has been a rather hard experience. Can you analyze why you feel the way you do?"

Mrs. Martin: "I am interested in the children. I suppose it's because I try so hard."

Leader: "Can you understand why you want the class to go just as you planned it?"

Mrs. Martin: "Well, I want to be a good teacher. I never believe in doing anything halfway."

Leader: "Do you see any possible good in the children feeling with Eddie and not allowing Jimmy to go too far?"

Mrs. Martin: "In a way, I guess that is the real point of the story after all, but I didn't see it then."

Answer 3. "I understand how you must feel. Sometimes I've felt that way myself, but if you resign what will be the effect on the children? How are they likely to feel about their next teacher? Would it be a strengthening or a weakening experience for you?"

Mrs. Martin: "I don't think I will ever try to teach again, at least not eight-year-olds."

Leader: "Can you see any way that you could redeem the situation, so that both you and they could learn from it?"

Mrs. Martin: "I might go and apologize to them for the way I acted, but that would be hard. I think

One person defined this threat as "growing teacherishness." He said he could sense a teacher a mile away. When I asked him to describe the role, he gave these characteristics:

1. A certain tidiness about dress.
2. A rather stiff and formal manner.
3. A reserved kind of dignity.
4. A lack of spontaneity and enthusiasm.
5. An authoritative, decisive manner.
6. An artificial see-beyond-you smile.
7. An attitude of know-it-all.

He said that some teachers were like this only in the classroom, but others seem to carry the teacher role over into life. Now, granted, he may be applying *his* teacher image to all teachers. (He admitted that he and his first grade teacher fought all the time.) Yet there is enough truth in his description to unmask any teacher.

THE DANGER OF COMPARISON

Another threat to the personhood of the leader is to measure himself by the abilities of another. Sometimes such comparisons have been used to motivate persons toward competence. The use of standards, patterns, and other incentives as rewards may cause the teacher to progress (?) step-by-step toward outside definitions and expectations. In the process his own uniqueness is canceled out, and he becomes a mechanical imitation of another. Could this be the source of the lack of spontaneity and enthusiasm just described—and of the artificial, see-beyond-you smile? His deeds may be very good and his actions close to perfect, but there is no "aliveness" about him.

When a person says, "Why can't I be like Mr. King?" he is denying the value of being himself. He is usually measuring his worst, which he knows, by the other person's best, which he has only seen from the outside. How often did Jesus ask people to imitate him? He was a "living presence" to them to help them to become themselves. The apostles maintained their individual strengths—and weaknesses—even after spending three years with Jesus.

---

they'd laugh, and I'd feel worse than ever."

Leader: "Now as you look at it, were they really at fault?"

Mrs. Martin: "Yes, they were as much to blame as I was. Maybe we could think together about the situation. I believe they would realize their faults as easily as I do mine. We might even learn better how to work together from this experience."

XI. How can one accept an effort as a failure, without feeling the self as a failure? Would you consider the man whose project failed, a failure?

XII. Are there things which a person cannot do, no matter how hard he tries? Are there times when maybe a person should quit trying to do some things? If so, how can he keep his sense of worth?

XIII. How does one distinguish between making a mistake and moral wrongdoing? If a person makes a mistake that harms another, should he feel guilty? How should he deal with such a mistake?

XIV. Make a list of scriptures that show God's plan for man as that of making his own choices. What do these imply about the teacher's responsibility?

XV. What is the source of the power of recovery? Why do some persons use trouble as a means to greatness, while others "cry the rest of their lives"?

XVI. Read Romans 8:37-39.

The final question will never be, "Why were you not like your famous uncle?" but, "Why were you not yourself?"

Each man should examine his own conduct for himself; then he can measure his achievement by comparing himself with himself, and not with anyone else. For everyone has his own proper burden. See Galatians 6:3-4, NEB.

COME TO TERMS WITH YOUR LIMITATIONS

Mrs. Martin had finally said good-bye to the last eight-year-old, and she sat tired and discouraged among the ruins of her plans. She knew that the children would be restless on the day after Halloween, and so she had planned a drama activity for the day. She had even brought some costumes along so that they could dramatize the Good Samaritan story. Then she planned to discuss ways that they could express the truth of the story at school.

But nothing went right. Some of the children brought their masks from the night before. She allowed them some time to tell of their Halloween adventures. Then they read the story and asked about the dramatization. Jimmy volunteered to be the robber. Eddie said he would be the man on the journey. Nobody wanted to be the Good Samaritan, but with some coaxing, they were ready to act. When Jimmy started his act he really put himself into being the robber. At first the class laughed, but when they saw Eddie helplessly taking a beating, they began to yell at Jimmy. Mrs. Martin lost her calm. She yelled at the children. She said if that was how they were going to act, they'd just read the story out of the Bible. When they were finally quiet enough to hear her, she told them how disappointed she was in their behavior. She said Jimmy was a naughty boy and that it seemed nobody in the class wanted to learn about Jesus.

Now that the children were gone she not only felt that the morning was wasted, but that she was a failure. Her image of a Sunday school teacher was that of one who is always calm and in control of the situation. She would never use her disappointment to punish the children nor embarrass them to get control. Yet she had done just that. "Why did I do it?" she asked herself.

Herbert Greenberg in the book *Teaching with Feeling*[1] holds that the humanity of the teacher is the vital ingredient if children are to learn, He says that teachers need to learn to face the reality of their own teaching behavior. They should accept the fact that their feelings are affected by the way the class responds. He says that the teacher can't love all alike, and to try to do so denies his own uniqueness and his own feelings. Certainly, the teacher may see and aim to develop the potential in each one and emphasize the desirable traits rather than the undesirable.

[1] Herbert Greenberg, *Teaching with Feeling* (New York: Macmillan Co., 1969).

Some people harbor an image of themselves that calls for a performance which they cannot reach.

What is the mask you are tempted to wear when you are teaching? When you meet the pastor? When you try to help someone? When someone comes to you for counsel? How do persons react to masks?

Whether we agree with Herbert Greenberg or not on every point, certainly we know that the teacher has to realize his humanity and learn to accept it. Perhaps it is not so bad not to be perfect. If adults can learn to admit mistakes and loss of emotional control and learn how to handle them, maybe children can too.

The real danger is that rather than accepting the unacceptable in one's self, admitting the situation, and setting forth on ways to redeem the experience, the person sets out to blame others and to justify self. Mrs. Martin needs some time to be alone, to pray, and maybe even to seek counsel. There is, however, within the maturing person emotional resilience, the ability to bounce back with added strength and zest for teaching.

HANDLING FAILURE

The teacher can learn to handle and overcome small failures because he knows his destiny. Mrs. Martin loves the members of her class, and they have had many good experiences together. She will seek to make the experiences of the past Sunday an opportunity for growth for all. She might have a personal talk with Jimmy to rebuild their relationship. She might ask the class to think about the situation and try to understand why they all acted as they did. It could be the means of a growing confidence in each other.

Fear of failure paralyzes action. It forces persons into playing a role. It drives them to conformity and compromise, to drifting with convention, to acting out of a sense of duty. Better to have some failure than to lose one's own awareness of being a particular person.

But some limitations and failures are big. They can't be overcome. Then they have to be accepted. A person may have to come to accept a certain effort as a failure. He must, however, make a clear distinction between the *effort* as a failure and the *self* as a failure. This distinction is the key to maintaining self-worth in the face of failure.

A large and worthy project had failed. People had suffered greatly, and some had lost their life's savings. It was the final dream of a great man. One day as he sat in the kitchen of his rented cottage, eating an onion sandwich, he said, "I've given my life for higher education in the church. This was my last great dream, but it has failed. Now, I'm getting to be an old man, and I doubt if I even have a place in the ministry."

For a year, he served as minister of a small rural church. There he had peace with time to think and pray. He regained his sense of selfhood. When next he stood before a large assembly he told the following story. "A great violinist stood before a large audience to give his final concert. After the welcoming applause, the audience waited in hushed anticipation. Just as he raised his bow to play a string broke. What should he do? Leave in defeat? No!

How do you feel when you compare yourself with others? Were you often compared with someone as a child?

Perhaps you have noticed that leaders in the church often hold others up as an example for you. Is this helpful to you? Why or why not? How does this make you feel?

When criticized, some people criticize back, some quit, some give up and conform. If a person receives too much criticism, he may become unworthy in his own feelings.

Others, when criticized, try to make an honest evaluation of their own actions. If they see mistakes, they try to learn from them, without feeling guilty. What is your most common reaction to criticism?

Immediately he improvised the music and played through on three strings."

Then he said, "A string in my life has broken. What shall I do? Quit? Give up in defeat? Never! I'll play through on three strings." He finished his life on earth with victory.

LEARNING FROM MISTAKES

Maturing persons come to accept their participation in the human condition with all its shortcomings, with all its discrepancies from the perfect image. They know they will make blunders and mistakes, and sometimes they may be guilty of actual wrongdoing. Surely all aware persons will feel the guilt of being a part and participant in a world of war and inhumanity.

But there is need for a clear distinction between errors in judgment and moral wrongdoing. In some people, conscience is a *biting conscience,* developed by experiences of condemnation and driven by the slogan "what will others think?" Such people live with an uneasy sense of guilt. If their efforts do not bring success, they beat themselves over the head with, "What is wrong with *me* that things turn out this way?"

Some psychologists today hold that there is room for guilt if the person is knowingly a moral wrongdoer. They say that there are times when individuals ought to feel guilty, and if they do not, perhaps we should help them to feel so! Moral wrongdoing and failure to do what one knows he ought require repentance and forgiveness. Mistakes, however, should not produce guilt; rather they should be used as an opportunity for learning, then forgotten.

Many teachers and parents feel guilty if their children do not choose the Christian life. They can never forgive themselves, and yet they do not know wherein they have erred. Such a nagging feeling of failure and guilt can eat away at one's sense of being until he feels weak and worthless.

The nature of God's plan for man is that each is created a choosing, deciding person. Parents and teachers create conditions to make the Christian choice inviting. They make every effort to communicate the gospel and to witness to their own choice and experience. But eventually each person chooses his own style of life and takes final responsibility for his choice. The leader will suffer greatly if he feels wrong choices are being made. He will pray and be sick with apprehension, but he cannot make the choice for another. He will be ready to forgive and restore fellowship, but he need not feel that he is guilty or that he has failed.

Thus, the teacher who can acknowledge his own mistakes and his humanity can stand beside his student before God. He can speak with humility, and he can witness to the forgiveness and freedom that have come to him. He is freed from the necessity of knowing everything. He can now join with others in the desire to grow and in the search for truth.

> How does one handle his feelings toward the one who has criticized him? Is it possible to see the situation through the eyes of the critic?

> As a teacher, should you feel guilty if all of your students do not become Christians? How do you find a balance between "caring" and "burden bearing," and feeling harried and anxious about the seemingly wrong choices of those you love.

> What is the meaning of the saying, "A man cannot die on every cross, nor is he expected to."[1]

---

[1] Thomas Kelly, "A Testament of Devotion" (New York: Harper and Brothers, 1941).

THE POWER OF RECOVERY

The human self is not easily destroyed, for the God-given power of recovery is strong and persistent. This survival power of the personal should bring great comfort when one is bruised by the criticisms, the failures, and the mistakes of life.

One day I met a charming, capable, and victorious woman. After we had been team teachers for a week in a Christian education workshop I asked her the source of her unusual strength. She told me this story of the crisis experience in her life.

"At fifty I found myself lonely and lost. My husband and I had been pastors of a large and effective congregation. We worked together closely, and I had charge of the Christian education program in the church. It was an exciting life filled with responsibility and involvement. Then suddenly he had a heart attack and died. The grief and aloneness seemed more than I could bear. The congregation was kind but of course soon began seeking another pastor. I moved from the beautiful, well-furnished parsonage to a small, inexpensive apartment. The new pastor had a strong outreach program but did not seem greatly interested in Christian education. The people said that they would no longer expect me to serve in Christian education, 'as they understood my grief.' So at the next election I was not nominated. At first, one of my married daughters would come to see me every day, but gradually they became too busy with their work and their families. I felt that my life was over. It had no meaning whatsoever.

"One day my oldest daughter dropped by for a cup of tea. Then the bomb fell! 'Mother,' she said, 'you always told us what a happy childhood and youth you had, and how much you enjoyed college. At twenty-five you married father, and you had twenty-five happy and useful years together. Now you probably have twenty-five more years to live. They could be the richest, most productive years of your life. You always deplored the incapable teaching in the children's department of the church school. With your abilities and experience, you could do much to improve this situation. You are free to move where you could serve best. Your life could be great—or *you could cry the rest of your life.*'

"When my daughter left, I cried for three days. I couldn't eat or sleep. At first I couldn't understand my own daughter saying that to me. But then I began to be reborn. I knew what she said was true. I volunteered to work with preschool children in the church. I enrolled in graduate school and finished my master's in Christian education. The State Council of Christian Education has now employed me to go wherever the need is greatest to help develop workers. There isn't much salary in it and I have my down moments, but I am alive again! I have found my place to serve and life has purpose and meaning."

How can we help people when their personhood is beaten to a pulp? Is the shock treatment used by this daughter usually wise? Read Galatians 6:2-4, Romans 15:1.

Being human, it is often hard to keep the real issues and values of life in the center. When the bumps of life come, the person is hard put to make the valiant choice. Some do escape into "crying the rest of their lives." Some place the blame on others or the circumstances and never rightly pick up responsibility. Others continue to carry a heavy load of guilt and anxiety. But some accept the fact that life has its hard knocks and that human beings fail and make mistakes. These determine, with God's help, to take into themselves suffering and pain and to use them for growth and power.

Surely no one could be treated more harshly than Paul had been, but his recovery song is, "For I am certain that nothing can separate us from his love: neither death nor life; neither angels nor other heavenly rulers or powers; neither the present nor the future; neither the world above nor the world below—there is nothing in all creation that will ever be able to separate us from the love of God which is ours through Christ Jesus our Lord" (Romans 8:38-39, TEV).

What is the source of the power to recover from feelings of failure and defeat? Is it possible for a person always to be on top of his "humanness"? What does it mean to be "teachers in process of becoming"?

~~~~~~

Life comes from life—the teacher is the living agent in the teaching-learning relationship.

"I have come in order that they might have life, life in all its fulness."

—John 10:10, TEV

What has hit you lately and moved you deeply? How long has it been since you cried bitterly because of some one else's suffering? When did you last become deeply enthusiastic about a cause or an adventure? In other words how much "aliveness" is there about you? How much "life" in all its fullness is a part of you?

There seems to be a striking correlation between effectiveness in teaching and *esprit de corps* in the teacher and in the group. The teacher needs to feel that life is interesting and worth while. The greatly beloved teacher, William Lyon Phelps expressed this attitude when he said, "Religion adds an enormous zest to daily life; it makes everything interesting and significant. It keeps alive the capacity of wonder. I, myself, am interested in everything in the world, from a sandlot ballgame to the nebula in Orion. But the mainspring of my existence, the foundation of my happy and exciting life is Christian faith."[1]

---
[1] From the book *Marriage* by William Lyon Phelps. Copyright 1940 by William Lyon Phelps. Renewal © 1968 by Dryden L. Phelps. Published by E. P. Dutton & Co., Inc. and reprinted with their permission.

CHAPTER 4

The Source of "Aliveness"

The Source of "Aliveness" / 31

What makes you feel deeply about the joys and sufferings of others? How is this a desirable mark for a mature Christian? Argue with yourself the dangers and advantages.

June Hart was a college girl from an affluent family. She had been given every privilege to make her life smooth and pleasant. Her family had a summer home at the beach with a boat, a tennis court, and everything that one could want. But June had grown weary of spending her summers in such uselessness. After her junior year in college she decided to invest her summer in the lives of junior high girls from the inner city. They were girls who had few privileges or opportunities. She got names through the social welfare worker and invited the girls, five at a time, to spend a week with her at the beach. It was to be a cooperative venture, with all sharing in the work and in the planning. There were rugged experiences, and often she had to do far more than her share of the housekeeping, especially during the early experience with each group. During the summer she came to a close, friendly relationship with forty girls, and the relationship still continued in many ways after she went back to college. When a reporter asked her about the experience she said, "Life sure can be fascinating when you jump right in."

It's something of this "jumping into life," this getting involved and growing in the meaning of it all that gives "aliveness" to the leader.

Make a list of your chief interests. Is it necessary that a teacher be an interesting person? How might you become more interesting to others?

The experience can sometimes be very devastating, and yet the person feels he is participating in life instead of standing on the side watching the parade of life go by him. Frankl, in his victory story, "From Death Camp to Existentialism," tells us that the inmates who could find meaning in their suffering and who had a purpose for living survived incredible stress.[2]

WHAT IS "ALIVENESS"?

"Aliveness" is related to the goals and purposes of a man's life—the meaning of his existence. It is not that external gaiety, which some people seem to be able to conjure up, nor is it the happiness, all-is-well syndrome. Rather, it is that high-level integrity which characterizes the person who seems to be making the most of his

---

[2] Viktor Frankl, *From Death Camp to Existentialism* (Boston: The Beacon Press, 1959).

Guidance for Session 4
THE SOURCE OF ALIVENESS

Aims for the Session

To examine our attitudes toward life, our motives for teaching, and to adopt the highest motives. To find God's unique call to the teacher. To open ourselves to be used of God, in order that we may be empowered by the Holy Spirit in our teaching.

Clusters of Learning Experiences

I. Ask each person in the class to write three synonyms for the word *aliveness* as it is used in the first part of the chapter.

II. Substitute the words listed for "life" in the scripture John 10:10. Do they enrich the meaning of the scripture? Do they change the meaning?

III. Have two or three persons describe a teacher who has "aliveness" as used here.

IV. Do an exercise with "aliveness" after the pattern of "Happiness is a warm puppy." For example: Aliveness is to reach the top of a mountain and see the other side after a difficult climb. Aliveness is the first pang of hunger after a long, threatening illness.

Now make it; be as creative and "alive" as you can. Share your sentence.

V. Give the following test on motivation. You may wish to make and pass out copies. There are no wrong or right answers, but such an exercise can be valuable for discussion.

32 / Basics for Communication in the Church

potential in a given situation. "Aliveness" means life sensitivity or "spirit."

1. "Spirit" involves motivation to progress toward a higher level of functioning. The person of spirit is motivated from within to expand his relationships with more persons and at a deeper level. He has emotional abundance. That is, he is secure enough within himself that he can afford to care deeply for others.

What exciting new service adventure have you experienced recently, or are you planning?

2. "Spirit" means an attitude of eager anticipation toward the future moment. The person of spirit dares to risk. He is open-ended and ever expanding into new and wider experiences. Although he cannot know the outcome of his efforts with others, he is strong enough to trust himself and others, that together they can make something meaningful out of any honest involvement.

3. "Spirit involves the ability to disclose oneself when with others. The person of spirit is real. He does not need to pretend that he knows more than he does. He does not play a role of self-righteousness. Since his goals and purposes are upward, he can afford to be just what he is. Such is the life which fosters life in the teaching-learning relationship.

How many new friendships have you formed during the last year? Consider whether you are able to share deep feelings with others. How do you listen to others and really "hear" how they feel?

WHY DO THEY DO IT?

Really to teach another person is one of the hardest things one can do. Yet thousands of Christians spend unnumbered hours in volunteer leadership through the church. Their work is largely unknown and often unappreciated. Sometimes they feel unprepared, frustrated, and discouraged. Yet they continue. Why do they do it?

Not all motives for such service are the highest. The honest leader will constantly analyze his motives in order that his relationship may strengthen another, rather than make his dependent. His task is twofold: to develop the student's integrity at the same time that he maintains his own. He cannot satisfy his own needs at the expense of the student's personhood, but neither can he allow the students to take away his freedom, or to use him for their wishes. What then are some of these lesser or, perhaps, even harmful motives for becoming a teacher?

Check yourself as to situations in which you are tempted to give a false image of yourself. Why is anyone tempted to do this?

Classify the following reasons for teaching as poor, fair, good, excellent.
A. The Bible demands service of a Christian. _____
B. A Christian must carry his part of the load. _____
C. Nobody else will teach this class. _____
D. I enjoy teaching the class. _____
E. It is an opportunity to share what God has done for me. _____
F. The class gives meaning to my life. _____
G. It provides a meaningful relationship with others. _____
H. It provides an avenue for sharing God's love. _____
I. Through teaching, I believe I can help others to find God and the meaning of life. _____
J. If I am faithful, I will be rewarded. _____

VI. Have members of the class share their feelings about teaching. Here, if it seems appropriate, you might have prayer, each sharing the joys and needs as expressed by others.
VII. Read together Ephesians 4:11-12. What is its meaning in relationship to this study?
VIII. Have a member of the class read chapters 7 and 8 of **Christy** and share in more detail with the class.
IX. Read Philippians 2:13. Discuss how God is working to make each teacher willing and able.

SERVING FROM A SENSE OF DUTY

Mrs. Marvin does not feel that she is a very good teacher. She does not understand youth and has had no preparation for working with them. She says that she works hard on her class preparation, for she knows the teaching of youth is important, but she dreads every session. The youth respect her well enough. But she does not find teaching them a satisfaction, and she feels certain the young people do not really enjoy her teaching. She has tried to resign, for she prefers working in the music program, but the superintendent says that it is her duty to work where she is needed most. He promises her that if she continues, it will become easier. She has asked for a replacement, but Sunday after Sunday goes by with no one to teach—so she has to keep on.

Serving from a sense of duty cuts the heart out of the self. Of course, there will be days when *duty* keeps one there, but duty is no proper motive over the long haul.

Mrs. Marvin's experience speaks to enlistment policies of the church. Every Christian should come to a growing stewardship attitude in life. He will feel deeply that he wants his life to be invested at its highest level for God and for others. He will assess his own abilities and limitations and working with other leaders, he will find the class to teach, or the place to serve where he feels he belongs.

One pastor had private conferences with every person in the congregation. After some honest discussion about the future of the church, he asked each one where he felt he could serve best. Many felt they were already serving at the right place. Some did not know of opportunities for service and for preparation. Several mentioned areas of service, which had not been opened. After prayerful consideration, and deep sincerity, persons made decisions as to their call. Some took several months to decide but most persons came through in a responsible way. Such persons serve with "spirit," for they serve from an inner call rather than from a sense of duty.

SERVING TO SATISFY ONE'S OWN NEEDS

There is a commonly accepted proverb in our society that if you are discouraged or lonely, the best way to overcome this is to go out and help someone who needs you. But some question whether helping others in order to meet your own need is justifiable. "But," you ask, "is there no pleasure in helping another?" Yes, there is! Really to enable another to find meaning in life is tremendous. But this satisfaction needs to come as a result of your helping, rather than being the reason for wanting to help.

THE NEED TO BE NEEDED

Every human being has the need to feel needed. Some who do

Sidebar notes:

Do you sometimes see others playing a false role in your presence? Identify something in yourself that might evoke this.

Do the students in your class sometimes give "expected" answers or act unreal? Why? How might you help them to be more themselves?

Consider: What are my real motives for teaching? Are my motives such as to strengthen the self-respect of the members?

not seem to be able to satisfy this need in the normal social experiences of life use their class to fulfill this need.

Mrs. Norman was a widow whose only child had been killed in a bicycle accident. After some time of grieving, she was asked to teach the junior high Sunday school class. She accepted the class as if every boy in the class were her own son. She asked the members to stop by after school. She always had popcorn, freshly baked cookies, or some other goodies. She never let the girls help her clean up, nor asked the boys to do her yard work. She was afraid they might not like it and would quit coming. When "her boys" got into trouble, or disobeyed their parents, or broke school rules, she always took their side no matter how wrong they were. She even planned evening activities on school nights, which broke some families' regulations about going out on school nights.

When the class moved on to senior high level, they refused to go unless Mrs. Norman could be their teacher. Most people, hearing this, said, "What a wonderful teacher Mrs. Norman must be. She puts her class above her own self." Others wondered why the members had become so dependent and were unwilling to progress on to the senior high level without her. The truth is that she had used them to satisfy her need to be needed, and the experience had weakened them into persons who were satisfied to take her food and favor and had not learned to take responsibility for themselves and their growth.

THE NEED TO MANAGE OTHERS

Nobody likes the words "control" or "manipulate"; yet some people seem to need to manage others. They feel that they know just how each life should be run, and in devious ways, some subtle and unrecognized, they make the other person's decisions for him.

The Christian leader is in a very strategic place, if he has this need to control others. In the very way he defines the Christian life and in his use of the Bible, he can control persons by creating a sense of guilt in them if they do not follow the path he sets out. Someone has called this "beating persons over the head with the Bible."

THE NEED TO FEEL SUPERIOR

Another poor motive for teaching is to build up one's own self-esteem. Some persons have such a low opinion of themselves that they have great needs to enhance themselves in their own eyes. They will accept a position of leadership, not out of a sense of stewardship, or even because they feel that they have a contribution to make. Sometimes they are joiners and "yes" people because any title or place of leadership helps meet their need to feel superior to others. The danger is that in order to satisfy this need they may feel highly threatened if anyone disagrees with them.

Consider: Do I allow the students to take advantage of me? If so, why? Under what conditions would I quit teaching?

What does a growing stewardship attitude toward life mean in your situation? Better preparation? Trying new methods? Sharing more deeply with each member of the class? Finding means of personal relationships? What _____?

Under what conditions is it right to find tremendous joy and satisfaction in your work with others?

Can you think of times when you may have used your teaching position to manipulate others? How do you distinguish between teaching, witnessing, and manipulating? What are the effects of manipulation on persons?

They become sensitive about their position and hold all the strings so that others may not take even their rightful responsibility. The more they are fearful of loss of control, the more tightly they hold to their authority. Then finally, the whole situation fails, and with the new feeling of loss, they have even greater need to feel superior.

THE NEED FOR REWARD

Even if the "stars in our crown" idea has lost some of its appeal, most persons apparently need some kind of reward, to keep them teaching away, Sunday after Sunday. In Chapter 2, this has been called "confirmation of others." The person of integrity needs to feel that others appreciate him and believe in him. He has a need for expressions of thanks and appreciation for his efforts. There is a relationship between the quality of a person's leadership and his sense of feeling appreciated. Yet, praise, special recognition, and rewards are poor substitutes for love and the stewardship of sharing.

TEACHING IS A RELATIONSHIP

What are justifiable rewards for teaching?

Such twisted motives for teaching as those just mentioned cut the heart out of effective teaching, for they set up the wrong relationship between the teacher and the learner. One cannot really help another if he is thinking primarily of satisfying his own needs. To put it bluntly, he is using the class for what he can get out of them. This sets up a wrong relationship between the teacher and the pupils and opens a gap across which there cannot be real communication.

Give some examples of I-it relationships. Show how they might become I-thou relationships. Do you believe teacher and pupil may be "I-thou" to each other?

The well-known theologian, Martin Buber,[3] held that all life is a meeting, but that there are two distinct kinds of relationships. There is an I-thou relationship and there is an I-it relationship. When a teacher treats each member of the class as a thou, he accepts him as a unique person worthy of respect, and he is not to be used to satisfy the needs of the teacher. When persons are used as *things* to satisfy the teacher an I-it relationship is formed. Then the relationship becomes strictly a one-way affair, and little learning can take place. Every teacher owes himself and each member of the class, a meeting—that each be known to the other as a person.

THE SOURCE OF POWER

PARTNERS WITH GOD

Read again the story in Chapter 1 of the leader who became a channel for the Holy Spirit. How do you think a teacher would become a channel for the Holy Spirit to reach members of the class?

To feel oneself a partner with God in helping another person to become his potential, is a powerful motive for serving. The scripture "We love, because he first loved us" (1 John 4:19) is a sound foundation for our motive for teaching. Jesus came to earth to make real God's love for man. That person who experiences the

---

[3] Martin Buber, *I and Thou,* trans. Ronald G. Smith (New York: Charles Scribner's Sons, 1958).

love of God in forgiveness, reconciliation, and power cannot do otherwise than want to find a way to lead others to the same experience. The real reason for teaching is in response to God's love. Because he has loved us, we feel within ourselves a burning desire to let others know of his love. Therefore, we teach.

Jeremiah expressed this deep feeling, even when he had been put in stocks for his prophecy. Still he said, "If I say, 'I will not mention him, or speak anymore in his name,' there is in my heart as it were, a burning fire shut up in my bones, and I am weary with holding it in, and I cannot" (Jer. 20:9).

It must have been something of this "fire shut up in their bones" that sent those early evangels of the American Sunday School Union out to face the unknown elements of a pioneer West. They pledged to plant a Sunday school in every town or hamlet where a wagon train settled. They met danger, disease, and sometimes death, but they still pursued the goal.

It is something of this fire that caused June Hart and thousands of other youth to enlist in work camps, summer work in the inner city, serving abroad and a host of other ministries of love. It must also be the fire that causes thousands of volunteer teachers to serve year after year, giving unstintingly of their best that others may come to know the Christ, who has meant so much to them.

PARTICIPATING IN OTHERS' NEEDS

To feel within yourself that you can help another to find the fulfillment to his deepest need is high motivation. Certainly, you cannot do this of yourself, but God, through you, may make himself known, and the students may respond in faith and love and become new persons in Christ.

Teaching, on this level, is no mere passing on of the Christian tradition. It is not only knowing the stories and facts of the Bible, as important as they may be. Rather, teaching is, through involvement and encounter, bringing the learner to the place where he hears God speak to him and knows he is dealing with the true and living God. When the teacher realizes he is dealing with eternal decisions, he will become motivated to teach at his best and to live life at its deepest. Teaching, on this level, becomes a joint effort. The teacher comes to see the needs from the learner's viewpoint, and they struggle together to find the answer to both their needs.

POWER THROUGH THE HOLY SPIRIT

Even though the motive is high and you feel the "fire in your bones," still you know you cannot really teach alone. The promises of God are that he will give power and make you able to accomplish the goal. "God is always at work in you to make you willing and able to obey his own purpose" (Phil. 2:13, TEV).

Read the Jeremiah story as told in the twentieth chapter. In what sense do Christians today feel this burning desire to tell others of the love of God?

How may one teach in such a way as to cause the pupil to hear God speak to him and to know he must make a decision?

Study scriptures which tell of the power of the Holy Spirit: Acts 1:8; Romans 8:16; 1 John 4:13; John 14:26; John 16:13; John 6:63.

There is great need for the teacher to examine his willingness for God to work through him. The human element of pride is an effective gate that closes out the Holy Spirit.

The story *Christy* by Catherine Marshall is an example of how pride locks the gate and how surrender opens it. Christy had gone out into the Appalachian Mountains to teach. There she found unbelievable misery, ignorance, and deprivation. In the cultural shock of it all, she questioned her ability and even doubted God's justice. She was about ready to give up and go home in defeat.

Miss Alice, the wise and strong Quaker missionary, challenged her:[4] "You see, Christy, evil is real—and powerful. And God is against evil all the way. So each of us has to decide where *we* stand, how we're going to live *our* lives. We can try to persuade ourselves that evil doesn't exist; live for ourselves and wink at evil. We can say it isn't so bad after all. . . . We can compromise with it, keep quiet about it and say it's none of our business. Or we can work on God's side, listen for His orders on strategy against the evil, no matter how horrible it is, and know that He can transform it." Then she left her with the question, "Who are you, Christy? . . . Were you supposed to come here, Christy? Or were you just running away from home?"

After a night of decision, Christy came to realize that she was supposed to come there. As she put her head on the cold wood of the windowsill, she prayed, "Dear God . . . when I came here, maybe I was partly running off from home for fun and freedom and adventure. But I have a notion that You had something else in mind in letting me come. Anyway if You can use me here in this cove, well, here I am."

The first condition for this power is the clear decision to live life as you feel uniquely called to live it. This is a call from God felt deep down within your being. It is a "burning fire in the heart" which cannot be shut in.

The next condition is a humble surrender to God, acknowledging possible wrong motives and weakness but opening yourself to be used of God. "Anyway, if you can use me here in this class (or town, or job, or whatever) well, here I am." The other condition is "to work like mad." Christy approached her schoolroom with new eagerness. She helped the children individually. She began studying her Bible and praying with real faith. She sat up half the night writing letters about the needs of her pupils. Now that she was willing, she found God working in her to make her able. Empowered by the Holy Spirit, she had power and "aliveness."

---

[4]From *Christy* by Catherine Marshall. Copyright, 1967. Used with permission of McGraw-Hill Book Company, pp. 95-98.

Sidebar notes:

Is it imperative that every Christian come to as definite a commitment as Christy made? Is it a "once for all experience" or must it be made over and over?

Do you agree with the three conditions listed for receiving the power to teach effectively?

Meditate on Acts 19:2.

CHAPTER 5

Explorations in Creativity

*Gratitude to God
Who created my spirit
Moves deep within me.*

*I begin to see
Every human being,
Is struggling to be.*

*How could I lock hands
With the eternal spirit
To set Spirits free?*

Haiku
by Robert McFarling

"If the Son makes you free, then you will be really free."
—John 8:36, TEV

CHOOSE SOMETHING LIKE A COMET

Every person born into the world represents something new that has never been before. He had his own uniqueness and his own purpose to fulfill. Every person was once creative and spontaneous and in his deepest roots still is. The teacher, more than others, has the opportunity and the necessity of fostering this creative potential in himself. Robert Frost entitled his poem, "Choose Something Like a Star," and he says, "To stay our minds on and be staid."[1] Most teachers would do better to choose something like a comet, a sudden moving flash, that would unsettle their staidness and give them a glimpse of their own creative potential.

CREATIVE LIVING IS FOR ALL

Choosing to grow; that is the essence of what in this chapter is called "creative living." To be human is to be creative. To the extent one has allowed his creative potential to wither, to that extent he has smothered his humanity. What then are essentials to the creative fire that is necessary to meaningful living?

---

[1] *Robert Frost's Poems,* Pocket Book Edition, (New York: Henry Holt, 1946), p. 262.

Welcome, O Life! I go for the hundredth time to meet the reality of this day, and to forge in the smithey of my soul the creative answer to the day's challenge.

Guidance for Session 5
EXPLORATIONS IN CREATIVITY

Aims for the Session
To understand creativity and to realize our own creative potential. To express creativity in attitudes toward life, in choices, and in relationships. To become more imaginative in teaching so as to evoke creativity in others.

Clusters of Learning Experiences
I. You might provide some experiences in creative imagination.
  A. Put nine dots on the board. See if any member of the class can touch all nine dots with four straight connected lines.

. . .

. . .

. . .

(Answer at end of Chapter 6. Neither teacher nor members are to see the answer before the class experiment.)

Explorations in Creativity / 39

"Where wast thou . . . when the morning stars sang together, and all the sons of God shouted for joy?
—Job 38:7

"Sing unto the Lord a new song, and his praise from the end of the earth!"—Isaiah 42:10

One of the first steps to the development of creativity is to swing the mind open to the charm, the challenge, the mystery of this wonderful world and to the interesting people in it.

For the creative person glimpses from everyday life open new pathways to understanding and relatedness.

THE CREATIVE ATTITUDE

To be creative means to consider the whole process of life as dynamic, moving, and changing. One does not take any stage of life as final, but rather as a step moving him forward to an even more meaningful time. The creative attitude is well expressed by those charming older adults who seem to feel that every stage of life had its values, but whichever one they are presently in is the best. They expect the future will be even better.

The creative attitude is to live keenly *aware* of persons with all their needs and potentialities. It is the ability to *see* new opportunities in a sometimes routine situation. It is a *leap* of the imagination that turns the combination of old forms into something entirely different and new.

The assumption is that all of us were once spontaneous and creative, having been made in the image of the Great Creator, who breathed into man the breath of life and he became a living soul. When man is creative, he is exercising that godlike quality within him.

It is well to think clearly about the meaning of the word *creative*. In some sense, the word has been used too freely, since only God can create the absolutely new from nothing. Some might prefer another word such as *questing* to describe the attitude. Yet, there is a realistic ring to the newness which comes to the situation when combinations of older elements seem to produce something entirely different. Or even more truly when the raw ideas are sorted and arranged in such a way as to bring an unexpected flash of insight. This is the context in which the word *creative* is being used in this chapter.

The creative attitude may express itself in the usual forms of writing poetry, composing music, or producing artistic objects. But it may be even more effectively expressed in daily activities. In this sense, there can be creative parents and creative teachers. Whatever one does can be done with certain spirit which arises out of the uniqueness of the person performing the deed.

THE CREATIVE POTENTIAL

Although man is endowed with creative potential, he can be encouraged in or inhibited from reaching his highest. Perhaps the

---

B. Make an ink blot on a piece of paper and have the class describe what they see. There is no right answer, of course, but the exercise can stretch the imagination.

C. You could have the class look at a drawing and tell what it communicates to them.

II. How do the scriptures used in the margin relate to a study of creativity? Read John 8:36; Isaiah 42:10; Job 38:7.

III. Divide the class into units of six and have part of the group work out a clear definition of creativity. The others can make a list of adjectives that describe the creative attitude. Share and discuss the ideas.

IV. Ask members of the class to share times when they feel that they were most creative. What were the conditions that evoked this creativity?

V. Write on the board the four marks which Dr. Mooney found common among persons judged as creative. See if the class understands and agrees with these marks.

VI. Have someone describe a creative person and ask the class to

first essential for creativity is that a person have an acceptance of himself and of others as creative. The one who cannot believe himself to be creative, rarely could be unless he has a narrow concept of the idea. Something of the wholesome self-acceptance discussed formerly (chapters 2 and 3) seems to be a basic requisite for the quality known as creativity.

It had been one of those mornings! The family had slept later than usual. In trying to help, Grant had spilled the milk all over the table. Mother had impatiently cleaned it up, and father had scolded him for his awkardness. Finally, when all three were holding hands around the table, father called on Grant to give thanks. He paused as if to try to find something or somebody for which to be thankful. Then he blurted out, "Dear God, thank you for myself." It is something of this self-appreciation that is an absolute necessity for creativity. He may be clumsy; people may be impatient with him and scold him, but he can still stand up and be thankful for who he is.

It seems to be true that all the qualities which characterize creative people occur to varying degrees in everyone. Yet, it is a fact that most people do not develop their creative potential to anything near their fullest. In order to develop creative ability, one must nourish a certain attitude of questing discontent in which improvement of conditions is always sought.

COMMON MARKS OF CREATIVE PERSONS

Ross L. Mooney[2] holds that man of necessity must ever be on a quest for positive values. Searching in every place, he endeavors to realize the good life as he understands it. Then he seeks to make things into what, to him, is beautiful, just, or good.

He compares man in this respect with all living things. The plant sends roots out into the soil and leaves into the air and draws into itself that which the plant can transform into a new and different form and substance. So, man reaches out into his environment and draws into himself that which he can change into something different but of value to man. By such taking in and giving out, living things are able to fulfill their purpose.

[2]Ross L. Mooney, *The Self*, ed. Clark Moustakas, Harper and Brothers, (New York: 1956) p. 262 ff.

"To the attentive eye, each moment of the year has its own beauty, and in the same field it beholds, every hour, a picture which was never seen before, and which shall never be seen again."—Emerson

Creativity requires willingness to risk, even to fail. It takes hard thinking and disciplined effort. Few are willing to pay the price.

Healthy, self-actualized, fully human personality and creativity may turn out to be the same. One cannot exist without the other.

Creative people can confidently face the future not knowing what is going to come. They can improvise in a situation which never existed before. The creative person is not a defeatist, for he finds ways of salvaging some learning value out of his relatively unsuccessful experiences.

---

judge whether Dr. Mooney's findings apply to him.

VII. Consider creative potantial. How does the class feel about every person being creative? Is creative living a part of being a Christian? Is it necessary for teaching?

VIII. List some blockades to creativity.

IX. If past experiences have caused the creative spirit to wither, how may the person begin to activate this spirit?

X. Discuss the process given by which a creative experience in teaching is born. Is it desirable for all teaching to be creative? Is it possible?

XI. Have someone read the description "A Teacher Experiments Creatively." Let the class react freely to this experience of a junior class.

XII. For a closing worship, class members might select and read a favorite quote from the marginal notes, with moments between for meditation and silent prayer.

NOTE: Certainly there are too many possibilities in this lesson for one session. Could the ideas spill over

Each person is born with creative potential. He learns to be uncreative by following directions, copying patterns, and waiting to be told what to do.

A great hindrance to creativity is to believe that one is not creative. How is it that one's belief about his own abilities, to a large extent, sets the boundaries of individual accomplishment?

An experience is creative and has reality and meaning only if it comes from within the individual.

This truth expresses the dynamic of creativity. There must be the reaching out for raw data and new experiences. Life is wide, but many people stay boxed in by fear and tradition. They never allow themselves to reach out and really explore alien ideas. They are asleep to large regions of their own potential.

There must also be a period of incubation. Time is necessary for thinking; for letting data or experiences fall into hierarchical order. Man has to do something with his experiences. He has to come to grips with value and insight. Such takes thought with relative freedom. The compulsively busy man can seldom be creative. Recently, I was recounting some of my activities when a high school fellow, with the insight and honesty of the young, said, "Some teachers are too busy to be human. My teacher says she's decided to be a human being first; then she'll be a teacher."

If, however, the person has reasonable self-acceptance, if he appreciates the abilities of others and is willing to risk possible failure in innovation, he can improve his creative performance.

In a search for what is common among creative persons, Dr. Mooney did not find commonality in personality pattern, in media used, or in the environment.

Rather, he found commonness in the way persons relate themselves to possible experiences. He points out four relationships which he believes are significant in creative productiveness.

1. THE OUTREACH OF EXPERIENCING

The creative person is open and consciously includes new and varied types of experiences. He gets out where the action is! He has a spirit of adventure and becoming about him. He is curious and willing to experiment, whether it be with planting a new kind of seed, concocting a new combination of foods, trying a new method, or traveling to an unheard of island. He is hospitable to new ideas and a fresh perspective. He is reaching out toward everything and everybody.

2. THE FOCUS OF EXPERIENCING

But the creative person does not try the new just for the excitement of it. He endeavors to put things in order by relating the new to the already tried. He does not care to be different in the insignificant, but he is willing to be different in that which really matters. He is courageous enough to live by his deeper convictions, even when his actions run counter to common expectations and when

into departmental meetings, observation, and laboratory experiences?
1. Possibly the teachers could take the next unit of lessons for their particular classes and let their imaginations fly as to how it might be taught in an exciting way. Perhaps this could be done in department meetings during the week.
2. Members of the class could go to observe some of the more innovative teachers in the church or in the city.
3. A laboratory situation could be set up where some of the more daring spirits actually teach, while others observe and evaluate.
4. Some members of the class may wish to try writing haiku, do woodwork or painting. The church might want to have a creativity table, a display board, or even an exhibit.

they may bring criticism, loss of place, maybe loss of job or even of life. He is making a persistent inquiry into the purpose and meaning of his own life. He has a deep feeling of identification with all human beings and finds that he can learn something from anyone.

3. THE DISCIPLINE OF EXPERIENCE

To the observer, the creative performance may appear spontaneous and easy, but not so to the producer. Writers, artists, explorers, and scientists, all testify to long hours spent in routine mastering of materials and tools. Madame Curie spent years over bubbling pots and test tubes before she discovered radium. Edison seldom got a full night's sleep. Charles Shulz, the creative inventor of "Peanuts," requires himself to stay at his drawing board until the idea comes and is communicated. Such discipline includes a willingness to stay with a baffling problem over an extended period of time and a capacity to be so consumed by his work that schedules may be forgotten.

4. THE EXPRESSION IN SOME AESTHETIC FORM

As the plant turns that which it has taken in into something different and useful, so the person seeks to express his creativity in harmony of form and order. He endeavors to show how things hang together, and what their relationships may be. The study found that the medium used was not significant. People can be creative whether the form is painting, writing, architecture, teaching, administration, scientific research, valuing, or social reform. However, the creative person derives meaning from his discovery or insight to the extent that he finds satisfying structural forms to catch up and express what has become meaningful to him.

Creativity can blossom best in an atmosphere which encourages sensitive, rich, and flexible relationships.

BLOCKADES TO CREATIVITY

On the other side, there are certain attitudes which hinder creativity. Perhaps the greatest of these is lack of trust in oneself. That person who says, "Why, I haven't a creative bone in me," needs to be awakened to his own potential. Another block is fear of the new. The person who would stimulate the creativity within him must be willing to try the untried. He will reject the temptation to freeze his behavior into repetitive patterns. He can become so absorbed in the present that it means more to him than either the past or the future.

Playing a role, doing the expected, drifting with convention, compromising for expediency's sake—these are effective hindrances to becoming creative. When a person's actions are determined by expectations, appearances, or the standards of others; when he is required to follow, to imitate, to conform, his creative potential is impaired and gradually withers and drops away.

Both children and adults become desensitized through being treated as an object to get things done. They become puppets when order, efficiency, skills, and content become more important than persons.

Catching glimpses of life and its deeper meanings opens new pathways of learning and relatedness. Creativity on its deeper levels demands freedom to choose; freedom to make decision and to take responsibility for one's actions. Such freedom within the context of moral and spiritual values inspires one to tremendous effort, especially if there is the deep feeling that here is something that desperately needs to be done, and I am the one to find the most effective, the most artistic, and the most creative way to do it.

THE TEACHER AND CREATIVITY

For creativity to be realized in any situation there must be an atmosphere in which persons can try novel ideas even though they fall flat. There must be a sense of tolerance that allows for experimentation, where the teacher can depart from traditional patterns without quickly having to retreat into conformity.

If the teacher hopes to encourage creativity in others, he should have a measure of venturesomeness himself. Now, just for example, suppose he feels that he has a meaningful idea which he wants to express in an artistic form. He might try sketching, painting, music, poetry, or some other art form. Suppose he chose poetry, then he could choose metric poetry, blank verse, prose poem or maybe haiku. (Haiku is a recently popular form of poetic expression, borrowed from the Japanese. It is a seventeen syllable verse, usually divided into three lines of five, seven and five. It often is a crisp picture of some nature subject with a subtle, hidden meaning. The reader feels the picture and brings his own experience to interpret the poem. The haiku given at the first of this chapter is the effort of a teacher to express the feeling within him in an artistic way.

There is a process out of which a creative experience in teaching is born. This process might be skeletoned as follows:

1. OPENNESS

The teacher will have an attitude of adventure, of getting out of the rut of trying some new way to help pupils experience what is being taught in the session. The teacher will survey many possibilities before a decision is made. Perhaps he will have the students give suggestions as to the approach to be used in dealing with a subject!

The best curriculum resources provide opportunity for creativity. The aim for the unit, the biblical resources, and a few seed ideas are provided. From there, teacher and class can go wherever their creativity leads them.

No real change is ever little; it is likely to be a big step for someone.

If man can feel within himself a sincere desire to be helpful, he has opened a floodgate of creative power.

2. REFLECTION

This will be a period of alternation between gathering data, serious thinking, and relaxation. The teacher will study biblical materials, the session aim and suggestions. He will think of meanings both for himself and for each member of the class. Then he may relax to come to the subject later. Some have called this the incubation period.

3. ILLUMINATION

The process of the birth of an idea—sometimes coming only after trial and error and sometimes as a sudden burst of insight.

4. FOCUS

The media for carrying out the idea are selected. A form must come out of the formless. For the teacher this is usually a session plan—or at least a point of departure and a supply of resources.

5. DISCIPLINE

Here is where the courage "to jump right in" is necessary. Teachers often have creative ideas when they are planning, but somehow they seem forced back into conformity when the class is present. Creativity requires willingness to risk, even to fail. Mostly there is a refreshing response if preparation has been adequate. But could failure be worse than the usual dull routine of some classes?

6. SHARING

Let the experience be a shared one. If the teacher freely gives his ideas and encourages others to share, the creative potential of the group may lead far beyond the original plans.

7. CLOSURE

There comes a time when the announcement is made, "It is finished." The judgment is to be made by the ones carrying out the experience. Closure must come whether the adventure is considered a high success or a colossal failure.

8. EVALUATION

The group summation of the whole experience is essential. Reasons for success and failures are to be explored. Honest sharing of insights and feelings will be inspiring. And after it is all over the teacher will lie awake and think—and arise a more creative person.

A TEACHER EXPERIMENTS CREATIVELY

1. OPENNESS

Both the teacher and the members of this junior class had an attitude of experimentation. During the past quarter, involving a study on Old Testament prophets, they had had a good experience by dividing into groups with each group being responsible to present one prophet to the class in a unique way. Now they were entering a study on stewardship. Frankly the teacher felt baffled on the "stewardship of money" part of the unit. These kids didn't know the meaning of money. They had far more "things" than were for their good.

2. REFLECTION

He pondered how he could help them understand the meaning of money in a Christian sense. He searched the teachings of Jesus about the Christian attitude toward money. He read again Michael Harrington's *The Other America*.[3] He learned that the welfare food budget in his city for each meal was eighteen to twenty-three cents per person. He talked to a welfare mother about her menu and how she feeds her family on the allowance.

3. ILLUMINATION

On the first Sunday of the unit he read to the class selected passages from the book *The Other America* and showed some poverty pictures. Then he had the class look up the sayings of Jesus about money. He told the story of Jesus and the Rich Young Ruler. He got the idea of having the class write a parable "The Rich Young Junior." It ended with the words "Go share what you have with the poor and come follow me." He told them about his talk with the welfare mother and put her menu on the board.

4. FOCUS

One member of the class said he thought he could live on that, and someone said, "Why don't we try it?" While he was gaining the cooperation of the parents, the teacher decided to try it with his family for five days. On the next Sunday he shared his experience and they studied the story of the Rich Young Ruler again and read their parable. He found that most of the parents were willing to cooperate for one or two days. Using the twenty-three cent budget they decided they would bring sixty-nine cents of the money saved to share with a needy family.

5. DISCIPLINE

He got in touch with each mother and explained the plan in detail. He encouraged them to let the junior help with the buying and planning. He asked for them to send a copy of the menu to the class.

6. SHARING

The experience was not perfect. Some mothers did everything, and the junior was hardly aware of any change in menu. Some forgot or failed to cooperate. But some seemed to begin to feel with the poor and to wonder how they could share. Then a thought

---

[3] Michael Harrington, *The Other America* (New York, Macmillan Co., 1962).

> Without caring deeply, we will always be mediocre human beings. Caring, whether for another person, a life of work, a field of knowledge, or a conviction is a hazardous experience.

struck the teacher. Let each person take sixty-nine cents, the allotment per person per day and buy all the food value he could with it. The children were excited about the idea. Now, they said, "What will we do with the food?" They asked their minister if there were needy people in the church. He suggested an elderly couple who, while not on welfare, were ill and also needed encouragement.

7. CLOSURE

Each child took his sixty-nine cents and accepted the challenge with enthusiasm. They studied food values, they looked for sales, and counted their pennies. On Sunday they brought their food and took it to the elderly couple. There they read the story of the Rich Young Ruler, and their own parable again. They sang their theme song, "They'll Know We Are Christians by Our Love," and the couple led in a prayer of thanksgiving.

8. EVALUATION

They met back at the church for sandwiches and to share their feelings. Their final question was "What are we going to do now?" In telling about the experience, the teacher said, "It's exciting to teach when you can teach that way, and I learned a lot too."[4]

---

[4] The basic ideas of this experience are true, though not every detail.

~~~~~~

The growing person will immerse himself in the richness of his own meaning, open to his own feelings and to the feelings of others.

"Live as free men; do not use your freedom however, to cover up any evil."

—1 Peter 2:16, TEV

The human personality is built around a system of values. If the personality is whole, there will be consistency between the professed values and the real values. However, with the experience of life, with constant change and outside persuaders it becomes difficult to maintain this consistency. The growing person seeks consciously to harmonize his ethical beliefs with deliberate acts in which his values are revealed.

The critical test of a person's values is whether they provide him with a rudder that guides him in decision making with regard to himself and his social and physical environment. Such values ought to be both personal and social. They are to be extensive in scope, dependable in action, and compatible with one another.

One's value system can be compared with an iceberg, where most of the ice is beneath the surface. That which is in sight is what he says and does when decisions relative to moral and ethical issues

---

Creativity is to be born again, born to new attitudes, new experiences, new potential. He who makes all things new is drawing upon us.

CHAPTER 6

Re-Creation of Values

Why is it necessary that a developing person must constantly re-examine his values?

are to be resolved. Even what he says and what he does may not be consistent. What he says is a value indicator—perhaps only a vestige of a former value or the beginning of a new one. What he does reveals his values.

The deepest level is the self-value. This is the reservoir of power. It is the value that shows how a person has decided to use his life. But between this value and the saying and doing are the constantly changing expectations of society. To keep the self-value and the expression of it consistent in the myriad of new issues in society today requires eternal vigilance.

Instead of keeping watch over values of the past, the maturing Christian accepts the difficult task of re-creating those values continuously in his own time.

THE MEANING OF VALUE

When we speak of "values," we mean the guidelines which give direction to our lives. The question is, "What is to be done with one's life and force? Which side are you on in matters that make a difference and why?" One speaker put it this way, "They say one person can't make much difference in this complex world. I never thought I could make a great difference, but I reserve the right to decide which side of the scales my stubborn ounces will be on." Such a matter is personal. Each person has to wrest his own values from the vast possibilities, but he will be weak as long as he is apathetic or uncertain.

Notice the theme of a call for decision running throughout the Old Testament, from Moses through Joshua and Amos. Jesus was insistent on choice and spoke of values when he said, "No one can be a slave to two masters: he will hate one and love the other; he will be loyal to one and despise the other. . . . You cannot serve both God and wealth as your master" (Matt. 6:24, TEV). It is evident in the sayings of Jesus that personal values may be either negative or positive. There are ample examples in society of persons who are highly motivated by negative values. Here, however, the discussion deals with Christian leaders, who seek a unique life-style, characterized by active concern for others. It is doubtful whether one can follow Christ effectively and be a member of the "silent majority" of Christians who don't stand up publicly for their convictions.

How may one determine what his values really are? Do one's values change as he matures?

What is the source of one's values?

Are values which have been considered high in the past necessarily high values today?

With the theme, "a call to decision," in mind, trace the idea through the Old and New Testaments. Note Exodus 32:26; Deuteronomy 30:19; Joshua 24:15; Ruth 1:15; 1 Kings 18:21; Mark 10:21; John 6:67; Hebrews 3:6, 15.

Can a Christian be silent about injustices which he sees in the social order? Can he be uninvolved? How does action relate to values?

Guidance for Session 6
RE-CREATION OF VALUES

Aims for the Session

To reexamine our values. To understand how we teach values. To introduce the value-clarifying method of teaching. To move through fact and concept levels in teaching to the values level.

Clusters of Learning Experiences

I. You could begin the session by reading again the story about Fred and Loren in chapter 1, with special emphasis on the covenant. Discuss the value of definite commitment to the right and good.

II. Have members share their life purpose, giving it in nontheological words. Maybe have them write it in one or two sentences.

III. Discuss the meaning of "value." How does value differ from interest?

IV. What is the source of one's values? How does one clarify and form values? What is the meaning of Matthew 6:24 in relation to values?

Use one or more value-clarifying

48 / Basics for Communication in the Church

THE NEED TO RE-CREATE VALUES

Why is it necessary for the effective Christian constantly to clarify and formulate his values? Surely he has chosen the high way and intends to live by those values which will result in the greatest good not only for himself but for all persons concerned and for society as a whole. Yet he finds that the keen edge of moral and ethical sensitivity may become dull.

1. That which is considered right may not have been freely chosen. Society, including the church, has constructed certain notions of right and wrong and expected that the adjusted person will conform. The conforming individual has formed a self-image that he is good, while the nonconformist often sees himself as evil. Good, thus created, does not become an intrinsic value, but one growing out of fear of the consequences. It is simply easier to go along with the expected.

Those who have worked in fields where Christianity is new testify to a definite "cooling off" in the second or third generations. Is it any less true for those who have grown up in the Christian community?

Think seriously about how your values have changed since you were twenty years old. Have they matured or become eroded by the ravages of time?

2. The gradual decay of ethical sensitivity. The ravages of time and the constant contact with differing values may wear away one's consciousness of moral injustice. Who cannot remember when to do the wrong thing brought sharp and swift judgment to mind and spirit? Then there followed a period when the soul seemed dull and numb. There was no marked or dramatic change—simply the wearing away of consciousness of wrong, until life lost its power and meaning. Unless some challenge causes one to clarify or formulate a value, he may not even realize his loss. In a recent televised interview, a well-known editor was asked what he considered America's greatest problem. Without hesitation he answered, "Boredom." He felt, he said, that many people have no clear vision of the purpose for their lives. They are tired and bored with trying to make up their minds about the many choices with which our changing world faces them. Thus they become drifters without either power or oars in the sea of life.

In adjusting the "ideal to the real," has life lost some of its zest and purpose? Are there areas where the keen edge of moral and ethical sensitivity may have become dull?

How do you distinguish between "educating the conscience" and "desensitizing the conscience"?

3. The difficulty of knowing right from wrong. Modern life is rich with opportunities, but it may become very confusing to sort out the implications of a value in so many new circumstances.

---

activities to demonstrate how these may help clarify and form values. You might, for instance, use a vote-taking activity. State a two-sided issue and have each person raise his hand or stand up in support of the side he is on. Discuss how this forces a person to think about where he stands and to act accordingly. Or, list on separate sheets of paper the names of several well-known persons. Ask individuals to arrange these sheets in front of the group in the order of importance of the persons listed. Discuss why the order was changed, helping members of the class bring out values they consider important. The same thing could be done on a continuum line, where class members place themselves on a line between two extreme ways of thinking.

V. Have an interview with an older person. Ask him what values seem important to him now.

VI. Discuss causes for the eroding of ethical sensitivity. Give room for

Re-Creation of Values / 49

> What do you see as the effect on personality of comforming to rules, doing the expected, serving out of fear?

Many people believe that values develop in and around the family, but recent changes in family life are dramatic and even frightening. Potent influences on values formation in the form of radio and television come daily into almost every home.

If values are a way of life and are those things that make a difference in living, one would expect more responsibility in the programming and in the listening and watching habits related to the new media. Yet, in order to hold interest (and to sell a product) little attention has been given to the way of life held up as desirable. In fact, so many different ways of life are presented that not only children, but most adults have a hard time delineating the right from the wrong, the desirable from the undesirable, the worthy from the unworthy, or the just from the unjust.

Consider the number of new social situations where the adult is not sure just what is the right, or what is ethical action. What is his responsibility to the new neighbors, who do not seem to want to get acquainted? How does he handle the "new freedom" which youth seem to expect? What shall be his attitude toward space trips, with the knowledge that thousands of children are starving? Where does a Christian stand on issues of population control, pollution, war, discrimination, violence—this need go no further. The changing times demand a hard, long struggle for every adult as he clarifies and formulates his own values in light of the situation.

4. Value formation is a lifelong process. Since values come from experience, a person who is actively living may be expected to modify his values. Even though the direction of life may have been set by a decisive act in youth, one may expect his values, as guides to action, to mature. Value formation is forged from the struggle of conflicting demands and difficult decisions. Complicated judgments are demanded, and risks are to be taken, To decide to try to do the right is only the first small step in the growing process of positive value formation.

> Some persons condemn themselves because they no longer have the sense or urgency to witness to the joy of the Christian experience which they once had. How does one distinguish between "cooling off" and maturing in Christian witness?

Freedom seems to be the theme song of the age:

> O Freedom, O Freedom, O Freedom over me
> And before I'd be a slave, I'd be buried in my grave,
>   and go home to my Lord, and be free.

Indeed, growth in freedom is one of the marks of the growing self, as has already been discussed in chapter 2. Freedom to choose one's way of life is a high value. Yet making such choices without moral and ethical sensitivity will result in chaos. Being free "to be"

---

sharing personal feelings and needs, if it seems appropriate. This could be a time of heart searching and prayer.

VII. Invite the pastor or some other mature Christian to tell how he decides what is morally right in a given situation. Or have various members of the class share their experiences.

VIII. Write the five steps under a "framework for freedom" on a chart. How valid do they seem as a criteria for deciding what is right?

IX. How does the use of the Bible fit into the criteria? Could the Holy Spirit guide through such a process? If not, how does he guide?

50 / **Basics for Communication in the Church**

means freedom within moral and ethical responsibility. It implies choice, but choice growing out of an understanding of the results of the choice both for oneself, for others directly concerned, and for the betterment of the whole society is also imperative.

Freedom within an ethical and moral framework means:

1. THE PERSON IS ORIENTED TOWARD THE GOOD AND THE RIGHT

To be one's self in the truest sense means to be rooted in the good, the just and the true. Yet the situation of man is such that his will enters in. He deliberately chooses to be good, true, and just. Out of this commitment decisions will be made. While there is a necessary direct relationship between a man's values and his action, we here also want to look at the importance of being, as well as of doing. A certain stalwart integrity is a prerequisite for freedom.

2. A PERSON CAN SEE POSSIBLE CHOICES IN A GIVEN SITUATION

In order for choice to be real there must be genuine alternatives. Ability to ferret out possible ways of acting in order to give each careful consideration is a mark of character strength. This ability comes through experience and through hard thinking. To help persons find alternatives for themselves is a task of parents, teachers, and counselors. For lack of time or patience, alternatives may be given too readily, thus depriving the learner of developing the ability to search out alternatives.

Do you weary with the struggle to determine right from wrong in the mass of new decisions that you face? What must be the reaction of the Christian? How are you dealing with this struggle?

3. A PERSON HAS THE ABILITY TO SEE CONSEQUENCES OF EACH ALTERNATIVE

It is not enough that a person wills to do right. It is a mark of strength to be able to see the result of certain choices, either on himself or upon others. Such understandings must be ever expanding in scope. Some naively believe that ignorance of the consequences removes responsibility.

Man cannot be really free in those areas where he does not have knowledge of consequences. Clear understanding is necessary for intelligent choice. Of course, life is not that pat, and where human beings are concerned the definite consequences cannot be predicted. Yet one can learn much about consequences through studying the Bible, through history, through counsel, and through experience.

*What help do you expect from the church in such new ethical and moral problems as population control, boycotts, genetic determination, body transplants, **space** rights? (Perhaps you can name many more.)*

How does the Bible give guidance in such issues?

4. THE PERSON ACTS ACCORDING TO HIS DECISIONS

This is the test of whether the choice has really been made.

X. Discuss the meaning of "model" as used here. Why do educators say that teachers are to be models, not merely examples?

XI. What is the meaning "the kingdom of God is within you" as related to values?

XII. What dangers do you see in the teacher sharing his values?

XIII. Give examples of experiences that aid children in forming values.

You might reexamine the lesson on stewardship from the last chapter. What values might it encourage?

XIV. Why is it necessary that the teacher constantly reexamine his values?

When you have an important decision to be made, how do you decide what to do? Some persons seem to overconform. They always decide according to how they perceive the dominant viewpoint of the moment. Others are overdissenters. They are always opposed to whatever is presented. Do you feel that you can freely and wisely make decisions?

There is a long step between knowing what is the highest desire and living by the choice.

Alongside freedom, the other high value is love. Love, too, is a theme song of the era, "They'll know we are Christians by our love." Yet where does love rank along with such modern values as success, prestige, glamour, money, power, and security?

5. THE PERSON TAKES RESPONSIBILITY FOR THE CONSEQUENCES OF THE CHOICE

Here is a subtle temptation even for the morally strong. Suppose he has followed conscientiously the process described here. If the consequences prove that his choices were wise, then all is well. But suppose the consequences are destructive? Then as he struggles with the whole situation, and with his own ineptitude, he may substitute some face-saving reason for the real reason. He may project the blame on someone else or on the circumstances. Moral strength requires that a man face his own failures and take responsibility for the results, even when his intentions were high. There can be no real freedom without moral responsibility.

Do you agree that freedom requires moral and ethical responsibility? How does one grow in decision making ability?

THE TEACHER AND VALUES

Teaching is essentially a series of interpersonal relations, in which growing persons take life experiences, both historical and present and use them as the framework for decision making. Teaching is helping persons to clarify and form values by which to act out a way of life, and to find their own destiny.

Perhaps in our weaker moments we would rather pass out content and tradition than help students clarify and form values. Maybe we prefer to seek some infallible rules or laws that persons can write down and follow, but Jesus would have none of it. He asserted that, "the kingdom of God is within you."

Why is it necessary that parents and teachers constantly re-create their values? Is this important for all adults?

THE TEACHER AS MODEL

Here I am using "model" in an entirely different sense than the usual meaning of "example." By model I mean a person who has experienced the process of valuing so that a clear sense of values permeates his personality. Furthermore, the process is dynamic and is operative in the experiences of life.

Take the Christian values related to "love." How does the church teach these to each new generation? How does it teach servanthood?

Students are not to become like the model. They are not to follow in his footsteps. They may not even choose the same values. But through relationships with one who has moral integrity they may come to form their own values and to see the meaning for their lives.

This is not to say that there is no basic truth. Christianity is based on eternal truth, personalized in Jesus Christ. But until this truth becomes prized by the person individually and freely chosen it does not result in values by which his life is directed. Direct attempts to transmit moral and ethical principles are apt to end in

Do you agree that it is more important to help persons learn "valuing" than to provide patterned sets of values?

failure. The student may learn to give the expected answers without a moral commitment to live by them. The result is a wide disparity between saying and doing currently designated as "phony."

THE TEACHER SHARES HIS VALUES

The teacher may not manipulate or control. He does not persuade or demand. He does not determine the values of others. But as a full participating member of the group, he may share with honest zeal those values which have meaning to him. It is doubtful if it is possible not to share, for moral and ethical convictions express themselves, if only subtly and indirectly. The ethically alert cannot be indifferent to the violation of individual personhood. He cannot pass lightly over injustice and cruelty. He cannot be indifferent to the inner feeling that a wrong moral choice is being made. Yet he knows that in the deepest sense, respect for others must allow them to form and examine their own values.

THE TEACHER PROVIDES VALUING EXPERIENCES

The teacher can create conditions that aid pupils in forming values. He can keep ethical and moral considerations at the center of attention. By his very method of dealing with historical material, he can focus attention on decisions and consequences, the "why" rather than the "what" of the incident. He can help persons think through casual relationships in biography and in everyday occurrences. The teacher can be alert to use what some educators call the clarifying response.[1] The idea is that the teacher responds to the student's statement in such a way as to cause him to think about what he has chosen, the possible results of his action, and whether the choice harmonizes with his goals. This stimulates him to clarify his thinking, his behavior and his values.

Some examples of clarifying responses might be:

Where did you get the idea? Are there people who disagree with you? What is their argument? What else did you consider? Why did you make this decision? Have you told anyone of your decision? What do you see as the final result?

Above all he can help persons follow through decision-making steps: (1) to desire the good, the true, and the just (2) to consider all possible alternatives (3) to project possible consequences for each choice (4) to act on the highest choice (5) to take responsibility for the outcome of the choice.

In a world that is changing as rapidly as ours, no patterned set of values will serve. Each person must develop the ability to re-create his goals, attitudes, feelings, and actions in light of new demands.

---

[1] Louis E. Raths, Merrill Harmin, Sidney B. Simon, *Values and Teaching* (Charles E. Merrill Books, Inc., 1966).

How may the church fill its role of sensitizing the conscience of mankind?

(Answer to the dot Puzzle of chapter 5)

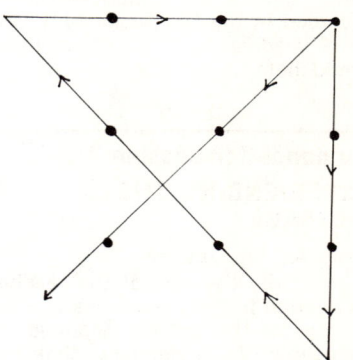

The idea is that in order to solve many problems you have to go outside the obvious, routine pattern and use imagination.

CHAPTER 7

Experiencing The Message

"He who tries to be without authority tries to be like God who alone is by Himself. And like everyone who tries to be like God, he is thrown down to self-destruction; be it a single human being; be it a nation; be it a period in history like our own."

—Paul Tillich, a marker in the Tillich Memorial Park at New Harmony, Indiana

"For we brought the Good News to you, not with words only, but also with power and the Holy Spirit, and with complete conviction of its truth."

—1 Thessalonians 1:5, TEV

Someone has described studying the Bible as a dialogue between God and the reader. Through the Bible God calls and man responds. How can one hear God's call as he reads?

Complete conviction of the truth of the gospel is a requisite for communicating the gospel. Some teaching seeks to be on the "word" level, where through a one-way effort at communication, pressure is exerted by one person to get another to think, feel, or act in a certain way. It is not very likely that an encounter with truth can be brought about by this method. For in this case truth is not an experience which confronts man. Rather it becomes a topic to be discussed by using the right words.

Other teaching is on the "concept" level. Here the effort is to come to an understanding of the real meaning of the gospel. The question is not only what does the passage say, but what does it mean for our situation.

How about trying the exercise of writing down the personal word from God to you, of each passage that you read?

However, even this does not go far enough. It is my firm conviction that one cannot communicate a truth well until he has come face-to-face with that truth and experienced it in his own life. Then he can "bring the Good News, not with words only, but also with power and the Holy Spirit," as Paul testified.

Can you draw out the "changeless truth" behind the historical events recorded in the Old Testament? Perhaps reading with a commentary would help.

Unless the gospel becomes meaningful to the teacher in the deep recesses of his own person, he cannot become a channel for the gospel as the good news of a personal God. He may be able to hang a few Bible stories, scripture verses, and moral maxims on the exterior, much like the glittering ornaments on a Christmas tree. He cannot teach in such a way that the fruits will be a genuine product of the interaction between the gospel and the person.

Guidance for Session 7
EXPERIENCING THE MESSAGE

Aims for the Session

To clarify the role of the teacher in relation to the gospel message. To search for the deeper meanings of the Bible. To understand that the gospel is valid only when experienced.

Clusters of Learning Experiences

Pick from among the following those activities and concerns most relevant for your study group.

I. Have each person share a verse from the Bible which has been a real source of strength in time of great need. In what sense is this part of the gospel? Discuss how the verse became meaningful to him. What is the meaning "word" level, "concept" level? Do you agree that a teacher cannot really teach something until he has experienced it for himself?

II. Read the poem "Between Two Fires" and discuss its meaning. You might draw two flames on a chart. In one have the class list man's persistent needs, and in the other the gospel's answer.

1. Who am I?
2. Relationships
3. Need for love
4. Forgiveness
5. Sense of purpose.
(Others)

1. Created by God
2. All men brothers
3. John 3:16
4. Colossians 3:13
5. Matthew 28:19-20
(Others)

54 / **Basics for Communication in the Church**

BETWEEN TWO FIRES

The teacher (who is also a learner) is between two fires.[1] As Harold Johnson says:

>   To teach and learn in the church
> is to be   between two fires.
>   It is
>   to face
>   to feel
>   to absorb the hurt of
>   the hunger in
>   the horror of
>   human existence.
>   It is to be caught up in
>   the heat and light of
>   sense
>   worth
>   and glory given to
>   the meaning of being human.
>   The first fire is torment
>   from which flight
>   (if no fulfillment is in sight)
>   is fervently sought.
>   It breaks the heart and separates
>   one person from another
>   making each person alone—sometimes lonely.
>   The second fire is ecstasy
>   for which eternity
>   is desired
>   and dreamed.
>   The first fire
>   writhes

[1] T. Franklin Miller, Beverly Welton, James Blair Miller, Harold Johnson, Kenneth F. Hall, *Basics for Teaching in the Church* (Warner Press, 1968), pp. 113, 114, 115.

III. Consider ways teachers may read the Bible so that it will gain freshness and vitality. What is the value of reading in the new translations? Have the students tried writing a passage in today's language and related to a personal problem? Have they taken certain themes or ideas and traced the thougut through the Bible?

IV. You could have the class experience writing a verse in their own words.

Step 1. Fold a sheet of paper in half and fold in half again.

Step 2. Select a verse such as Ephesians 4:11-12 or Galatians 6:7-9.

Step 3. Read the Bible verse slowly and distribute Bibles.

Step 4. Have them write the text reference on page 1.

Step 5. Ask each student to paraphrase the verse on page 2. He is to use his own words and his own situation.

Step 6. List on page 3 at least one problem or concern related to the verse.

Step 7. Divide the class into triads and allow ten minutes to share the problem, think through, and attempt a solution.

Step 8. Write on page 4 the most helpful solution.

Step 9. Come back to the total group and share feelings about the experience.

V. List the five learning tasks so that all can see them. Discuss the real meaning of each one for the teacher. How does this relate to the idea that the teacher is a full participant in the learning experience?

Experiencing the Message / 55

>   and spirals
>   into
>   question
>   marks.
> The second fire
>   leaps
> and flashes
>   into
>   exclamation
>   points!
> Each is one factor, one side
> Of the algebraic equation of existence.
> On one side
>   the ache, the thrust, the yearning
>   for survival with worth.
> On the other,
>   the promise fulfilled
>   by God in Jesus Christ.
> Between them is = (the equal sign)
>   the daring act
>   the church engaged
>   in resolving the equation —
> the church teaching and learning.

Not only do the students have lifelong persistent needs such as interpersonal relations, affection, usefulness, security, forgiveness, self-image of worth, and a sense of destiny; the teacher has every one of the needs just as potently as does the student. Before the teacher can become = (the equal sign) which brings together these needs and "the promise fulfilled by God in Jesus Christ," his work is enriched if he experiences the gospel deeply in his own life.

THE MESSAGE FOR THE TEACHER

How does the teacher experience the message of the gospel in such a way as to appropriate it to his own life needs? What is the source of life-changing power and growth in his own life? How does the gospel come alive for the teacher?

Five learning tasks have been identified for the learner.[2] I propose that the teacher (who is a learner, too) follow the same tasks on his level of maturity and need.

---

[2] *Ibid.*, p. 42.

Sidebar (left margin): What do you see as some of your own deep needs? Do you find help through studying the Bible? In what ways?

(If you use this possible experience, you may want to supplement resources from **Basics for Teaching in the Church**.)

VI. Discuss the meaning of "crossing point." Have members give examples of crossing points in their own lives. What conditions brought these about? (Again you may want to refer to **Basics for Teaching in the Church** for additional resource in this area.)

VII. What are some of the issues about which God seems to be trying to speak to us today? How is he speaking?

1. LISTENING WITH GROWING ALERTNESS TO THE GOSPEL AND RESPONDING IN FAITH AND LOVE

"Listening to the gospel with alertness" may be a difficult task for the teacher. Perhaps he has studied the Bible and heard its central message explained from childhood. Because it is the "old, old story" he may not be able to listen with alertness to its message for him today. Certainly "listening" means that God speaks through the gospel for each stage in life. An adequate and true childhood faith may not be strong enough to command grown-up worship and love. Teachers may need to discard the childish and inadequate in order to hear the gospel for their present needs. Listening is not passive. It means becoming engrossed with the gospel. It means getting involved in value determining decisions. It means identifying with Moses, Abraham, or Paul in the struggle to find one's own highest destiny under God. It means a person becomes Job (or J. B. as the modern play interprets the problem) trying to solve the problem of evil if an all-powerful God is good.

Of the modern speech versions, which is your favorite? Why?

2. EXPLORING THE WHOLE FIELD OF RELATIONSHIPS IN LIGHT OF THE GOSPEL

As the teacher studies with new awareness God's word, he explores all his relationships in light of the teachings he finds in the gospel. As the truth becomes known to him, he examines his own treatment of others and from such exploration he learns what is morally and ethically right.

3. DISCOVERING MEANING AND VALUE IN LIGHT OF THE GOSPEL

Here is his key to his own system of values. Through such a study he can come to know what is just, good, and true in ever widening relationships.

4. APPROPRIATING PERSONALLY THE MEANING AND VALUE DISCOVERED

As he listens to the meaning of the gospel with growing alertness he takes the message to heart personally. This is not something that he is merely to teach and to discuss. The gospel is burning truth and when it speaks of the sacredness of persons, of reconciliation, of justice and destiny it means to be taken personally by the teacher.

Can you think of ways your beliefs about God have changed as you matured? Your beliefs about the Bible? Your faith? Your ethical sensitivity?

5. ASSUMING PERSONAL AND SOCIAL RESPONSIBILITY IN LIGHT OF THE GOSPEL

The teacher can do no less than is expected of the learners. Personal appropriation issues in assuming personal and social responsibility. It means that the teacher will "live the gospel" as he teaches it. The understanding of the gospel in his own relationships will be a part of the growing process for the teacher. This is the true meaning of the idea that the teacher is to be a full participant

What does it mean "to be a full participant in the learning experience"?

Experiencing the Message / 57

in the learning experience. In his struggle to "respond in faith and love" to the gospel in all his relationships, he becomes the "model" for others in their attempts to "listen with growing alertness to the gospel" and to respond on their level of understanding and maturity.

THE LANGUAGES OF THE MESSAGE

There are two languages of teaching. The first is the language of relationships and after these are strong, then the language of words can have meaning. The depth of meaning of the words may be dependent on the quality of life and relationships within the Christian community.

If the teacher hopes to teach the words of the Bible, he ought to know what it says. He should know well the stories, the history, and the teachings. But it is even more important that he understand the true message.

How important is it that the teacher know the content of the Bible? How does one come to sense the meaning in life?

One may, for example, commit Bible verses to memory and understand the historical background. He may even be able to argue theologically, but only when one senses the meaning in life and makes a meaningful response does learning really take place. The content must be so related to the life needs of the learner that he makes a positive response to it and becomes changed by it. If beliefs are to be effectively authoritative, it will be not because of some prior, exterior claim of an authoritative nature but because of a process whereby these beliefs become a person's own and an effective commitment by which to live. How is it possible to use "content," not for its own sake, but for the spiritual growth and direction of the learner?

Look at the great truths of the Bible listed in number VI under Clusters of Learning Experiences. Do you agree that these are the basic truths? Can you add others?

In order to deal with this question the teacher will seek to understand the central message of the Bible. He may come to understand the Bible as a lifting out of the story, the proclamation of the good news that in Jesus Christ God has entered human history, seeking and saving men.

He may understand the Bible as a record of God's mighty acts and the ways he has revealed himself in history in relation to his people. He will find meaning as he studies the Bible, not only as history dealing with particular events, but as great truths or themes running throughout the Bible. These themes show some aspect of truth which persists more or less prominently. Each of these truths deals with some profound need common to man in all ages. As Lewis Sherrill has said, "Revelation is God's disclosure of himself in creation, in lordship, in vocation, in judgment, in redemption, in re-creation, in providence, and in the life of faith; the Bible contains these themes, and each of them is correspondence with some profound human predicament."[3] When a long series of

---

[3]Lewis J. Sherrill, *The Gift of Power* (New York: Macmillan Co., 1955), p. 110.

revelatory events speaks to a persisting human need this becomes a theme. Something which hangs together is being said in many ways, through many events, through centuries of time and is still pertinent today. This is what is meant by getting behind the words, and even the events of the Bible to the revelatory truth that God is trying to disclose to man.

These great truths relate to such eternal questions as: Who am I? What is the meaning of life? How do I relate to others? When I become separated by sin, how do I find forgiveness and reconciliation? What is my responsibility to my neighbor? What values are eternal? What is my final destiny?

The "story" is that in Jesus Christ, God has entered human history, seeking and saving men. The story is to be told not only in its parts, but in its entirety and in such a way that every person will feel himself involved as a part of the whole great drama and will respond in terms of decision, commitment and faith.

Such a depth understanding of the Bible gives a new dimension to life. Through emotional participation the present moment can be seen in the context of God's loving and victorious acts in history. As one comes to feel a part of this whole movement and plan of God, he has hope and strength for the present. He feels, "This is my situation and the personal God who made himself known to the prophets in their problems now is present with me." Such an encounter is the point where learning at its highest level takes place.

The teacher is to struggle with the meaning of the Bible "until he hears God call his name" then commit himself to whatever the meaning is, in faith. The Holy Spirit is present in enlightening power wherever such honest struggle is taking place.

Such an experience has sometimes been called a "crossing point." When the teacher comes to feel the meaning of the content in his own situation and knows that he must make a personal response, a crossing point has been reached. The goal is that he will respond in faith and love. The personality is not coerced or forced. The person is free to respond as he will.

This is what is meant in the poem:

> On one side
>   the ache, the thrust, the yearning
>   for survival with worth.
> On the other,
>   the promise fulfilled
>   by God in Jesus Christ.

Teaching is bringing about this = (the equal sign), the crossing point. It is providing those experiences where persons come to recognize God speaking to them here and now, in relation to their decisions on the issue being discussed, and responding to and interacting with him.

Can you think of some high crossing points in your life—times when God spoke to you and you changed as a result? Some have felt strength and courage. Some have been comforted. Some have been called to work for moral justice. Some have been forgiven. How have you experienced his voice?

We are all called to become learners. When we know all the answers, or all the answers are given, we die in that moment.

Experiencing the Message / 59

If our religion has become the crystalized form of a past relationship with God, then we must continually give up the form so that the true substance, the relationship may grow.

No living person has yet plumbed the depths of meaning of the Bible. Its possibilities are as exhaustless as the God whose written word it is. Yet every living person can find, through the Bible and the good news it brings us, the meaning of his life and the direction he must go.

Such teaching calls for teachers themselves to experience the "story" in a dynamic way both historically and in the present. It requires a depth study of the Bible with a growing understanding of those great recurring themes which run throughout the Bible. Teaching of the Bible is effective only if the teacher has the insight and ability to help pupils feel the relevance of the biblical theme in their present situation.

The two languages—that of relationships and that of words, become one when the "story" is shared in the context of interpersonal relations of acceptance, trust, and love.

CHAPTER 8

Being— Behaving— Becoming

Take a fresh look at your own life. Do you experience the excitement of feeling you are a real person, making progress toward your intended goal?

"Being the teacher: is not only a function but a stance in the stuff of life."

"No pupil is greater than his teacher; but every pupil, when he has completed his training, will be like his teacher."

—Luke 6:40, TEV

There is nothing so exciting as sensing what one is intended to be, knowing what one is trying to do, and then feeling that one is making progress toward his goal. The purpose of "Teachers in Process of Becoming," this part of the book now coming to an end, has been to help teachers to take a long, deep look inward and to find understanding and grace to become authentic persons and "great" teachers. The hope has been that through this study each person will come to understand more clearly what he is intended to be, know what he is trying to do in teaching and feel that he is making progress.

BEING

The teacher is to be a center of aliveness. Such aliveness grows out of a sense of rightness about himself and his style of life. He feels that he is in a measure in the place prepared for him from the foundation of his life.

Guidance for Session 8
BEING—BEHAVING—BECOMING

Aims for the Session
To discover how being, behaving, and becoming operate together without separation. To grow through openness, risk, and commitment, thus calling learners on toward their own potential.

Clusters of Learning Experiences
I. You may wish to study the prose poem "How can I teach," as a summary of Part I of the book. What does each stanza say about the special need of the age? What does it say about the teacher? Can one be a teacher even though he has "not yet learned the answers"? What do the last two stanzas say about teaching? Do you agree that this is teaching?

II. Discuss: What does it mean to be a person? Review "Dimensions of Selfhood" as given in chapter 2. You might ask in which of the areas each has found help through the study. They might be ready to share areas of need yet remaining.

III. What does it mean to be "a center of aliveness"? How does this come about? Why do some people appear more "alive" than others?

In reading the biographies of outstanding leaders, I have been struck over and over again with the sense of divine destiny many of these men and women seem to feel. So many have faced strong opposition, even persecution, and in the face of it they have come up with a renewal of their call. They have felt the quiet assurance of an inner voice saying, "I am with you. Do not fear to stand for right and truth."

So often these persons found themselves leading lives they really didn't expect to lead. But the force of events piled up on them. Leadership was thrust into their hands. They had to give themselves entirely. Their values have become quite clear and compelling to them as they have acted on once privately held, even tentative inner thoughts. There is strength in such a sense of destiny and in such a growing dedication. Not that many of us are going to be thrust into leadership of vast national and international scope. But the same sense of destiny applies to all who answer calls to serve in and through the church.

Surely, Jesus in his words recorded in Luke 6:40 did not mean that the learner would be like his teacher in personality, in destiny, or in actions. But each person can find his own personal "being." He can know what he is intended to be and do, and he can give himself fully to nurturing that self in its highest expression.

Do you feel a sense of rightness and satisfaction with your style of life? Are you sometimes tempted to follow others rather than being true to your own uniqueness? What is the result on personality?

Even so, such a person will be a strange synthesis of hope and disappointment, success and failure, assurance and doubt, individuality and cooperation. All life is of this mixed nature. A person is wise to know that this is so; therefore he is not too distressed when the darker parts are most in view. Neither is he confused because he knows his direction, who he is, and what are his purposes.

BEHAVING

The self that one is becoming emerges in appropriate patterns of behavior. Yes, one takes into consideration his abilities and the social situation which seems to confine him. Yet values will some way find expression in action.

Such actions will be both social and personal. They will be social so that one takes informed action relative to the grievous problems of the day. They will be personal in that he comes to

How do you interpret the person who has a great gap between what he says he believes and how his actions correspond? What is the source of behavior? What is the test of actual values?

What do you see as the Christian responsibility in such social problems as poverty, racism, injustice, war, pollution? How far does his responsibility reach?

IV. What do you see as the meaning of Luke 6:40? How are pupils to be like their teacher? Discuss the idea: "The teacher does not try to have his pupils to become like him, rather he hopes to evoke them to become their true selves."

V. Discuss why life must be made up of opposites such as: hope and despair, success and failure, assurance and doubt. Can one learn to live above the negatives of this description?

VI. Give examples of values being expressed in social behavior. In personal relationships.

VII. Discuss: The Christian is to become a change-agent in the society, rather than merely adjusting to the changes in society.

VIII. What are the implications of living life meaningfully now but with a thrust toward the future?

IX. What kind of "risk" is the teacher expected to take today? Are "shrinking back," as we use it here, and "backsliding" synonymous terms?

X. What is the meaning of "making life our own" as given in Hebrews 10:30?

understand and act out the true meaning of love in every relationship with other persons. Thus he becomes an agent of change both in his personal relationships and in society. Some teachers seem to see as their prime duty the preservation of the *status quo,* or at best the return to a past ethic. The change-agent can never be a passive onlooker. He takes the significant of the past and uses it to understand and re-create the present. He feels deeply with people who suffer from man's inhumanity to man. His behavior grows out of his deep sense of justice and personal caring.

Increasingly his way of doing and responding will be less dependent on outside teaching or rules. His behaving will be the natural expression of his inner self and related to his values and goals. Thus harmony and creativity in life come from the increasing capacity to relate to others and to act according to that which seems good in the depths of one's own being.

BECOMING

People are inclined to think of maturity as a definite state to be reached much as if it were the end of a journey. It would be better to think of it as an ever-receding goal toward which we begin to march at birth and go on to the end of life.

Such a journey is exciting, for the journey itself is seen as important as well as the goal. The maturing person accepts all experience as worthwhile and he finds the entire process of pursuing or moving in the direction of the goal, as much a value as the goal itself.

The emphasis is on living life meaningfully at the present time with a forward thrust into the future.

Dr. Sherrill holds that in every person there is this inward propulsion to grow, that is "to pass through certain stages as one moves toward the complete fulfillment of life."[1] This is obvious in the physical realm, but it is also true of the self in its development. This forward thrust is very strong, but within the self is another very strong tendency; that is the fear of the risk and hardships. There is a pull to shrink back from new challenges and opportunities. In the tension between the need to grow and the unwillingness to take the risk, man is required to make a decision. He can take the usual, lower way and shrink into the routine of ordinariness, or he can take the daring risk and go forward.

---

[1] Lewis J. Sherrill, *The Struggle of the Soul* (New York: Macmillan Co., 1963), p. 21.

Is it possible for one to live in a love relationship with every other person? What do you understand the I-Thou relationship to mean? What does it mean in a Sunday school class?

Consider: "Your greatest teaching is through your deepest relationship."

"Involvement with persons is the riskiest thing known to man." Why may this be true?

XI. Discuss the quote from Gordon Cosby. Is there a danger that we take too good care of our health and strength? What is the chief cause of tiredness? How much truth is there in the idea that "nothing makes a man so strong as a call for help." Are there words from Jesus that give guidance here?

XII. How can one be both **present** and a **presence** in those situations where he is most needed?

XIII. Why may it be preferable to think of one as "a maturing person" rather than as "a mature person"? What is to be the attitude of the maturing person toward the journey of life?

The letter to the Hebrews expresses this idea clearly. "But my righteous one shall live by faith, and if he shrinks back, my soul has no pleasure in him. But we are not of those who shrink back and are destroyed, but of those who have faith and keep their souls" (Heb. 10:38-39, RSV). Or, "But we are not among those who shrink back and are lost; we have the faith to make life our own" (Heb. 10:39, NEB). It is something of this making "life our own" that the teacher in process of becoming feels.

This spirit expressed itself in Gordon Cosby, pastor of the dynamic Church of the Savior in Washington, D.C. At one time he made a target of the notorious Junior Village, where 902 deprived children were crowded together. The challenge was to find a suitable foster home for every child in Junior Village. Gordon Cosby said, "If you don't find me in the march, look for me over in the graveyard for that's where I'll be. We so carefully watch the limits of our health and strength, for some of us are very tired. We measure out the love that we give to others from a medicine dropper. But under the baptism of the Spirit, I have seen limits disappear. People walk who can't walk—the too old, the too young, the too responsible, are all at it in the most irresponsible and refreshing way. I am deeply sympathetic with the limits—I understand them, but the power of the Spirit when the limits disappear is heady stuff."[2]

The real person is not a fixed entity but a center of experience involving this inner desire to grow, and this continual pull backward. But each person has the power to decide, to assert his own direction, and to determine by the power of the Spirit to make his life his own.

True, he cannot remove all his limitations. He may not be able to change all the circumstances, but he can develop essential capacities and make his own contribution. To the extent that difficult experiences foster personal growth they are desirable. Growth can come through failure, conflict, and suffering, as well as through victory and love. The growing person responds to all the experiences of life. He takes the risk of courageous witness and living. Then he weaves both the agony and the ecstasy into the person he is becoming.

A STANCE IN THE STUFF OF LIFE

We have come to understand that there are two languages of teaching, the language of words and the language of relationships. We have been studying about the language of being, behaving, and becoming—the language of relationships. We have said that teaching is not only what one says and does, but it is also "a stance

[2] Elizabeth O'Connor, *Journey Inward, Journey Outward* (New York: Harper and Row, 1968), p. 144.

It has been said that conscience is sensitized through deeply caring. Do you agree? How does the conscience develop beyond what one has been taught? Is this one of the elements of maturing?

How do you respond to challenges to do new and risky things? Do you feel that you "make life your own"?

Do you feel that you are a change-agent in your society?

Could you say with Gordon Cosby that you intend to be in the "march," in some significant way, until you're in the grave? How do you measure out the love you give to others?

How would you interpret "becoming" as used in this chapter? How do you feel about the past experiences in your life? Do you enjoy the present and find it meaningful? What is your attitude toward the future?

What does "teaching as a stance in the stuff of life" mean to you?

*How can a teacher be **present** with the pupils? Give examples of ways one may be absent to pupils, even though he is physically present.*

*How may he also be a **presence** among them? How does the Holy Spirit work in the teaching-learning process?*

in the stuff of life." It has to do with the quality and purpose of the life of the teacher. It requires that he be not only *present* with the pupils but that he be a *presence* among them. Too often the teacher is absent to the pupils' real feelings and needs. Sometimes he is absent in conversation and especially in listening. To be *present* means that he lives in the experience. It has meaning to him. He feels the excitement of the search and hears the deep cry for love and understanding. No person can be a *presence* within himself alone. But as he opens himself to others and to the Holy Spirit, he may claim the promise of the risen Christ. "Teach them to observe all that I have commanded you and, remember, I am with you always, even to the end of the world" (Matthew 28:20, Phillips).

Such may be the power and presence of the teacher!

HOW CAN I TEACH?

How can *I* teach
    A child?
So questioning, curious, and open
Seeking to learn to trust,
Persons and God.
Asking, "Why am I me?" "Where is my world?"
I, who am so human,
So lacking in trust.
Such a new pilgrim on the journey.
How can I teach
    A youth?
The searching, unfolding, potential youth,
Looking for a model.
Striving to answer, "Who am I?"
"Where is my place?"
"How do I join with the Creator?"
I, who am struggling to be real
So far from the goal.
How can I teach
    A man?
The busy, driving, uncertain man.
Looking for meaning in life.
Asking the ultimate questions
About life and death,
God and man.
I, who face the same questions
And have not yet learned the answers.

How can I teach
    The aging?
Seeking honorable existence
In preparation for leaving,
Sorting out eternal values,
Maintaining worth and dignity
And loving and being loved.
I, who can not yet know
What it means
To be near the end of the journey.
I can
    Open my heart as I journey
    Be honest in my humanity
    Believe in the integrity of each person
    Be *with* and *for* him regardless
    Share the hope forged out of suffering.
This I can do.
We can
    Search together for meanings
    Share truth as we find it
    Open our lives to the gospel
    Trust the Holy Spirit to guide us
    Learn the joys of the journey
This we can do—
    Is this teaching?
        —Irene Smith Caldwell

PART II

Communication, the Teacher's Tool

By Richard A. Hatch

"Communication? Why I'm an expert at that—I do it all the time! I can talk to my family and be clearly understood; I teach in the church; in fact sometimes I think I talk all day! I know all about communication."

And indeed you do. We spend a major part of our lives communicating. Think back over the last day. How much time did you spend talking, listening, reading, writing, watching television? Most of us spend hours every day in communication. And we think we've come to be pretty good at it.

But think again over the last day—if you can bear to do it—and chances are you'll find that at least some of your tensions and irritations arose from situations in which you really did not understand what someone was trying to tell you—or they did not seem to understand what you meant.

The irritating thing about communication failures is that *we* can understand what we meant quite clearly; it's just that the other fellow seems to be doing such a terrible job of it. After all, it should be perfectly easy for us to understand each other in our everyday home and business and church life. Maybe the other fellow just isn't paying attention!

Sometimes it's really important for us to get a very difficult message through, and the responsibility is all on our shoulders. We *have* to make ourselves understood. When we:

—ask the boss for a raise.

—explain to our thirteen-year-old why he ought not start smoking.

—try to help an adolescent to a more mature understanding of sin.

CHAPTER 9

How Communication Works

What are some of the causes of communication failures?

An Introduction to the Study of Part II

About This Part

This section of the book concentrates upon the role of communication in teaching-learning. It considers how the process of communication works and reviews the contributions of many experts and researchers in the communication field as they apply to teaching-learning. It considers the teacher as a communicator and the learner as a communicator, and it discusses the interaction between teacher and learner in terms of the series of processes that are communication. It identifies some of the common problem areas in teacher-learner communication and suggests some of the directions in which solutions to these problems may be found.

Some Issues This Part Faces

What part does communication play in the interaction of teacher and learner? How do people communicate? How can the research findings of social scientists and communication theorists be applied in church school teaching-learning? What part does perception play in communication? What kinds of communication sensitivities does the teacher need to bring to teaching-learning? What kinds of things can the teacher do to communicate more effectively? How can the teacher help the learners to communicate better in the learning situation?

Does knowing how something works usually make us better at using it? Does knowing how your automobile engine works make you a better driver? If so, how?

At such times we must muster every bit of communication skill we have and just do the best we can. These are the situations in which a more thorough understanding of communication can really be useful. Maybe—just maybe—knowing a bit more about the principles of communication can help us to be enough better at it to get our meaning shared. And that's what this section is all about.

THE TEACHER'S BASIC TOOL

The carpenter spends many years in his apprenticeship learning to use the tools of his trade: his hammer, his saw, his plane.

The accountant's basic tools are mental skills, but he too spends many years in college and in the early part of his career developing his skill at using the basic tool of his profession: his knowledge of efficient methods of solving problems of financial record-keeping.

What is the teacher's basic "tool-of-the-trade"? It must be communication. For the teacher is most basically a communicator.

He communicates facts with those he teaches, of course; but more importantly, he communicates with them meanings—meanings about themselves, meanings about other people, meanings about God. The teacher is a communicator; the good teacher is an expert communicator.

GOOD COMMUNICATION IS COMMUNICATION THAT WORKS

As a teacher, you communicate for a purpose; you communicate to accomplish something. The measure of your success at communication can be stated in a word—*effectiveness*. Good communication is effective communication. It succeeds in getting meanings shared.

How can we evaluate our effectiveness in communication.

Some people seem to have the idea that if only they could develop a deep, resonant, well-modulated voice and a talent for elegant phrasings, they could communicate much better than they do. As we'll soon see, however, *effective* communication depends much more upon the thought behind what you say than

---

Some Purposes for This Part

To gain a new awareness and appreciation of the importance of communication in teaching-learning. To become more fully informed about the way meanings are shared in communication, and to understand the important role of perception in the communication process. To develop a conceptual framework for analyzing situations in which there is a lack of communication. To begin to think about ways to improve the teacher's effectiveness in communication and ways to guide the learner toward more effective communication. To become more critically sensitive to the implications of various kinds of communications techniques, and to develop skill at selecting techniques that are suitable for a variety of teaching-learning goals.

A Note about the Session Guidance

This material is designed, by and large, for group study. The various suggestions that go with each chapter are not intended necessarily to add up to an exact sequence of study for a session, although they usually may be used that way. Sometimes a study group could use but one or two of the suggestions for a session. Sometimes sequences could be changed. Occasionally, you will find a suggestion that would be carried out largely in individual study. Because of the multipurpose use of this book, the session guidance has been kept relatively fluid.

upon the sheer beauty of your presentation. Certainly a pleasant voice and reasonably good diction can make people enjoy listening to you, but the crisp delivery of a radio announcer is unnatural to most of us. We'd have to strain our voices and we'd have to devote nearly all our attention to precise diction if we thought the key to effective communication lay in this direction.

For most of us, a much better way of increasing our communication effectiveness is to develop a thorough understanding of how communication works. In the process we may find that many of our common-sense notions about communication are inadequate. Their inadequacy may show the clearest when we get into just those situations when communicating effectively is most important —when we are teaching.

We tend to think, for instance, if we're not very careful, that communication involves simply lifting an idea out of our heads and popping it into somebody else's head. We say, "He surely knows that; why I just told him all about it this morning!" But as we'll soon see, communication hardly ever involves such a simple transfer of knowledge from your head to somebody else's head. What really happens is much more complex than that.

We need to begin, at least, to be able to predict consciously how other people will react to what we say, and to do this we need to know something about the mental processes that determine how people react to messages. We need to develop, for instance, some more sophisticated notions about *perception* and about how we can use *feedback* to be sure we are communicating.

> What do you already know about how communication works?

HOW COMMUNICATION WORKS—AN OVERVIEW

Communication is a *process* rather than a simple (and easily describable) object, like a chair. Since it is a process, it consists of a whole series of related actions which together serve the function of getting meanings shared among people. If we are going to understand how communication works, we need to describe each of the component parts of the process, and we ought to see how each of the component parts fits into the process as a whole.

So as we begin thinking about communication, we shall try to concentrate our attention on one very specific detail of the process at a time, without losing track of how that detail fits into the overall scheme. We'll want to keep in mind the details and the whole process all at the same time—a difficult thing to do.

To make things easier, communication theorists have developed a simplified model, or mental picture, of the communication process. The model tells us what the individual parts of the communication process are, and it shows us how these parts are related to each other. It lets us concentrate upon explaining some detail and at the same time it provides an easy way of remembering how that detail fits into the process.

> What are some other simple processes?

Think of some communication situations that are important enough that we'd be willing to spend some time analyzing them.

In addition to helping us learn about communication, our model will help us think through those particularly difficult communication situations and figure out how to deal with them. It identifies for us the really crucial points in the process, so that in thinking about some specific situation we can know where to begin analyzing what we should do to communicate effectively. It helps to keep our attention on the important things, so that we don't get bogged down in trying to figure out where to begin in our thinking.

SOMEBODY WITH SOMETHING TO SAY

Picture in your mind this simple communication situation, and let's see how we can begin to apply a model of communication to it.

> Stanley and his friend Sidney are walking to church together this Sunday morning. Suddenly Stanley glances up and notices Mr. Everett, their teacher, walking toward them. Mr. Everett has a big black eye this morning. . . .

Guidance for Session 9
HOW COMMUNICATION WORKS

Aims for the Session
To assess the importance of communication in teaching-learning. To develop a framework of understanding from which to view each of the parts of the communication process. To begin examining some common-sense assumptions about communication.

Questions to Ponder
What is communication? Why do I, as a teacher, need to understand the communication process? How much of the responsibility for clear communication rests upon me in the teaching-learning situation? How can I evaluate whether I have communicated well or not? What kinds of things do I need to know in a specific teaching-learning situation that will help me analyze ways to communicate better?

A Study Plan
I. Consider the importance of communication for the church worker.

A. How much of your day do you spend communicating? Try to figure out, in rough proportions, how much time you spend communicating compared with the amount of time you spend in noncommunication activities. Include in communication time at least all of the following things: talking, listening, reading, writing, watching television, listening to records or to the radio, reading labels on packages. Be sure to include the time you spend preparing to communicate, the time you spend thinking about what you'll say when you see so-and-so, for instance.

B. Of all the time you spend on your church leadership responsibilities, how much do you spend communicating? Again, try to figure rough proportions. Be sure to include at least all of these things in your communication time: talking and listening to learners, preparing what you'll say, preparing ways to get the learners to say things, reading session materials, reading background materials, reading this book and other materials in teaching-learning, discussing church educational activities with your fellow workers, thinking about things that happened during class sessions (communicating with yourself).

II. Discuss: How are teachers good and poor communicators?

A. Have you ever studied under a good teacher who did not communicate very well? Why do you think he was a good teacher? In what ways did he communicate poorly? Why do you think he was able to teach well even though he didn't communicate well?

68 / Basics for Communication in the Church

Our model of communication must begin, of course, with a person who is going to send a message. We'll call our person *Someone* and we'll label him S in our diagram.

Someone has something to talk about. He sees Mr. Everett's black eye. We'll call our something-to-talk-about an *Event* and we'll label it E in our diagram. We're using the word *Event* to stand for something-to-talk-about because it is such a general word. It can stand for literally anything you could talk about. In the context of our model, for instance, Mr. Everett's black eye could be an Event: a rainstorm could be an Event; the chair you're sitting on could be an Event; the history of the United States from 1776 to yesterday could be an Event—literally anything you can think about is an Event. Actually our very general use of the term *Event* probably won't be very difficult for you to understand if you just remember that an *Event* is *anything that somebody might talk about.*

Now we are ready to state the first little piece of our model of communication in a formal way:

Think of a message you received today. Who was the Someone who sent the message?

Name some Events.

B. Have you ever studied under a poor teacher who communicated very well? What makes you think he communicated well? In what ways was he a poor teacher? Why didn't his expertise in communication make him a good teacher?

C. Were most of your good teachers good communicators? How did they communicate that makes you conclude they were good communicators?

III. What other "models" of a process like our Model of Communication have you seen before? Is the United States Constitution a model for our federal government in the same way that the statement in this chapter is a model of communication? Is the organization chart of a company a model of interaction in that company? Does the instruction manual for your automatic washer include a model of a process that is like our Model of Communication?

IV. If you had sat down to describe the process of communication before you read this chapter, how would you have described it?

V. One of the ways in which people often think about communication is that it consists simply of plucking ideas out of one person's head and inserting them into somebody else's head. Why isn't this a very good description of how communication works? What characteristics would the messages that carry these ideas have to have? If this model were true, the teacher's job would be much easier. In what ways?

VI. Apply the Model of Communication to a communication situation in which the communicator was successful. To one in which the communicator was unsuccessful. To one in which the communicator had a clear goal in mind ("Please close the door"). To your answer to this question. In the beginning, practice applying the Model to simple communication situations; as you develop some skill at applying it, you can use it to analyze any communication situation. As you think about each communication situation, ask yourself:

A. Who is the Someone?

B. What is the event that he perceived? (Try to be as specific as you can.)

C. How did he react to the Event?

D. What is the situation in which he reacts?

E. What form does his message take?

F. What is its content?

G. What consequences does he expect as a result of the message? As you answer each point, try to figure out how that factor influenced his communication, if at all.

Someone perceives an event *and reacts in a situation*. Of course, there's more to communication than just somebody looking at something. To have communication, he must do something or say something as a result of his perception. He has to *react*. And Stanley has decided to react by telling Sidney about the fire.

But Stanley doesn't react in a vacuum—he reacts in the context of a specific *situation*. It is a situation that includes him and Sidney, Mr. Everett with his black eye, the street they're walking along and the church they're all approaching, and a lot of other details that we just haven't paid attention to. The *way* Stanley reacts is partly shaped by the situation in which the communication takes place. Stanley would react differently, for instance, if Sidney hadn't been there for him to talk to or if he had noticed Mr. Everett's black eye during the church service.

What other kinds of differences in the situation would make Stanley react differently?

. . . Stanley says to Sidney, "Hey, look at that shiner!" . . .

Someone perceives an event, that is, Someone has some kind of representation, or picture, of the Event in his mind. In his mind, Stanley has an image of Mr. Everett's black eye.

. . . Stanley thinks, I better tell Sidney about it. Mr. Everett is still too far away to hear us talking. . . .

Are there other kinds of images in people's heads than "picture" images?

Someone perceives an event and reacts in a situation *to make available materials in some form conveying content*. To put it simply, Someone sends a *message*. (In our model, we use the more general language so that we can apply the model to more complex situations like those involved in the teaching-learning process.) We'll label the message M.

Notice that the message is divided into two parts by a vertical line. We've divided it this way so that we can easily remember that there are two important attributes of a message: first, its *form;* and second, its *content*. The idea that a message has some content is one we're all familiar with. But the form a message takes is important too—maybe nearly as important as the content. It is important because the form a message takes can put some very real limitations upon the content that it can have. To take a simple example, if Stanley had written to Sidney in a letter about Mr. Everett's black eye, the message would have been quite different from what it was. The form, or medium, of letter writing is different from the form of conversation in the ways we use it and in the things we say with it.

What are some of the forms we use in teaching-learning?

Now, finally, we arrive at the end point of all our communication effort:

. . . Sidney hears Stanley's comment. . . .

Someone perceives an event and reacts in a situation to make available materials in some form conveying content *of some consequence*. What kind of consequence do we ordinarily hope to obtain when we communicate? We hope somebody hears what we say, don't we?

AND SOMEBODY REPLIES

Now we have followed one communication situation and we have seen how our model of communication applies to this situation. Common sense tells us, however, that the situation has not ended yet, even though we have followed it clear through our model. The conversation between Stanley and Sidney certainly will continue, won't it?

Do some communication situations end after one message?

How Communication Works / 71

You're probably jumping ahead now—you've probably already noticed that we've arrived at a point that looks very much like the beginning of our model. Of course you're right. After Someone has sent a message, *someone else,* we hope, perceives it. We'll label the second someone, Sidney in this case, S2.

. . . Sidney says, "Wow! Look at that! We're sure going to have some fun teasing him about that, Stanley!" . . .

Can a person who receives a message sometimes also perceive the Event that the message is about?

Someone (Sidney, this time) perceives an Event (Stanley's comment) *and reacts in a situation to make available materials in some form conveying content of some consequence.* That is, Sidney answers Stanley's message by sending a message back to him.

FEEDBACK

. . . And Stanley replies, "Yeah. I'll bet he'll try to tell us he ran into the edge of a door." Sidney says, "This will be fun. That black eye is a beauty. It really must hurt, though." . . .

And so on and on the conversation goes. Stanley hears Sidney's message and replies to it, and Sidney hears Stanley's reply and answers it. In each exchange, we can follow the action in our model through the perceiving process and the reacting process, going around and around the circle as each boy replies to the other's comments.

We call this circular conversational pattern *feedback*. Specifically, feedback occurs when somebody communicates something *in reaction to* a message he has received. When you make a comment and somebody reacts to it, by commenting back, by yawning, by shrugging, he is giving you feedback. He is letting you know what he thinks of your comment.

For the teacher, feedback is one of the most important parts of the communication process. You find out whether your communication has been effective when you get feedback from your students. You find out whether they *understood* what you said; you find out whether they were *convinced* that you were right in what you said; you find out whether they were *persuaded* to act upon what you said.

If effectiveness is the communicator's goal, then feedback is the communicator's measuring instrument, his way of evaluating his success.

But probably an even more important thing for the teacher to remember about feedback is that it lets you know what the learners are thinking about. Feedback makes it possible for the teacher to hold dialogue with learners. It lets us "close the feedback loop," following the idea of figure 7, to get the full benefits of two-way communication. If effective communication is the sharing of important ideas among people, then it can only come about through a process that includes listening to feedback as an important part.

> What do you suppose the phrase "Closing the feedback loop" means?

BEGIN USING THE MODEL OF COMMUNICATION

Someone perceives an event and reacts in a situation to make available materials in some form conveying content of some consequence.

During the next few days, try to apply the model of communication to a variety of kinds of communication situations. As you watch television, try to follow the model to analyze the TV program: Who is the *someone?* What is the *event* that he *perceived?* How did he *react* to the event? What is the *situation* in which he reacts? What kind of *form* does the message take? What is its *content?* What *consequences* does the writer of the program or the speaker expect?

As you watch your friends, your spouse, your children communicate, try to follow those communication situations in the model. As you sit in a meeting, analyze the speaker's communication using the model. As you teach, analyze what you are doing by using the model, and use the model to think through some things your learners say to you. In short, get used to seeing communication situations in terms of the elements of our communication model.

You may find that it's worthwhile to memorize the model quickly. If you stop right now and repeat it to yourself ten times,

> What kinds of things do you find out when you apply the Model of Communication to a communication situation?

making yourself look at the page less and less each time, you'll probably have it nearly memorized. After all, it only has eight parts:

1. Someone
2. perceives an event
3. and reacts
4. in a situation
5. to make available materials
6. in some form
7. conveying content
8. of some consequence.

And as you're getting used to seeing communication situations in terms of these elements, you'll also be learning, over the next several chapters, a lot about how each element works in the process of effective communication.

Use the Model to analyze the communication between the authors of this book and you.

CHAPTER 10

Someone Perceives an Event...

Why did the four members of the family make such different comments?

The family was driving home together after church on Sunday morning. "That really was a good sermon this morning," said ten-year-old Kevin. "Our minister sure is good at telling funny stories!" "It was a good sermon," said mother. "We're lucky to have such a good minister. He's so inspirational. I always feel a lot better after the Sunday morning sermon." Eighteen-year-old Elizabeth thought to herself, I'll never understand how mother can feel so good about the things that minister says. He just makes me feel guilty by pointing out to me how far I am from measuring up to Christian standards. After a pause, father commented, "You know, I don't think I ever really understood what salvation is all about until this morning. The sermon led me to think carefully about something I hadn't considered in years. We all should really appreciate the work our minister is doing."

Guidance for Session 10
SOMEONE PERCEIVES AN EVENT

Aims for the Session

To develop a more detailed understanding of how human perception affects the communication process. To become acquainted with the concept of a Map of the World in Our Heads. To begin to see some of the important implications of this concept in teaching-learning.

Questions to Ponder

What effects does perception have on the communication process? What do we mean when we say that the meanings of Events are in our heads, not in the Events? What does it mean to the teacher that every learner's perceptions are at least a little bit different from anybody else's? How can the teacher cope with the selective perceptions of learners? What can the teacher do to stimulate meanings in the minds of learners?

A Study Plan

I. Describe in some detail the patterns of nerve impulses that would be generated in your body and interpreted by your Map of the World as "sitting in church during a sermon," as "eating an ice-cream cone," as "driving a car," as "participating in a group discussion on teaching-learning in the church school." What patterns of nerve impulses would be present in your body during these situations but be ignored by your selective perception?

II. Try to list all the things in the room that you could perceive, but that you've ignored while you're reading this question. If you're in a group, only include the things that nobody in the group was aware of for the moment. When you finish, try to estimate roughly the proportion of sensations available to you that you were actually conscious of.

Four people were exposed to the same Event. They even sat in the same place in the sanctuary, and yet we can easily see that the four people left church on this Sunday morning with four very different impressions of what happened in church. Each person perceived a different thing in the minister's sermon.

How can this happen? How can four people who know each other so well, who agree so completely on life's basic values, who share the family fellowship, see such different things in this Sunday morning sermon? How can four people perceive this Event so differently?

Why is it that *no two people ever perceive the same Event in exactly the same way?*

The answer to this important question lies in an understanding of how perception works.

THE PROCESS OF PERCEPTION

Our knowledge of Events in the world around us is not directly connected with the actual Events themselves. We find out about the world only indirectly. In fact, there are three intermediate steps between an Event itself and our *conscious perception* of that Event. In these three intervening steps, each person impresses his own individuality upon the perceptions he has of Events. We'll call these three steps (1) the nervous system, (2) the "mapping" system, and (3) the selecting system.

THE NERVOUS SYSTEM

Every sensation that reaches your brain must be translated by your nervous system into nerve impulses from whatever form it takes outside your body. The various kinds of nerve endings in your body do the translating. Let's look at some examples:

Vision. Light waves in the world around you strike the retina of your eye. Nerve endings in the retina translate patterns of light waves into patterns of nerve impulses.

> When you're inside the house with the windows closed, in what sense can we say that you can only find out about the weather outside **indirectly**?

If your proportion is more than five or ten percent, keep looking for more sensations that you could have been aware of, but weren't.

III. Leaf through an old magazine or newspaper and tear out a picture—what meaning does it have for you? Show it to other people and see what it means to them. When you can't contain your curiosity any more, look at the caption and see what it "really" means. Is its "real" meaning any more real to you than the story you made up? If you wanted to illustrate the story you made up, is there any reason you couldn't use that picture?

IV. Have two members of the group stage a short conversation about some topic, carefully concealing the topic. Then have each of the other members of the group write a short story telling what led up to the conversation and what it was about. First share the meanings the group saw in the conversation, then let the actors tell what "really" happened. Whose meaning is the correct meaning?

V. Suppose you have to go to the supermarket to buy a can of shortening, a dozen eggs, and a package of frozen peas. From your own Map of the World, try to describe each action you'd take to get from the place you're sitting right now to the store, inside the store to pick up the items you need, through the check-out counter, and home into the kitchen. Try to remember all the visual cues you'd actually use to guide yourself along the way. How will you go about finding these items in your grocery? Make a little script of the things you'd say to the check-out girl. If you drive to the supermarket, how do you get into your car, start it, drive out of the driveway? Next time you go shopping, check your inner Map to see if you've planned this trip accurately.

Hearing. Sound waves in the world around you strike your eardrum. Nerve endings in your inner ear translate patterns of sound waves into patterns of nerve impulses.

Touch. When there is some pressure on your skin, nerve endings in your skin transmit patterns of nerve impulses in response to the pressure.

Taste. Certain nerve endings in your mouth are sensitive to some chemical properties of the food you eat. When these nerve endings contact certain chemicals (for instance, salt), they transmit patterns of nerve impulses.

Your other senses work in similar ways: In response to some condition outside your body, nerve endings transmit nerve impulses inside your body. Information that may eventually reach your brain exists in a wide variety of forms outside your body; inside your body all of this information has been translated into one form—nerve impulses.

The translations that our nerve endings make are generally accurate enough for most purposes. We do, after all, manage to live reasonably secure lives with the information our brains have available in the form of nerve impulses. But our nerve "translators" can be fooled—in fact they commonly are fooled in everyday situations.

Optical illusions, for instance, are humorous devices in which we more or less knowingly trick our eyes into "seeing" something that is not really there.

> What are some of the other kinds of translations between Events outside your body and patterns of nerve impulses inside your body that your nervous system makes?

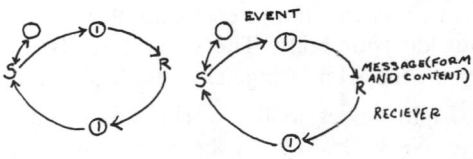

Stereophonic sound systems, for another example, trick our ears so that we seem to hear things we know are not really there. You may have had the experience of listening to a stereo phonograph and "hearing" a singer's voice coming from a place between the two loudspeakers that are actually making the sounds. The fact that you knew where the sound was coming from didn't make the apparent source of the voice one bit less real. You knew that your perceptions were being tricked, and yet the trick worked anyway.

And anybody who has lived in a cold climate has had the experience of coming indoors on a sub-zero day and washing his hands in cold water that felt very hot. In the same way, dry ice burns if you touch it—it really feels hot!

Many of the situations in which your nerve translators are fooled are not so apparent. Let's perform an experiment. Without moving at all, try to feel the clothes that cover most of your body. Chances are you can hardly feel your clothes even when you try. Although your clothes are pressing against your skin, the only time when you have very much sensation of pressure is during the first few minutes after you change clothes. Very soon your nerve endings simply stop registering the pressure.

Place this book flat on your hand. How long does it have to rest motionless there before you can no longer feel it clearly?

The point that we need to understand is that there is a discontinuity, a disconnection, between Events outside you and the patterns of nerve inpulses through which your brain finds out about these Events. You don't experience the world directly. All you experience is a complex series of nerve impulses that were generated inside your body. And these patterns of nerve impulses that reach your brain may not have any direct connection with the Events themselves; your nervous system can be fooled, and it commonly is.

But it's not enough for our brains just to receive patterns of nerve impulses. It's obvious that what we perceive is not made up of nerve impulses; it is made up of pictures of events, images, *meaningful* sensations. We must consider, then, how meanings become attached to the patterns of nerve impulses that our brains are receiving.

What's the difference between patterns of nerve impulses and meaningful images in your mind?

THE MAPPING SYSTEM

Consider for a moment the patterns of nerve impulses that would reach your brain if you were watching a house burning down. The flickering pattern of light striking the retina of your eye would produce patterns of nerve impulses. The crackling and hissing sounds striking the eardrum would produce patterns of nerve impulses. If you were standing close enough, the heat on your face would produce patterns of nerve impulses. Inside your head, you put these patterns of nerve impulses together and come up with the meaning, "burning house." Where did you get that meaning?

What patterns of nerve impulses is your brain receiving as you read this book?

Authorities in this field have found that an easy way of understanding what happens is to imagine that you have a "Map of the World in Your Head." This particular map contains all the meanings that you know—all the things you know about—and shows you which of the meanings to attach to a given pattern of nerve impulses. When you're watching a burning house, for instance, your brain receives the complex patterns of nerve impulses from your eyes and ears and skin, and your Map of the World supplies a meaning, burning house, that matches those patterns of nerve impulses.

Think what would happen if you had never known anything about burning houses, if you had never seen a house burning down and had never heard of such a thing. What would those patterns

Can you remember being in a situation that you just couldn't supply any meaning for the things that were happening?

Someone Perceives an Event / 77

of nerve impulses mean to you then? Probably nothing. It is only because you already have the meaning, burning house, in your head that you can perceive the actual Event of a house burning down. The meaning, burning house, is part of your Map of the World.

You began to develop a Map of the World in Your Head soon after you were born, when you first came to realize that the particular pattern of eyes and nose and mouth that floated in and out of view from time to time belonged to a wonderful, warm, comforting mother, who provided food and other good things. Before a year had passed, you were able to make sense out of many other patterns of nerve impulses—those corresponding to your bed, to your bottle of milk, to a cookie, to your favorite rag doll, and so forth. Watching an infant begin to develop his Map of the World is an exciting experience!

Maps of the Physical World.—The idea of a Map of the World in Your Head is easy to grasp if you imagine a blind man trying to find his way around your neighborhood. Since he cannot see, he must take his cues from the texture of the surface beneath his feet, from the sounds around him, and from the small cues he gets from his red and white long cane. If he is to learn to get around your neighborhood with very much efficiency, the blind man has to make himself a very real mental map. He must be able to interpret the meaning of various kinds of ground surfaces; he needs to know where he is likely to hear the various kinds of sounds; he learns where a telephone pole has been set into the sidewalk, where a tree is dangerously close to his path. In short, he consciously builds himself a set of meanings ready and waiting to be attached in a moment to the few patterns of nerve impulses that are available to him. His Map of your neighborhood is required to be detailed indeed.

You have a map of your neighborhood in your mind, too. Since you can see, and you don't have to find your way on the tenuous cues the blind man has available, your map of your neighborhood may be less detailed. But think for a moment—if you suddenly found yourself walking on a sidewalk a few blocks from your home, how would you identify where you were? First, you'd look around you to see what your surroundings looked like. Then you'd search your mind—your Map of the World—for a place that looks like this one. You'd use your Map to find yourself. And your map would tell you which way to go to get home.

Think of all the other places you have "mapped" in your mind. Your home, your office, your car, your church, your route to and from work (this is so well-mapped that you could follow it in your sleep—and sometimes you nearly do!), the arrangement of goods on the shelves of your supermarket. Your Map tells you that the long yellow pointed things at the fruit counter are bananas.

Maps of Social Relationships.—You use the Map in Your Head to attach meanings to places and to physical objects, but you also use it to make sense of your relationships with other people. When six-year-old Johnny says his head hurts at eight o'clock on a weekday morning, does it mean that he may be catching cold or does it probably mean the school nurse has announced she will give measles vaccinations at school that day? When dad comes home from work with a big smile on his face, does it mean very good news or does dad always come home from work with a smile? When the announcer on television says that Ed's Used Car Lot has the finest cars in town, can you take his word for it?

Once again, let's begin at the beginning and consider the kind of information your brain has available to it when you're talking to somebody. Let's say you're talking to a good friend about something. As he talks, your ear receives sound waves from the air and translates them into nerve impulses. As you watch him, your eyes receive patterns of light waves and respond by transmitting patterns of nerve impulses. And so it goes. All of the information your brain is receiving consists of patterns of nerve impulses, and the Map in Your Head is attaching meanings to these impulses.

Your mental Map of your close personal relationships is a very complex thing. When you're talking to your husband or your wife, to your children, to your best friend, you can read a thousand subtle shades of meaning into comments that another person might take at face value. A great deal of the "territory" of your Map is concerned with attaching meanings to the actions and statements of the people who are important in your life.

And another large section of your Map provides the meanings you need to maintain casual relationships. Buying a sack of potatoes, taking a taxi to the doctor's office, asking directions to the shoe department of an unfamiliar department store—all these are situations in which you must interact meaningfully with other people. Think for a moment how you expect to be able to identify a salesperson in a department store—think of the subtle cues you must be able to understand: a salesperson will not be wearing a coat or hat, for instance; a salesperson probably will be wearing a certain kind of clothes, a suit or dress rather than sport clothes; a man in a suit who has several pencils in a holder in his shirt pocket may be a salesman; certainly anybody who is fairly well-dressed and has a store badge pinned on his shoulder may be a salesperson. Finding the salesperson is harder than you thought, isn't it? But in fact you seldom have much difficulty in finding one because the Map in Your Head makes these small cues meaningful to you.

Maps of Christian Meanings.—Finally, your Map provides you with the moral and spiritual meanings that you use in your life. It tells you which Events are good and which Events are bad. It tells

> What are some of the facial expressions or gestures you can recognize in your best friend that nobody else would notice?

> How do you decide whether to go ahead and find a seat or to wait for the hostess to seat you in a restaurant?

How do you teach a baby not to play with electric cords?

What different things does this chapter mean—to you? to the author? to the editor? to the typesetter? to the mailman who delivered it?

you when you are acting in a moral and Christian way and when you should consider your actions more carefully.

It is this part of the Map that we work so hard to develop in our children. We provide instruction to them directly and by example to help them build moral and spiritual understandings. As you think back over your own childhood, the things you probably remember most vividly are situations in which your parents made it clear to you that certain kinds of actions were unacceptable or unchristian. It is no small wonder that some of the most powerful and meaningful understandings that we have as adults resulted from these childhood experiences.

Meanings Come from Within the Perceiver.—To summarize for a moment, the information that reaches your brain is entirely in the form of nerve impulses, meaningless in themselves. Before you can have any understanding of the Event that caused the nerve impulses, your mind must supply a meaning for them. An easy way of visualizing the meaning-supplying process is to pretend that you have a Map in Your Head of the world around you, and that this Map contains the meanings that you could apply to the bunches of nerve impulses. When your brain receives some pattern of impulses, your Map supplies a meaning that matches the impulses.

The important thing to remember is this: *The meanings you attach to Events are not inherent in the Events themselves. The meanings come from within you.*

Now we can begin to understand clearly why four people can listen to the same sermon in church on Sunday and have such different impressions of what the sermon meant. Each of the people was receiving rather similar nerve impulses—they all witnessed the same Event. But each was supplying meanings from his own Map of the World in His Head. All four saw the same things, heard the same things, and each supplied different meanings from his own mind.

As a teacher, you will try to help your learners discover or clarify certain meanings. You will aim to get them to share understandings. You must be very aware as you teach that each of your learners brings a slightly different map of the world into the class. Sometimes the differences may be very important in shaping how the learner perceives the learning situation and the understandings you're trying to help him develop.

THE SELECTING SYSTEM

There is one more part of the process of perception that is quite important in the teaching-learning situation—one that creates a perennial problem for the teacher. This is the fact that perception is *selective.*

There is so much going on around you all the time that your brain would be literally flooded with sensations if you perceived it all; it's just too much. Your nervous system is generating an avalanche of impulses all the time. You must necessarily have some way to filter down this flood of sensation to a manageable trickle, and of course you do.

The first set of filters that helps to reduce the flow of impulses is right in your nervous system, where the weak and usually unimportant kinds of impulses get low priority. Signals from these weak sensations are simply overridden by the much stronger impulses that succeed in reaching your brain. At six o'clock in the morning, for example, you can hear the chirping of a robin whose nest is in a nearby tree. By seven-thirty or eight o'clock, when the sounds of traffic and of the neighborhood have increased, you can no longer hear the friendly robin. The robin's sound is still there—it still strikes your eardrum and creates nerve impulses—but now other stronger sound impulses are overriding the weak impulses from the chirping.

Have you ever had a headache that nearly disappeared as soon as you had something interesting to do?

Even of the patterns of impulses that do reach your brain, however, very few are ever consciously perceived. Consider for a moment the room you're sitting in right now. Look around you and see how many things there are that you could be seeing: furniture in a number of interesting shapes, walls and ceilings with various patterns of texture and light reflections, floors with all kinds of interesting markings on them, perhaps other people who would be fascinating to watch, and a hundred little objects of various kinds that you could look at. How many of those things were you consciously perceiving before you thought about it? Almost none of them? Listen for a minute to all the sounds you can hear where you are sitting. Sounds of people, sounds of traffic outside, sounds of the building itself. How many of those sounds were you conscious of a minute ago? Almost none of them? Feel carefully; feel the pressure of the chair you're sitting on. Were you aware of it? No? Think how many things right in this room you now notice that you weren't aware of just a few minutes ago. All of these things were there then. And you didn't perceive them. You were busy reading.

Reread the last paragraph. What did you see in it this time that you missed the first time you read it?

Selective perception can do amazing things. It can let you read a book or watch a TV program so intently that suddenly you notice that somebody has been talking to you for several minutes and you haven't heard a thing he said. It can let a high school student look out the window and daydream and completely miss everything that happened right in front of him in a forty-five-minute class. It can let you get so involved in thinking about some point a speaker has made that you miss everything he says for the next five minutes.

Most of us can only concentrate on one thing at a time. When we're reading, we miss nearly everything else that happens around us. When we're listening to a speaker, we don't pay very much attention to the people around us (and if we get distracted by the people around us, we don't hear much of what the speaker is saying).

What do you suppose determines which things people will pay attention to and which they will ignore?

As teachers, we must be particularly sensitive to the selective perceptions of learners. In the first place, we must make ourselves very aware of the need to keep attention on the teaching-learning situation, to make things interesting enough so that learners pay attention—this is obvious. But in addition, we must be aware of the fact that the learner's mind may continue along one train of thought after the class has gone on to another idea. Be sure the learner is making the transitions right along with you or you may find that he is still thinking about your interesting example ten minutes later.

NO TWO PEOPLE PERCEIVE AN EVENT IN THE SAME WAY

We began our discussion of perception by posing an interesting problem: How could four members of the same family sit through the same sermon on Sunday morning and leave church with four very different impressions? Let's try to follow what happened that Sunday morning now that we've begun to appreciate how their perceptions of the sermon could vary so much.

To begin with, each member of the family was exposed to the same Event. Each sat in the same part of the church; each listened to the same sermon preached by the same minister; each had the same distractions during church. Although there may be small individual variations between the family members in how sensitive their hearing or their eyesight is, each had roughly the same nerve impulses transmitted to his brain in reaction to the Event.

How does your Map of the World affect the things you notice in your minister's sermons?

Here's where the resemblance between family members ends, however. Each family member brought with him his own Map of the World—a Map that is different from anybody else's. Each interpreted the nerve impulses that his brain received differently because his Map was supplying different meanings. And each was paying close attention to different things in the sermon, too. Mother was selectively perceiving the parts of the sermon that reassured her; Elizabeth was selectively perceiving the parts of the sermon for close attention that made her feel guilty. Kevin heard the pastor's opening story and apparently couldn't get very interested in anything else that was said.

If you were Kevin's church school teacher, how would you try to communicate meanings to him?

No two members of the family perceived the sermon in the same way. And just incidentally, no two people in the whole congregation perceived the message in exactly the same way either. Every person in the church that Sunday morning brought his own problems, his own background, his own interests, his own values—his own Map of the World—to bear on the same sermon and each picked out his own meanings.

What lesson can the teacher learn from this description of the process of perception? The most important lesson is this one:

The meanings that a person attaches to an Event come from within him.

The meaning of an Event is not part of the Event itself. The only meaning an Event can have is the meaning that some person attaches to the event. The meanings that learners carry away from a session are not part of the session itself; the meanings that learners carry away from a session come from within the learners. The most that a teacher can do is to *stimulate* the learner to perceive important meanings.

That morning in class, sixteen-year-old Jimmy Hendrix had asked, "What did Jesus mean when he said, 'Blessed are the meek?' Does that mean that we should just let people get away with anything they do to us? Should we let people walk all over us?" Sitting in the living room after the Sunday dinner dishes were washed, Mrs. Brainard wondered, "What could I have said to him? I know what I think Jesus meant, but how can I give this idea some real meaning to Jimmy? How can I lead him to understand? How will he react when I try to explain this to him?"

This is the important question in communication, isn't it? How will he react if I explain it this way, or that way? Will it have real meaning to him if I use this particular example? How can I make this meaning so vivid in his mind that he will act on it? How can I predict how he'll react?

Actually we make predictions all the time about how people will react to things we say and things we do—we couldn't lead stable and secure lives if we weren't pretty good at predicting how people will react. When you

> ask the salesman the price of a pair of new shoes, tell the serviceman to "Fill'er up with high-test," ask the usher to give you a seat on the aisle in church, request a double-dip, butter crunch ice-cream cone,

CHAPTER 11

...And Reacts In a Situation...

What advantage is it to the teacher to be able to predict how learners will react to the things he says?

How do you feel when somebody doesn't react the way you expected?

In what kinds of situations is it so important to predict accurately how a learner will react that we'd be willing to take some time to work out our prediction?

you are assuming that the people you're talking to will react in predictable ways.

We make these predictions without particularly thinking about them because we've learned through years of experience that such reactions are predictable. We predict almost by intuition. And for most purposes, this works well enough. And just because we predict, this does not mean that we force or trick someone into acting contrary to what he really wants to do.

LEARNING TO ANALYZE OUR PREDICTIONS

Under some circumstances, it becomes very important to be able to make an especially accurate prediction about how the learner will react. His reaction may affect his life in important ways. If we make a mistake in our prediction, as we may do if we work entirely by intuition, then we may do more harm than good with the guidance we are giving the learner in such a situation.

As we work to guide a teen-ager toward a growing concept of God, for example, we must be particularly sensitive to the possibility that in providing new meanings to him we may undermine too quickly the childish understandings that he has already developed. We may, with the best of intentions, of course, be trying to guide him toward meanings that he is not yet ready to accept, and at the same time we may begin to weaken for him meanings that he still needs very much. In a situation like this one, we need to have a plan for analyzing how he may react. We need to have a way of thinking through the various reactions he may have and deciding whether a given kind of guidance is likely or not to get the desired reaction.

In this chapter, we will be thinking through the ways we make predictions about how people probably will react to the things we

Guidance for Session 11
... AND REACTS IN A SITUATION ...

Aims for the Session

To develop a more thorough understanding of the ways we predict how people will react to the things we do and the things we say in communication. To examine very explicitly the underlying assumptions of the ways we make these predictions. To analyze some of the factors that contribute to determining how people react to Events.

Questions to Ponder

Why does the teacher need to be able to predict how learners will react to the things that happen in teaching-learning? What kinds of reactions does the teacher need to be able to predict? What kinds of factors help to determine how somebody will react to something you say to him? What effect will the communication situation have upon the learner's reaction? What effect will the situation in which you're asking him to change his behavior have upon your communication? What are some of the things you know about the people you communicate with that help you to predict how they'll react?

A Study Plan

I. Try to think of some situations, imaginary ones if you can't think of any real ones, in which you understood what somebody was saying to you but you weren't convinced they were right. In which you were convinced they were right but you couldn't understand the idea they were trying to explain. In which you were persuaded to act in a certain way even though you didn't understand why you should act that way. In which you were convinced that an idea was right but you didn't act upon it anyway. Why did you react the way you did in these situations? Briefly explain your reaction in each case.

II. What differences would you expect in a learner's reactions if you communicated with him in a formal class meeting? in a class discussion? in a conversation just between the two of you after class? in a conversation that included three or four of his friends? in a conversation that included his parents?

III. Make a list of meanings you might try to communicate to a learner that you'd expect him to

84 / Basics for Communication in the Church

do and the things we say. We'll be very explicit, just this once, about a process we carry on subsconsciously all the time. Then once we've thought the process through very clearly and considered in some detail how we ordinarily go about making these predictions, we'll be in a better position to think through some particular very important prediction about how somebody might react. We'll see how to analyze consciously, and we won't always have to rely on intuition to make these predictions.

Since we're being very explicit about a process that each of us carries on many times a day, it may sometimes seem that our discussion is belaboring the obvious by dwelling at some length on something "everybody knows." I hope you'll bear with me when you get this feeling, because even though the ideas that we're thinking about may seem familiar, I think you may see some new twists in them, as you try to make them very clear to yourself, that will be useful to you as you communicate. And you just may discover that one or two of the things that "everybody knows" aren't such sure things after all, when you think very carefully about them.

We must be careful to remember throughout this discussion that we'll never be skillful enough to predict perfectly how anybody is going to react. We can never be completely sure of our predictions. What we can do is to learn to predict better than we do. We can develop skill at predicting, even under difficult or very important circumstances, even though we understand that we'll never develop 100 percent accuracy.

Can you ever predict with absolute certainty how you will react to a situation?

As we discuss the problem of predicting how people will react to our messages, we must be aware that there is a difference between considering how people will react on the one hand and try-

react to only after some time had passed. Can you think of any meanings you could communicate about that the learner would react to as much as twenty years later? fifty years later?

IV. Think of a simple situation that you could stage for a friend, a situation that you could arrange to have happen to him while you watch. Before you stage the situation for him, write down in some detail how you would react to that situation—be careful to say how you would react and not how you expect him to react. Now stage the situation and see how he reacts. What do you suppose caused the differences between the way you'd react and the way he reacted?

If you're in a group, select one group member and send him out of the room. Then have everybody else make up a simple situation that would be easy to stage for him when he returns. Now as you write down how you'd react if you were he, remember that he'll be reacting in front of a group of people—how would you react to that situation in front of a group of people?

V. Brainstorm to produce a list of differences between people that would make a difference in the way they'd react to some messages. List every possible difference you can think of, even if some sound a little silly. After five or ten minutes, stop and read through your list underlining the dozen or so of the differences that you think would be most useful to know in predicting how a person would react to a wide variety of situations.

VI. How many different subcultures can you name that are represented in your community? For each of the subcultures you name, think of at least two or three ways you think members of that subculture would react differently from the way other people would react to things you might say.

VII. Name as many specific ideals or beliefs as you can think of that you and your best friend, or you and your husband or wife, can agree on. If you're in a group, name all the ideals anybody can think of on which everybody in the group can agree on. Think about all the kinds of religious and spiritual beliefs, moral ideals, political beliefs, ideals concerning child-raising, and any other ideals and beliefs you can think of.

ing to manipulate people on the other—trying to force every learner into some tight mold that we may personally hold up as our ideal. Sometimes the difference is subtle, but always the difference is important.

On the one hand, as responsible teachers we owe it to our learners to consider them as individuals and to think carefully about the kinds of discussions and explanations that will be most beneficial to them. But on the other hand, we must be responsible to them by not trying to manipulate each of them into a carbon copy of ourselves.

Frankly, some of the ideas and techniques we'll discuss in this chapter could be used to manipulate learners in small ways. But a responsible teacher will try not to use these ideas in that way.

WHAT WE'RE TRYING TO PREDICT

When we make our predictions about how somebody will react to the things we say, what do we really want to know? What kinds of answers are we looking for? Let's consider three kinds of reactions that we may, in some particular circumstances, hope to get.

Will he *understand* what I say? First, we're looking for understanding, aren't we? If the learner doesn't understand your meaning, then his reaction may be quite unpredictable indeed. When you have led him to understanding, you have succeeded in stimulating in his Map of the World an image that corresponds to the image you have in your own Map. His image and your image may not be exactly the same—in fact they may be different in important respects—but their general outlines, at least, will have some similarities.

Will he be *convinced* that I am right in what I say? It's quite possible that someone will understand very clearly what you're telling him and at the same time think you're entirely wrong. So to understand is not necessarily to be convinced. But ordinarily you're not likely to be able to convince somebody that you're right unless he can understand what you're saying. When you convince somebody of something, you have succeeded in changing his Map of the World. You've changed some image in his Map so that it corresponds at least partially to the same image in your Map.

Will he be *persuaded* to act on what I say? It's not unusual for a person to be convinced of something and yet not act on it. You might be convinced, for example, that the Super Gazelle Eight is the finest automobile on the road and yet you may continue to make do with your old Stallion Six for another year or two. No matter how strongly you may be convinced of the superiority of the Gazelle, you still aren't ready to act upon your belief. You'll wait another year before you're ready to buy a new car. Being persuaded to act in a certain way is different from being convinced that the action is the one you should take.

We've seen that being convinced is no guarantee that somebody

Once a person understands you, what more do you have to do to convince him that you're right?

will be persuaded, but it is also quite possible that a person will be persuaded to act the way you want him to act without being convinced that you are right. We expect very young children to do this all the time, in fact. We may punish two-year-old Tommy for reaching into the goldfish bowl to touch the pretty fish, and thus we may succeed in making him stop reaching into the goldfish bowl. But we hardly expect to convince him that it would not be fun to touch the fish.

Ordinarily, however, we recognize that a person who is convinced that a thing is right is more likely to be enthusiastic about acting upon his belief. And as a result, we spend considerable effort in trying to convince Tommy that he'll injure the pretty fish if he touches it, and we expect that when he finally becomes convinced of this idea, he'll be very much less likely to sneak his hand into the goldfish bowl. A person who is persuaded to do something without being convinced that it is the right thing to do usually will not be very enthusiastic in his action. But if we can convince him that the action is right, we may find that he is much more strongly persuaded to do it.

As we try to predict how people will react to the things we communicate, then, we're trying to answer one of these three questions:

Will he *understand* what I say?
Will he be *convinced* that I am right in what I say?
Will he be *persuaded* to act on what I say?

PREDICTING REACTIONS: A FORMAL APPROACH

Now let's begin to develop an approach to answering these questions. Our approach, of course, is going to consist of asking more questions. If we can agree on a set of questions that we feel are useful and productive in a wide variety of situations, then we'll have an approach that is almost as valuable as if we could provide a set of ready-made answers that would fit all situations. Certainly each set of circumstances is different enough so that no set of pat answers will ever cover them all. It's more important to know how to analyze each one as it comes up. And that means knowing the right questions to ask.

WHAT SITUATION WILL HE REACT IN?

You remember that in our Model of Communication, we found that the situation in which a person reacts is important in helping to determine how he will react. As we agreed, a person may react to the same message in very different ways under different circumstances. So our first question as we begin to try to predict how someone will react to a message we may send is this: What is the situation in which I want to influence his reaction?

The answer to this question is often very easy. You and the person you wish to influence are together in the same situation

---

Do you ever do things just because somebody asks you to?

What kinds of differences in people's reactions can the situation make?

and you expect to get an immediate reaction. Under these circumstances you really don't have to think very carefully about the situation factor, since it will usually be pretty obvious.

Don't lose sight of the fact, however, that even in the same situation, you may be perceiving quite different things from the things he is perceiving. It's easy to imagine, for instance, that in most situations, your perceptions of the situation and four-year-old Jennifer's perceptions of the situation are quite different. You attach meaning to the things around you according to your Map of the World, and nobody else has a Map of the World in his Head that is exactly like yours. So you must be sensitive to the possibility that even in the same situation, you may be seeing some things and your listener may be seeing some very different things.

Much of the time you'll be trying to predict how your listener will react in a situation that is different from the situation in which you're doing the communicating. When you write a message to somebody or when you telephone somebody, you and he are separated in *space*. The two of you aren't in the same place. You must consider as you begin to predict how he will react, then, what the situation will be in which he reacts.

In many other cases, the situation in which the listener will react is separated from the situation in which you actually send the message by the passage of *time*. Sometimes you and your listener are actually separated by the passage of time when you are communicating to him, as is nearly always the case when you are writing a message rather than talking directly to him. Sometimes you may both be in the same place at the same time when you are communicating, but you are trying to motivate him to react in some certain way later on; for instance, you may be giving him some instructions on how to use a certain machine that he'll actually use a week from now.

Predicting the listener's reaction when his reaction will occur later is a basic problem for parent and teacher. The idea that you are trying to help the learner understand now may be one that he will use to guide his reactions twenty or even fifty years from now. The teacher must sometimes try to help students understand material that they have no strong, immediate use for, but which they will find more useful at some later time.

We'd like to know, then, what situation the learner will be in when he reacts to our message. If we can know with some certainty what situation he'll be in, then we can shape our message to fit that specific situation.

This idea is illustrated by the experience of a large direct-mail sales company that was trying to sell a very useful small item to top executives of large American corporations. To a selected list of executives, the mail-order company sent a letter ending, "To take advantage of this attractive introductory offer, take a minute right

---

What kinds of differences in perceptions of the situation would you expect when the seller of a house and the buyer are sitting in the living room discussing the price of the house?

Are the writer and reader of a written message always separated both by time and by space?

In what ways can a teacher shape his message to fit the situation the learner will react in?

now to dictate a quick note on your company letterhead letting us know you'd like to try the amazing 'Whatzis.' In less than a week you'll be enjoying the 'Whatzis' at your desk every day." Even though the product was very saleable in the company's experience and it was priced quite attractively, the letter resulted in very few sales. When the mail-order company began to analyze the reason for the low sales, it found that its mailing list had contained home addresses rather than office addresses of the executives. The sales letter had assumed that the executives would be reading it in the wrong situation. A follow-up letter with a postage-paid card in it got the sales that the mail-order company expected; by keying the reaction that the message aimed to get to the situation in which the reader was asked to react, the mail-order company improved the accuracy of its prediction about reader reaction considerably.

LOOK INSIDE: HOW WOULD I REACT IN THAT SITUATION?

Most of the time we stop the formal analysis at this point, if we have even carried it this far. We simply stop and ask ourselves, How would I react to this message in that situation? That is to say, we look inside ourselves, or *introspect,* and we predict that the listener to our message will react the same way that we would react to it in that situation.

> Under what circumstances is introspection likely to give accurate predictions?

Introspection is often a very productive way of predicting listener reaction, especially in situations where very accurate predictions are not absolutely essential. Introspection works because in many ways people are similar to each other. In a wide variety of situations, most Americans would react in similar ways. So the way I'd react to a given message in a given situation and the way you'd react might be nearly the same, and we could predict each other's reactions fairly accurately by introspection.

But we must be very careful to recognize that everybody does not react the same way in all situations. All people are not exactly the same, except perhaps in spirit, and life would be very dull if they were. Differences between individuals and differences between groups of people are the things that make people so interesting to each other. And we must take account of these differences in predicting reactions.

> What kinds of differences are there among people that make them react differently?

Sometimes we can allow for individual differences and say, Even though he and I are different in some respects, I think we are alike in the ways that will determine how he will react to this message in this situation. And this is an entirely legitimate line of reasoning which may be even more productive than assuming that everybody is the same. Just be careful that you're not being too optimistic about the basic similarities between you and the listener just to make your analysis a little easier. Be sure you're not fooling yourself.

Let's suppose that you don't feel very confident that your

What kinds of patterns?

listener will react to your message the way you would react to it. How can you continue your formal analysis to allow for the differences you think might appear? Fortunately, people exhibit patterns in the ways they react. There are regularities in a person's reactions. And if we know what kind of regularities to look for, we can often predict with fair accuracy how a person will react to our message. Often we can identify key reaction patterns from a very small amount of information about a person. Once we find out a few facts, we can infer more wide-ranging patterns from those few facts. Of course we won't always be right, but we may be right more often than we would have been right if we had simply guessed.

WHAT KINDS OF REACTION PATTERNS SHOULD I TRY TO FIND IN MY LISTENER?

What we'd like to know about our listener is this: What does his Map of the World look like? How does he ordinarily attach meaning to certain kinds of Events? Are there consistent patterns in the way he attaches meanings? What kinds of consistent patterns am I looking for?

What kinds of patterns would you like to know about in a person whose behavior you'd like to predict?

Social scientists have concluded that certain kinds of patterns make better predictors about a person's behavior than others. For a variety of kinds of predictions they may consider a wide range of kinds of patterns, but certain kinds of patterns suggest themselves for our purposes. Let's consider four kinds of consistencies that we may look for in a learner whose reactions we'd like to be able at least partially to predict: (1) age patterns, (2) psychological patterns, (3) cultural patterns, and (4) social patterns.

Age Patterns.—Educators, child psychologists, and pediatricians like Dr. Spock tell us that most children can be expected to go through certain "stages" in the course of growing up. That is to say, at certain ages children consistently exhibit certain kinds of behavior. We can expect the three-year-old to behave in such-and-such a way in a given situation, and by the time that child is seven years old we'd expect him to behave in another way in the same situation. The reaction patterns of children, then, are partly predictable if you simply know how old the child is.

How are most six-year-olds alike? Are some behavior patterns fairly similar in most six-year-olds?

We need to be careful in applying this idea of consistencies. If you spend very much time around children, you're surely protesting already that a child's reaction patterns are not entirely determined, by any means, by his age. I think you'll agree on the other hand, though, that you can at least begin to predict, a bit tentatively, how a child will react if you know how old he is. This illustrates a basic truth that we can keep in mind all the time when we are working with these patterns: No single pattern is a complete predictor of how a person will react in a given situation. Knowing something about a person can give you some clues about his reaction patterns but a little bit of information can never tell you all about his reaction patterns. So the kinds of information we're using here can never permit you to make perfect predictions. These kinds of information, however, can help you to make better predictions than you'd otherwise be able to make. Sometimes the difference can be very significant.

Age may be a rather good predictor of behavior in a very small child. But as the child grows older, his age becomes less and less important as a guide to his patterns of reaction. By the time he is an adult, his age is no longer very useful in helping us predict how he'll react. Of course an eighty-year-old man probably will react differently from a twenty-five-year-old, but the differences are much smaller than the differences between a two-year-old and his ten-year-old brother.

The more you can learn about the patterns of behavior commonly associated with children the age of the children you're working with, the better you'll be able to use age as a predictor. As you become intimately familiar with the mind processes of children at a certain age, you begin to find that you can almost intuitively predict how they'll react in given situations. Then you won't have to take time to think so explicitly about age patterns in your analysis of how your learners will react. So, the more you can learn about "stages" of behavior in growing children, the less you have to think about it as you teach. It will begin to come naturally to you.

Psychological Patterns.—We all tend to attach labels to the people around us—labels that refer to the person's individual approach to life, his psychology. One person is gregarious and enjoys being around other people; another person is more introverted and gets his enjoyment in solitary tinkering with tools, or maybe with ideas. One person is easygoing; another person is nervous and high-strung. One person is very meticulous and careful. Another person often lets well enough alone and doesn't worry about the details.

Think of your two or three best friends—try to describe the consistent patterns in their behavior in a few words. Chances are the words you used really describe psychological patterns that you ordinarily use to predict how they'll react to the things you say to them: Harry doesn't like crowds; he isn't going to enjoy going to the Auto Show. Margaret is bothered by heavy traffic; maybe I'd better plan to take our vacation early in the season when the roads aren't crowded. John likes to spend his evenings quietly at home in front of the TV; I hope he doesn't mind going to the PTA meeting this evening too much.

This kind of psychological patterning is demonstrated most clearly in cases of mental illness. A person who is paranoid, for instance, organizes his Map of the World in terms of a series of vast plots against him by nameless villains who intend to harm him. And we recognize mental illness in a person when we can see this

Are these labels in a sense predictions in themselves?

assumption behind the ways in which he reacts to the things people say and the things people do to him. A person who is mentally ill carries some unrealistic pattern of mapping and of behavior to extremes.

Once we begin to watch for various kinds of psychological patterns in the people around us, we can consciously begin to predict their behavior and their reactions, partially at least, on the basis of the patterns we've seen in them.

Cultural Patterns.—Most Americans hold certain ideals, or moral beliefs. Among them: A nation should be governed by laws that apply the same to everybody and not by capricious men who can change laws as they see fit. A person should be rewarded for having abilities and for working hard. A man should be faithful to his wife. A person should not spend more money than he earns. There are thousands more. And all of these ideals put together are the *culture* of our society. Nearly everybody in our society holds some of these ideals, and nearly everybody in our society gets upset when somebody violates them.

> What are some more American cultural ideals?

Although we believe in these cultural ideals very strongly, there is certainly nothing universal about them. Of the ideals I've mentioned, some society on earth believes exactly opposite on every single one. So the ideals that undergird the culture of a society are different from society to society. One society holds one set of ideals; another society may have quite a different culture.

Many of the areas of our Map of the World are determined almost entirely by our American culture as it was brought to us by our parents and our teachers. The moral feelings that we have associated with sexual behavior, the feeling that we should believe in God through some religious organization, our patterns of dress, even our language and communication patterns come to us from our culture. It's easy to see, then, that cultural ideals are very important determinants of the ways in which a person is likely to react to a given set of circumstances.

> Is the way you behave in church a cultural pattern?

But since most of us spend our time talking to Americans, and very few of us expect to teach somebody from another culture, the fact that a person raised in the Japanese culture or the Ibo culture in Nigeria may have a very different concept of the Supreme Being in his Map of the World from yours isn't a very useful thing to know.

What is useful to know is that in any society, including ours, there are subcultures of various kinds with cultural ideals that are slightly different from the main stream of culture. Children in these subcultures are brought up to believe in ideals that are subtly different from the ideals the rest of the people in our society hold. In the United States, for instance, we have subcultures based upon the nationality backgrounds of families who immigrated in the last generation or two; we have racial subcultures; we have

> What are some subcultures or counter-cultures?

religious subcultures (people raised in your own church body may be members of a subculture or counter-culture of sorts); we even have subcultures based upon age, of which the subculture of college students is the most visible example.

A member of each of these subcultures shares a Map of the World in his Head that is, in some respects at least, similar to the Maps held by other members of that subculture. Certain of the ideals that he holds are very likely to be similar to ideals held by others in his subculture and a bit different from the mainstream ideals.

As you begin to become sensitive to these subcultural consistencies, you can begin to use them to predict—partially—how a person may react to what you say. One of the easiest things to find out about a person is whether he belongs to some sort of subculture. He may volunteer this bit of information in a casual conversation. Sometimes this single piece of information can give valuable clues about that person's consistent patterns of reaction.

Social Patterns.—In many areas of our beliefs, our culture allows us a whole range of possible ideals rather than concentrating upon one single ideal. That is, we may feel that it is entirely moral and legitimate to hold one or another ideal within a certain range rather than feeling upset with ourselves if we do not stick to some particular ideal. We feel, for instance, that an American can hold political beliefs that are conservative or that are liberal, but we feel that it is not legitimate for an American to be a monarchist and wish for the establishment of an American king. Nor do we feel that it is legitimate for an American to be a communist. For another example, we may feel that it is more or less proper for somebody to dress in a variety of ways in public, but hardly anybody in our society believes that we should go nude in public.

Even in these areas where the culture permits a range of legitimate beliefs, each of us holds some specific ideal within that range, and sometimes we hold that ideal very strongly. Our culture, for instance, permits quite a range of attitudes toward organized labor ranging from strongly prolabor to strongly antilabor. The culture does hold certain beliefs to be immoral or illegitimate, of course. We perhaps all agree that violent strikes are immoral, and we all agree that calling out the National Guard to shoot strikers down in the streets is immoral. So there is a wide acceptable range. But each of us holds some specific belief about labor unions within that range, and many of us have very strong beliefs in this area. Where do these ideals come from if not from the culture?

One of the important sources of these ideals is the people in our lives who are important to us—our parents, our husbands or wives, our very close friends, our co-workers. Social scientists call these people our *reference groups.* They are the people we compare ourselves with, the people with whom we discuss our ideals and beliefs, the people who influence our lives.

> But don't get carried away! Are **all** students hippies? Are **all** black people good athletes?

> Can you think of other areas in which the culture allows us a range of ideals?

> Name some people who are reference groups to you.

. . . And Reacts in a Situation / 93

There is a very strong pressure among people who are very closely associated with one another to agree on important ideals. Perhaps you've felt this pressure. Have you every sharply disagreed with a close friend on some ideal that was very important to both of you? What happened as a result? Very likely one of two things took place: Either you tacitly agreed to ignore the topic on which you disagreed and avoid discussing it, or you found yourself drifting away from close friendship with that person. The pressure to agree is ordinarily so strong that a friendship cannot withstand the heated conflict that must result from friction over the disagreement. Only if both friends are willing to compromise their strong feelings about that topic can the friendship continue.

Who influenced you to become a Christian?

Think for a minute how much your ideals have been influenced by the people who are close to you—your parents, your husband or wife, your friends at church. Perhaps you can easily recognize areas of your beliefs that are very much shaped by their influence. When political scientists began to study the influences that shaped people's voting patterns, they found very quickly that the way a man voted depended most upon the way his father voted. In fact nearly 70 percent of the time, a person will vote for the same party he remembers his father voting for. The family is a person's most important reference group.

"Like father, like son"—how true is it?

Since a person's patterns of ideals are shaped by his reference groups, mainly his family, his close friends and his co-workers, knowing what a person's friends are like, can give us some clues about what he is like. As a very rough rule of thumb, a person's pattern of behavior is likely to be similar to the behavior of his family, his friends, and his co-workers. So now we know of a fourth kind of information that has some predictive value—to know what a person's reference groups are like is to have some clues about what he is like. If you know his family or his friends, you may be able to predict, partially, how he will react to something you say to him.

A REVIEW

In these last two chapters, we've taken a detailed look at the two basic processes in communication; perception and reacting.

We saw that the meanings that a person attached to the Events around depend upon the way he conceives of the world around him, or in other words upon the shape of the Map of the World in his Head. And we came to understand that the meanings a person supplies for things that happen around him come from inside him—that they are not determined by the Events themselves.

How do a person's perceptions and his Map of the World affect the way he'll react to things others say to him?

In this chapter we've tried to find ways of predicting the shape of somebody else's Map of the World and ways of predicting, as a result, how he will react to the things we say to him. We've begun to develop a very specific and explicit procedure for analyzing a given set of circumstances and predicting how the learner will react. Our procedure turned out to be a series of questions about the set of circumstances:

1. What is the situation in which I hope to influence (but not not manipulate) the learner's reaction?
2. What kinds of consistencies can I observe in the learner's normal patterns of reacting? Can I find:
   a. Age patterns?
   b. Psychological patterns?
   c. Cultural patterns?
   d. Social patterns?

Begin right away to develop your skill at predicting by asking yourself these questions in simple, familiar situations in which your listener is someone you know very well. See how accurately these questions can lead you to predict how that person will react to something you say. As you begin to develop your skill, I think you'll find that you can begin to make predictions about people who aren't so familiar to you. If you're a very good predictor of learner reactions, you're probably a very good teacher!

CHAPTER 12

...To Make Available Materials in Some Form...

Now that we've explored two of the basic processes involved in communication in some detail—perceiving and reacting—let's take a very close look at the part of the communication process that most people intuitively feel is the basic problem in communication —the message. Since we understand something of how the message works, by stimulating another person to think about some part of his Map of the World, and since we've considered how the message may accomplish our goal of changing another person's Map of the World and influencing his behavior, we now have a much better foundation upon which to build some ideas about the kinds of messages that may be most effective.

What do you think are some of the implications of the perceiving and reacting processes we've considered for the kinds of messages that are likely to be effective?

Be very careful to keep in mind as we spend the next two chapters talking about messages that the message is hardly ever the end point in the communication process. Only when we write a poem for the sheer beauty of the way we've put together our words or when we sing a song for the sheer pleasure of hearing a delightful melody does the message itself become the goal of communication. Nearly all the time, we communicate with the goal of stimulating somebody's perceptions or influencing somebody's behavior. And we judge the consequences of our communication in terms of whether we have accomplished our goal—whether we have been *effective*.

So communication is a goal-oriented process. Each part of the process must be judged according to the goal we're trying to reach. And we measure the outcome of the process in terms of effectiveness with respect to some goal. The finest, most splendid message

What kinds of goals do teachers have? What need do you see for the teacher to make his short-term and long-term goals explicit, perhaps by writing them down?

. . . To Make Available Materials in Some Form / 95

in the world just might be quite ineffective in a given set of circumstances. And the most simple, homely, common message might be very effective in that particular set of circumstances. Only if we know what the communicator's goal was can we judge whether he has been effective.

Of course, there can be a variety of different kinds of goals. Often the goal of the church leader is to stimulate people to think more carefully about a part of their Maps of the World. In these situations, the leader or the teacher may serve as a provider of new ideas and of facts, as a catalyst, a stimulator. In these situations, the teacher's messages are effective if the teacher succeeds only in getting people to think carefully. He has been effective when he gets people to think even if their thinking leads them to conclusions that are different from his.

So we can see that being effective often doesn't have to mean that you're making people agree with you—often that isn't your goal at all.

FORM IS IMPORTANT

You probably remember that in our model of communication we described the message this way: ". . . to make available materials in some form conveying content. . . ." We purposely described the process of message-making from two separate points of view. First, we pointed out that a message has some structure, some form. And second, we saw that the message says something; it has some content. We wanted to make it very clear that the *way* you say something may be as important as *what* you say. The structure of the message may be as important as its message.

What kind of limitations?

Why do we need to be so careful to make this distinction clearly? We need to be very clear in our minds about it because the form a message takes puts some very real limitations upon what it appears to the listener to say. That is, the form that a message takes limits what you can communicate in that message. It limits the *kinds* of things you can communicate.

Guidance for Session 12
. . . TO MAKE AVAILABLE MATERIALS IN SOME FORM . . .

Aims for the Session

To learn why form is an important attribute of messages. To investigate some of the limitations that form puts upon what can be communicated. To explore the biases of some of the common teaching-learning forms.

Questions to Ponder

What are the unspoken ground rules during the class sessions when I teach? How can I find out what they are? What kinds of biases are implicit in these ground rules? How can I change the ground rules to avoid some of the biases that may be hindering learning? How can I change some of the ground rules so that I can get more feedback from learners?

A Study Plan

I. Try to formulate the beginnings of a set of ground rules for television situation comedy programs. What consistent kinds of structures do these programs have? What kinds of things appear in nearly every TV situation comedy? What kinds of things almost never appear in TV situation comedies?

II. Discuss: What are some of the reasons why it is useful to employ a variety of forms in teaching-learning? What are some of the forms that could be used together, either at the same time or one after the other, in a series of class sessions? Why not just find the best form and stick to it?

III. List a group of message forms you use in teaching. What are some

Since a message's form is such an important attribute of the message, and since most people are not conscious, as they communicate, of the limits that the form of the messages puts upon what can be said, we'll think very carefully about form as a part of the process of communicating in this chapter. In the following chapter, we'll concentrate upon some interesting aspects of the content of messages.

WHAT IS A FORM?

To put it most simply, a form is a generally accepted set of ground rules by which we structure messages. A poem, for instance, is a form. A poem happens to be a very formal kind of form in which the ground rules are consciously prescribed in advance rather than being just taken for granted. Ordinarily a poem consists of a certain prescribed pattern of phrases, or lines of type, arranged in some certain sequence, with extra space between certain lines to set off what we call verses or stanzas. Each of the lines has a defined internal structure that is ordinarily based upon the fact that the English language accents certain syllables in a sentence more than others, so that each line has a rhythm in a prescribed pattern. Finally, a poem often has a prescribed rhyme structure; that is, the last syllables in some of the lines must sound similar to the last syllables of certain other lines. So when we think of some very explicit form like iambic pentameter poetry, we have in mind a very clear set of ground rules for structuring a message.

Do other communication situations have ground rules like these?

The more common message forms also have ground rules very much like the ones we'd use to write a poem, except that the ground rules for most forms aren't so conscious to us. A conversation among acquaintances certainly has many ground rules. How many of them can you think of? Let's name some of them.

Why do you suppose the ground rules of most message forms aren't very noticeable?

—Whoever is talking may continue to talk for a reasonable amount of time or until he appears to be finished.
—Nobody may interrupt the speaker unless he agrees to be interrupted.

---

of the important biases of the two or three basic message forms that you use in class sessions? Begin with the suggestions in this chapter, and see how many additional kinds of biases you can think of. Are there certain subjects that are taboo in your class sessions partly because of the way you've structured the teaching-learning situation? Are there certain kinds of comments that learners might be thinking about but that they wouldn't feel free to say? Try to identify the unspoken ground rules that cause these biases.

IV. Make a list or collection of printed resource materials. What is the place of printed materials in teaching-learning? What are some of the printed materials that are available to the church school teacher? Begin your list, of course, with the Bible and add as many kinds of materials as you can think of. What are some of the communication biases of these materials? How can you structure your use of them to minimize some of the biases that may interfere with their usefulness?

V. Discuss in small groups: Another set of forms, like talking-listening and writing-reading, are the nonverbal forms—facial expressions, body posture, gestures, symbolic actions, and so forth. What kinds of biases do you think these forms might have? For instance, how complex a message can you communicate in these forms? Do you think that communication in the form of facial expressions is likely to be more honest or less honest than verbal communication in representing a person's true feelings?

—When a silence occurs, each participant has an equal opportunity to begin talking; that is, nobody is intentionally excluded.

—No speaker should talk for "very long," a time which may vary from a few seconds to a minute or two, depending upon the circumstances.

—Anybody may change the subject while he is talking without getting permission from other participants.

These ground rules really do apply when you're having a conversation. If you don't believe it, try violating one of them. Try to insist, for instance, that every participant in a conversation stick to the subject; object when anybody makes a comment on another topic or asks a question that would lead the conversation into another subject. What response will you get?

What happens when the ground rules of a form are broken is interesting. People get upset. People notice immediately that we're not behaving the way we should behave in that setting, and they don't like it. The literary world was upset when poets began to experiment with free verse, haiku, and other forms new to western literature. The world of serious music was outraged when composers began to experiment with the new forms of dissonance and atonality. You may have been a bit upset when your favorite radio station began playing that new form of popular music, rock music. Although few people ever think very much about the forms messages take, they do more or less subconsciously expect, and strongly so, that certain messages will take certain forms. People have an emotional attachment to the forms they're used to.

The important thing to remember is that messages are communicated in structured situations. The fact that you don't particularly notice the structure doesn't mean that there isn't any structure; it just means that you are so familiar with the structure that you don't have to think about it any more. You probably learned the structure when you were so young you don't even remember learning it. These structures are the things we call forms.

EVERY FORM HAS SOME BIASES

Each of the message forms that we use in everyday life and in teaching-learning situations has some kinds of things that it can communicate well and some kinds of things that it can communicate only poorly (or maybe not at all). We call these things biases. It may be easier for you to picture what we mean by the word *bias* if you can imagine that each form is "prejudiced" against communicating certain kinds of information well. Or it is "prejudiced" against being useful in certain kinds of situations—it is biased against these situations.

To take an obvious example, if you want to send a message and you want to have that message recorded for future reference, you

Think of some situations when it upsets you for people to break the ground rules of a message form.

What kinds of meanings can a poem communicate well, and what kinds of meanings can it communicate only poorly?

probably won't use a telephone conversation as your message form. Telephone conversations disappear into thin air as they happen, and you'd have to go to a lot of trouble to keep a complete record of what was said over the phone. If you want a complete and accurate record, you'll probably write down what you have to say—perhaps you'll send a letter instead. One of the biases, then, of a telephone conversation is that it doesn't leave a record for future reference.

Often a detailed description of the form itself, its ground rules, can give us some valuable clues about what it can do well and what it does poorly. Knowing that in a conversation anybody can change the subject who wants to suggests to us right away that if we need to talk out some subject completely, then we may use some other form than conversation to do it. We may try to use a structure that gives some leader a little more control over the direction of the conversation, or we may just informally agree at the outset that we'll limit our comments to that subject. Knowing this ground rule of a conversation at least warns us of the possibility of difficulty.

SOME BIASES OF TEACHING-LEARNING FORMS

Since we're especially concerned in this book with communication in the teaching-learning situation, let's consider some of the forms that are commonly used in that situation and let's try to identify some of the important biases that these forms have. We certainly cannot cover, in this short chapter, all of the forms that a teacher might use, although we'll try to consider some of the important ones. And we certainly cannot discuss completely each of the forms we'll consider, by any means. Experienced teachers gain new insights after many years of thinking about the message forms they use. What we'll try to do here is to help you become sensitive to the kinds of biases that our forms have so that you can begin to explore the message forms that you use from a more informed point of view.

What are some of the kinds of message forms that teachers use?

TALKING-LISTENING FORMS

The teacher, beginner or expert, probably spends more of his teaching time talking and listening than he spends doing anything else. And certainly the individual learner spends more time listening than he spends any other way. So the biases of the various talking-listening forms are ones the teacher must be especially sensitive to. In this section we'll consider three types of talking-listening forms, although you should be aware that these three are rather arbitrarily chosen from the nearly infinite number of variations that we could have considered. We'll look at one very informal form, the conversation, that we've already begun to map out. Then we'll consider the lecture, the most formal of the forms that are commonly used in teaching-learning. Finally we'll think

What are some of the other talking-listening forms that a teacher could use? What are some of the differences between the one's you've thought of and the ones mentioned here?

> Think ahead a bit. How do you use conversations in teaching-learning? Why does the conversation work well for your purposes?

about the biases of the leader-group discussion, a kind of compromise between the extremes of formality and informality.

Conversation.—We've already begun to think about some of the characteristics of the informal conversation as a message form. It can be a very useful form in the teacher's repertory for certain purposes and under certain circumstances. Let's try to see what these circumstances might be.

The conversation is the most democratic of all message forms. As we've seen, any participant can guide the direction of the conversation as he wishes. Any participant can contribute any time he wishes. Every participant has an equal say in the course that the conversation will take. The democracy of a conversation can be its greatest advantage to a teacher, or it can sometimes be a disadvantage, depending upon the circumstances.

Conversational democracy can be advantageous to the teacher in this way: Before a learner can "understand" an idea, that is, before he can fit it into his Map of the World, he has to perceive that idea in terms of meanings that he already has available in his Map. This means two things:

First, he needs to pay attention to the idea. If we can manage to say the things we have to say during a conversation, we have a rather high likelihood that the participants in the conversation will pay attention to our ideas. That is, since the participants are listening voluntarily, they could change the subject any time they wish. The very fact that they aren't busy changing the subject may very well mean they are paying attention to what is being said, and they find it interesting. Of course, it isn't always possible to keep the conversation on the topic we'd like for the participants to think about, but if we can get them to listen to an idea, then they may have considerable motivation to pay attention to it and to try to understand it.

> Try a little experiment. Some time in the next few days, when you know you'll participate in a conversation among four or five people, decide in advance on some specific thing that you'll try to work into the conversation. Then keep trying until you get it in. Can you work your comment into the conversation without just artificially breaking in? It takes a little skill, doesn't it?

Second, it means that he has to make the effort to fit it into his Map. The most important single communication problem facing the teacher is to explain ideas so that the ideas can just be "plugged in" to the learner's Map of the World. If you can provide a learner with a meaning that already fits right into his Map, then you have a very large chance that he will consider that meaning carefully. But if you explain your idea in terms of meanings he's not familiar with, you're asking him to make quite a large jump in understanding. You're asking him to do a very hard job.

> Is this one of the reasons that we try to use a fairly simple vocabulary when we talk to our children?

When you're getting a lot of immediate feedback from your learners, as you very likely will in a conversation, you have a pretty good chance to evaluate whether you've succeeded in explaining your idea in a way that has meaning to the learners. When your idea is a difficult one, your learners have a chance to ask questions about it, to let you help them reshape it so that it will fit into their Maps of the World. So you don't have to get the idea explained just perfectly the first time you approach it. You may have more opportunities to communicate after your initial attempt. Knowing you'll get plenty of feedback gives you freedom to experiment with new ways of explaining your ideas. If your listeners don't understand you the first time around, you know you'll get another chance to explain more clearly.

There are two major disadvantages for the teacher in using the conversation as a message form. The first relates directly to the fact that the conversation is the most democratic form. Since a conversation is so democratic, you as the teacher cannot always steer it in the direction you think it should go. If you get a chance to say what you have to say during a conversation, fine! But you may spend a long time in conversation with your learners before you get an appropriate opening to explain some specific idea that you have in mind. So a conversation can be a rather inefficient way to convey some specific idea.

What other forms are also fairly democratic? Do they also have this disadvantage?

The second disadvantage of conversation as a message form for many teaching-learning situations is that you may not be able to communicate a very complex idea in a conversation. Conversations are usually too informal for complex ideas. To consider a really difficult and complex idea, such as the meaning of the crucifixion, we'd like to be able to structure the learning situation so that at least the participants feel some obligation to stick to the subject. It's easy to imagine, and in fact we'd predict, that a conversation that started on the subject of the meaning of the crucifixion would have drifted off into some other subject before fifteen or twenty minutes had passed, and long before any of the participants had been able to think through even a few of the complexities of this meaning.

Of course these "disadvantages" may not always be real disadvantages. Under some circumstances, for instance, we may not need to communicate a terrifically complex idea, and we may decide that the informality and quick feedback of a conversation is just what we need. And many teachers find that the conversation form has enough advantages that it is well worth tolerating its relative inefficiency in return for its important advantages. The point we need to be clear about is that the more we know about the strengths and weaknesses of the various forms we might use in teaching-learning, the more intelligently we can make selections among the various forms that we might use under some specific set of circumstances.

In what kinds of teaching-learning circumstances might the teacher use a conversation as his message form?

Lecture.—The formal lecture is the form that some people think of first when they think about teaching-learning. Certainly the lecture as a form has a very real place among the forms available to the teacher. Under certain limited circumstances, the formal lecture may be a very useful way of communicating if the teacher is aware of its biases as a message form.

. . . To Make Available Materials in Some Form / 101

The teacher who uses the lecture as his message form ordinarily uses it for one of two reasons. First, the lecture is an easy way of saying something to a very large group of people at one time. The lecture, more than any other talking-listening form, however, puts the full responsibility for paying attention squarely upon the members of the audience. People who are highly motivated to learn may pay very close attention to a lecture. People who are not so highly motivated may find it easy to let their attention wander during a lecture. The result is that they don't actually hear or understand what was said. With this fact in mind, we might question the efficiency of the lecture as a way of sharing ideas—you can't share an idea if the learner is thinking about something else.

The second reason that people use the lecture form is that the teacher can explain a very complex idea in a lecture. Assuming that the listeners pay close attention throughout, the teacher can explain a more complex idea in a lecture than in any other talking-listening form. The teacher can consider and explain all of the complex aspects and ramifications of an idea without having to worry about whether somebody will change the subject. Keep in mind, however, that you can only explain something to somebody who is listening, and that the entire responsibility for paying attention falls upon the members of your audience. When they aren't interested in what the lecturer is saying, even the most entertaining lecturer may not be able to hold their attention—and most of us are not naturally highly-skilled lecturers; it is a very difficult art.

Aside from the difficulty of holding the audience's attention, the lecture as a message form has one additional problem: You get very little immediate feedback from your audience. Of course, you do get some feedback. Your minister, for example, finds it fairly easy to tell when his congregation is interested in his sermon by the expressions on people's faces and by the postures of their bodies. People who are interested and who are agreeing with him are sitting up straight and looking intently at him, and people who are not so interested may be beginning to slump and get glassy-eyed. So the lecturer does get some feedback, but it is not the most useful kind. It does not tell him *how* he could change his explanation to make it more understandable to his listeners.

Leader-Group Discussion.—Many public school teachers and college professors, as well as many church leaders, have concluded that the disadvantages of the lecture as a message form are so important, and the advantages of the conversation as a form are so inviting, that it would be a good idea to try to find some form that would combine the inherent interest and high feedback of the conversation with the ability to handle complex ideas that the lecture has. Very often the compromise that these people arrive at could be called the leader-group discussion.

Could you work the ideas on this page into a conversation? the ideas in this chapter? the ideas in this book? Could you explain the ideas in Part II of this book in a series of lectures?

As you teach, how much feedback do you get purely from the expressions on the faces of your learners and the amount of fidgeting that is going on?

This form is more structured than the conversational form, and because it is more formal, it is easier for the teacher to guide the discussion into the areas that need to be considered. Participants agree in advance, if only subconsciously, that they will stick to the subject, and they agree in advance that they will accept a certain amount of guidance from the teacher. The teacher, on the other hand, relinquishes some of the control that he would have in the lecture form and accepts a certain amount of guidance from the feedback he gets from the group. The teacher and the learners do not regard each other quite as equals, as in a conversation, but the learners are certainly more nearly equal to the teacher in their ability to contribute ideas than in the lecture form.

The teacher will often begin a session of leader-group discussion by asking some basic questions for the learners to explore. Then as the learners begin to discuss possible answers to the question (for instance, "What do we mean when we say that Christ died for our sins?"), the teacher occasionally asks additional questions that he thinks will guide the learners toward some useful answers. The teacher may contribute quite a bit, by suggesting possible answers and by summarizing things the learners say, or he may contribute very little, only posing additional questions as the discussion begins to bog down.

The teacher who begins to use the leader-group discussion as a message form must learn to exercise a lot of patience. He may find that the learners are unfamiliar with the idea that they can contribute their ideas to the class, and they may be reluctant to say very much at the beginning. And the teacher who has been accustomed to talking for the full session may find it difficult to be quiet so that the learners have a chance to talk. So both teacher and learners must *learn* to participate in the leader-group discussion. Many teachers have found that the effort is worthwhile because the form is so useful under many circumstances. It combines some of the important strengths of the conversation with some of the efficiency of the lecture form.

Do people have to learn to participate in a conversation? in a formal lecture?

The really experienced teacher will know how to use several of the talking-listening forms during class sessions. He'll know how to lecture as interestingly as he can in the occasional situation when he must lecture; he'll be ready to contribute to a conversation when the opportunity presents itself; and he'll have some skill at guiding a group discussion when he feels that the discussion would be useful to the learners. He realizes that no one form can possibly be best in all situations, and so he is prepared to adapt his teaching to the circumstances.

WRITING-READING FORMS

It would be difficult to imagine a church school program without written materials. Certainly the wide variety of written materials that the church school teacher has available to him both simplifies

How would it change your teaching if no written materials were available?

Communication expert Marshall McLuhan says that the typewriter is an extension of the mouth. What do you think he means by that?

and enriches his work. Published materials widen our horizons and expose us to the ideas of people all over the world, and through thousands of years of time, whom we could never hope to meet and listen to personally.

Writing-reading forms allow us to make our own ideas clear to people who are too far away for us to talk to them. And they allow us to put our ideas in a convenient form so that somebody can read about the ideas at his leisure rather than having to listen to them only when we're ready to explain them aloud. As teachers, we can continue to support our learners spiritually even when they are off at college, or perhaps in Vietnam, with our letters. And even while they are still in the church school class, we may be able to make some ideas clear by mimeographing them so that the learners can read them after a class meeting is over.

We can see that all the writing-reading forms share one basic and important characteristic; they allow us to communicate even when the writer and the reader are separated by great distances or by the passage of time. Once we've written an idea down, the learner no longer has to be actually in our presence to be able to understand the idea. He may read the idea four years later in a book or a pamphlet. But the teacher and the learner don't have to be physically together to communicate with each other. Writing-reading extends greatly our ability to communicate.

Writing-reading also extends the abilities of other people to communicate with us. It makes it possible for us to bring messages into the teaching-learning situation from people who couldn't possibly be present. We can, in effect, "hear from" the foremost experts in any field simply by opening a book and reading. And we can be guided in our teaching by people who have devoted years of study and practice to explaining the very ideas we'd like to make clear to our students. When you use the various kinds of written and printed classroom materials that are available in the teaching-learning situation, it is like having a dozen expert teachers at your side helping you to communicate with your learners.

All of the writing-reading message forms share one additional bias: they permit only delayed feedback. In a conversation, you say a few sentences and then your listener responds immediately. You know right away whether he has understood you or not. But when you write a letter or a note to somebody, you have to express yourself fully all in one long message. And you may not get a reply for weeks. Even when you do get a reply, you may not be able to know for sure whether your reader really understands what you wrote. Unless he specifically happens to comment on something you said, he could very possibly be misunderstanding your idea without your knowledge. Hardly ever do you get as much feedback or as useful feedback from writing-reading as you do from talking-listening, and your feedback is nearly always delayed.

Because you get so little useful feedback when you communicate in writing, you must formulate your message with much greater care than you usually take in conversation. You must be much more careful to be perfectly clear. And you must devote much more thought to the problem of explaining your ideas so that they will fit easily into the reader's Map of the World. Since your reader isn't telling you as you write what kinds of meanings he is perceiving, you must supply from your own imagination what you think are the meanings he'll get. You must predict his reactions much more accurately and explicitly.

The writing-reading forms share one more bias that makes them extremely useful to the teacher: they can handle ideas of almost unlimited complexity. Hardly any idea is so complex that it can't be expressed in writing—in a mimeographed pamphlet or in a book or in a whole shelf of volumes. Nearly anything that the mind can conceive of can be written down for somebody else to share.

In a book like this one, we can consider a group of ideas that we couldn't possibly cover in a conversation, or even in a whole series of conversations. There's just too much to talk about. We'd even have a difficult time sharing all these ideas in a long series of lectures, although I suppose we could probably do it if we really wanted to. But here in this book, it is easy to share all these ideas—it comes naturally to us. Writing-reading makes it relatively easy to think together about complex ideas.

My high school composition teacher liked to say, "You don't really understand an idea until you've written it down." And there's a certain validity to this point of view. When you've thought through an idea well enough that you can put it down on paper so clearly that somebody else can read your words and share your idea, then you have taken an important step in your own understanding of it. You are certain, when you've written an idea down, that you have at least thought it out well enough so you can share it with another person whose Map of the World is a bit different from yours. Writing makes you discipline yourself in a way that talking does not.

CONTROL THE FORMS YOU USE RATHER THAN LETTING THEM CONTROL YOU

As you teach over the next few weeks, begin to analyze the forms that you use during class sessions. Try to discover the hidden ground rules by which they operate. Of course, it won't be easy to see the ground rules—they're ordinarily hidden to the people who use them. In fact, in a certain sense, we could say that the forms actually use you. They ordinarily control you much more than you control them.

But the ground rules of the forms you use are like many other half-hidden behavior patterns. Once you recognize them and

How much preparation time does it take to participate in an informal conversation? to give a formal lecture? to write a book?

Do other cultural patterns work like this?

understand them, you can control them. You can modify them to fit the circumstances as you need to, or you can take care to use a form that will let you do what you need to do in a given situation. Only knowledge and understanding can give you this power.

Sometimes it can be a bit difficult to begin recognizing the ground rules of a form that you know very well; you're so familiar with it that you don't know where to start. Here's a little trick that can help: Watch very carefully for the times when you begin to get irritated at somebody who isn't behaving right while you're using that form, or watch carefully for the times when things start to go wrong. Then ask yourself what ground rule of the form somebody has violated. Why does that irritate me? Why is this going wrong? You can gain valuable insight into the forms you use from your own mistakes. You're almost tricking your subconscious mind into telling you things you need to know.

As long as you're a teacher, you'll continue to learn more and more about the forms you use. And as a result, you'll become a better and better teacher. You certainly won't learn all there is to learn about the forms you use in the next few weeks, though you can make a lot of progress once you begin to think carefully about them. But you can, at least, begin to exercise your own control. In this case, indeed, knowledge is power!

What are some of the ground rules of book writing? What are some of the things I could do, as the author, to make you upset as you're reading? Use phrases and half-ideas, rather than sentences? Use potfuls of groovy mod slang?

CHAPTER 13

...Conveying Content...

What is communication?

"Aha!" I hear you saying to yourself. "Now that we've finally dug through all the preliminary ideas, now that we know all about Maps in Our Heads and predicting listener reactions and forms and all the other things we've read about, now we're finally to the chapter on content. Now at last we're going to get down to business and talk about 'communication.' "

But wait. Let's step back for a moment and see what we've already learned about how the message really does fit into the process of communication. Maybe we've arrived at a point where we can begin reexamining some of the commonsense assumptions about communication that we started out with. For instance, the assumption that communication really *is* the message—that the message is the important thing in communication.

Now certainly nobody can possibly say that the message isn't important in the process of communication. Of course, it is. But there are other parts of the process that we must consider *along with* the message if we're going to make sense out of how communication works.

The message is only one of three absolutely necessary parts of the communication process. The three parts are these: the perceptual process, the reacting process, and the message. Any communication situation includes (1) somebody who reacts to some set of circumstances (Event) to produce (2) a message,

106 / *Basics for Communication in the Church*

which (3) somebody else perceives. It is meaningless to think of a message without thinking at the same time of the other two important parts of the process which go along with the message.

Let's look at an example: Think of the message, "It's raining outside." It might mean, "I've been telling you all day it was going to rain, and I was right all along." It could mean, "Please go check to be sure all the windows are closed." It could mean, "I knew it; I just knew it; if I washed the car, I just knew it would rain!" It could mean, "Those people in that play on TV are going to get wet." It could mean, "Wonderful; now the crops are going to be saved." But so far we just don't know what it means, do we?

*Go ahead and commit yourself— what **does** it mean?*

What will we have to know before we can know what it means? We'll have to know
—who said it
—to whom
—in what situation.

This sounds familiar, doesn't it? It sounds like another very simplified way of saying, "Someone perceives an Event and reacts in a situation to make available materials in some form conveying content of some consequence." And in fact that's just what it is.

A statement is meaningful only in the context of the whole communication process of which it is a part. It is only *one* of the parts. As soon as we can see the statement in the context of the whole process of communication, which includes all of the parts, then we can begin to attach some meaning to the statement. Of course in most everyday situations we *do* perceive messages in the context of the other important parts of the communication process. When somebody says "It's raining outside" to you, you subconsciously take into account all of the circumstances of that communication as you make some meaning of it. You do consider *who* said it as part of the meaning of it. You do consider the fact that he said it *to you* as part of the meaning of it. And you do consider the *situation* in which he said it as part of the meaning of it. Every message has meaning only in the context of the whole communication process.

Would the meaning of this book be clear if you didn't know who said it to whom in what situation?

EVERY STATEMENT IS A STATEMENT ABOUT "ME"

One of the reasons that it is so easy to forget that messages are not all there is to communication is that our messages *appear to be*

Guidance for Session 13
... CONVEYING CONTENT ...

Aims for the Session

To understand clearly that the content of a session is only one of the ways in which the session communicates. To develop some more sophisticated ways of conceptualizing the relationships between content and meanings. To investigate some specific kinds of relationships between symbols and their meanings.

Questions to Ponder

What does **meaning** mean? What is the relationship between a symbol and its meanings? Is the meaning of a symbol something that happens in the symbol? in the Event the symbol refers to? in the speaker? in the listener? What kinds of meanings do symbols have? Are the meanings of symbols precise and tight? Are they vague and ephemeral? What kinds of symbols are there beside words? What is the relationship between nonverbal symbols and their meanings?

How is "It is raining" a statement about something that happens in our heads?

directly connected to the real world so closely. When we say, "It is raining," we appear to be simply confirming something that already exists. And yet actually, the real meaning of "It is raining" has much more to do with something that is going on inside your head than with anything that's happening outside. The real meaning is a meaning about *me* much more than it is a meaning about the state of the weather. When we say, "It is raining," what we really mean is something more like this: "*I have noticed* that it is raining, and *I think* there will be such and such consequences of the fact that it is raining." Very often the consequences part of this meaning is implied by the situation (since the windows are open, saying "It is raining" means "I think you should shut the windows").

Let's look at another statement. When we say, "John is stupid," or, "Sue is smart," it would appear on the surface that stupidity and smartness were characteristics of John and Sue. But if we think very carefully about what we mean by these statements, it's something more like this: "When I perceive John's behavior, I am disappointed or distressed or frustrated or disgusted. The statement that I use to express *my* perceptions and evaluation of these Events is 'John is stupid.' " When we say "John is stupid," we're saying more about ourselves than we're saying about John. We've just forgotten to get the *I* into the sentence.

Is there any simple way to change this sentence so that it more clearly indicates that we're talking about "me" more than about "John"?

Actually, when we begin talking about John, most of what we're saying refers to my Mapping of John rather than to John himself. And certainly it is my Map of the World that supplies the meaning "stupid" in reaction to all the Events that I've perceived in which John was a participant. John acted this way on this occasion and he acted thus and so on that occasion, and I have perceived those actions and supplied the label "stupid." When I say "John is stupid," I'm really talking about something I've done.

When we say
—It's hot in here
—That TV program is scary

A Study Plan

I. In a small study group (groups) work out a series of written definitions.

A. Define the symbol **storm**. Begin with the dictionary definition and work on from there. Keep trying to work the definition around to something you could actually point to. Consider this: If you were struck mute for an hour and you had to describe the mental category "storm" to somebody, what would you do or point to that would make him understand what things are included in "storm" and what things aren't.

B. Define the symbol **Christian love** in the same way.

C. Try to define the meaning of a smile (not what a smile is, but what it means) in the same way. Since a smile is a symbol, it ought to have a meaning that you can specify—what is it?

II. Discuss: How is the statement, "John is wearing a yellow shirt," more a statement about me than a statement about John? Describe in some detail the mental processes that led to the statement. Is yellow an abstract category, one that exists only in your head? Are you sure the shirt wasn't orange, rather than yellow? And are you sure it wasn't a light jacket or a sweater rather than a shirt? How can you define the meaning of the symbol **John**?

III. Build a scale of increasing abstractions (usually called an abstraction ladder) from "the chair you're sitting on" to "Events." Take your time and go into some detail in your list. Your list will certainly include symbols like **chairs, furniture,** and **nonliving things.** See how many more levels of abstraction you can find— you ought to be able to discover the first fifteen or twenty fairly easily.

IV. Work on some lists using words that carry strong connotative or emo-

108 / Basics for Communication in the Church

—Sunday's sermon was really inspiring
—Jeffrey is a good student,

or nearly anything else, we're really talking about ourselves much more than we're talking about anything that happened outside ourselves. We're putting little parts of our Maps of the World into words.

SYMBOLS: OUR LABELS FOR ENTRIES IN OUR MAPS

We communicate with each other through symbols, labels we agree upon that stand for little sections of our Maps of the World. All words are symbols. But some other things are symbols, too. Since some symbols can't be expressed in single words, people have to use phrases or sentences to express them: "Law and Order," "Peace in Our Time," "The Priesthood of All Believers," "God is Dead." Some symbols aren't even expressed in words at all; sometimes they're very formal symbols, like our flag or the shape of the United States Capitol Building. Sometimes they're quite informal, like a smile or a shrug or a wink. But in the interests of efficiency, we usually find a word, or invent one, to symbolize the things we often want to talk about. Most of our symbols are words.

What part of your Map of the World might a wink stand for?

Although everybody's Map of the World is different from everybody else's in some important ways, still there are similarities among our Maps of the World. These similarities correspond to the symbols we use to share our ideas. That is, when we use symbols meaning *rain, John, sermon, stupidness, green,* we succeed in sharing ideas because our Maps of the World more or less agree upon the significance of these symbols.

The fact that the entire range of meaning for the symbol *rain* in my Map of the World is not exactly the same as the meanings you have in your Map doesn't keep us from talking about rain, because there is some common ground, some sharing, some community of meaning that allows communication. When we say rain, no two people in the world have exactly the same image in their

tional meaning, using several scales or dimensions of meaning that such words can take. The most common one, of course, is the good-bad dimension. The differences between the symbols, **statesman, politician,** and **demagogue** illustrate the good-bad scale of connotative meaning; statesman is very good, politician is nearer neutral, and demagogue is very bad in the good-bad dimension.

Another one is the active-calm dimension; the connotative meaning of **stormy** doesn't really have very much flavor of "bad"—it's more like "extremely active." A "stormy romance." Make a list of other words that have strong connotative meanings in the active-calm dimension. Begin with **stormy, shriek, atomic, whiz,** and add as many others as you can think of. Some of your words may also have some degree of good-bad meaning, but right now we're interested in the active-calm meaning.

V. Explore the complex code of facial expressions by standing in front of the mirror and trying to keep an absolutely straight face. If you're in a group, let somebody volunteer to stand in front of the group who thinks he can keep a "poker-face" for a minute or two at a time. Now watch the tiny changes in expression that creep in—one muscle moves just an imperceptible amount and the expression changes completely. Now try to smile without moving your mouth; smile with your eyes only. Can you feel your change of expression? Can you "read" the change easily?

The expressions on our faces and the feelings inside us get so closely associated with each other that when we smile, we really feel better; when we frown, we really feel worse. Try it. Try to smile with your eyes and frown with your mouth. How do you feel?

Maps of the World of what the symbol means, but anybody who understands English shares enough of the common meaning that he can understand the symbol.

It's easy to see how we can still manage to communicate even though we don't share exactly the same meanings for the symbols we use if we consider that we can carry on a perfectly reasonable conversation with a blind man about rain. Now your image of rain very likely is a predominantly visual image. When you think of rain, you think of *seeing* the rain falling. His image of rain can't possibly be just like yours, or even very near yours. His image probably consists of sound images, and perhaps of tactile images, the sound and feeling of being out in the rain. When he says the symbol *rain* he means the sounds and feeling of rain; when you hear the symbol, you interpret it to mean the way rain looks to you; and communication goes on pretty well considering that the two of you are talking about such different things.

Sometimes, though, our images of some of our symbols are so different that after we've been talking for a while we find that we aren't talking about the same thing. When parents and teen-agers talk about *love,* for instance, they sometimes have to conclude that they aren't referring to the same sort of thing. When our diplomats discuss *democracy* with the representatives of foreign governments, sometimes the word doesn't mean the same thing to everybody who uses it. And the wide variety of meanings that people have in their minds when they use the word *God* can be startling.

SYMBOLS AND THEIR MEANINGS

The first thing we ask about a symbol is this: What does it mean? It's an easy question to ask, but often it isn't a very easy one to answer. The meanings of symbols are difficult to pin down for several reasons. First, symbols often have several dimensions of meanings. A symbol may simply refer to something in the world, for instance, but it may at the same time convey an emotional aura to the thing it's referring to. Along with these meanings it may have other kinds. It may mean a reaffirmation of belonging to a group, as certain hymns do when we sing them in church.

Second, symbols may have very vague and slippery meanings. The word *democracy* and the word *love* are difficult words to pin down. After we've spent several minutes (or several hours, for that matter) talking about the various kinds of specific things and activities that democracy refers to, and after we've tried to express the emotional feelings that democracy as a symbol arouses in us, we still may not be very satisfied that we have described the symbol very completely. But even fairly simple symbols may be slippery to define. Take the word *cat* for instance. Even my little desk dictionary gives twelve separate definitions for "cat," and it doesn't try to cover all the kinds of emotional reactions that people may have to the symbol.

What are some of the other symbols that mean different things to you and to somebody who is blind? to somebody who is deaf? Can you still communicate to them about these things?

What does **meaning** *mean?*

Can you think of other kinds of meaning?

Check to see how many definitions your dictionary has for the symbol **make.**

Third, many symbols don't refer to anything that actually exists outside our heads at all. They may refer entirely to inferences each of us may make in our heads, for instance; there are no logical relationships outside those we draw in our heads, and so the whole realm of symbols relating to logic point only inward, to things that happen inside us. Or they refer to emotional reactions, like fear or pain. You can never know what pain feels like to anybody else; you can only experience it yourself. Of course, you can see signs of pain in the behavior of others, and you can certainly sympathize with them when they say they feel pain. But you can never know if it feels the same to them as it feels to you. How, then, can we ever pin down the relationship between the symbol "pain" and its meaning?

Does pain hurt you the same amount that it hurts other people?

With some of these difficulties in mind, let's consider some of the kinds of relationships between symbols and their meanings.

SYMBOLS AND THEIR "POINTING" MEANINGS

Part of the meaning of most symbols lies in the fact that the symbol refers to some object, action, or quality that we could (in principle, at least) point at. The symbol *chair,* for instance, has as part of its meaning a reference to a chair or a number of chairs that we could point to. We call this kind of meaning of a symbol *denotative* meaning.

The denotative meaning of some symbols is very easy to specify. *This book,* for instance, is something you can easily define. You can hold up the actual book and let everybody see what you're talking about. You can fairly easily show somebody what I'm talking about when I use the symbol, "the chair that you're sitting on." When we use a symbol to refer to something that we're actually looking at or doing, then the relationship between that symbol and its meaning can be extremely clear. The symbol "points at" something that everybody can look at and understand.

Define "this book."

As soon as we leave behind the small group of symbols that actually point at some specific thing, then we begin to encounter some difficulties in defining the relationship between the symbol and its meaning. The symbol, "this cat," is one everybody can understand. But as we saw above, the symbol "cat" doesn't have the advantage of this simplicity. We can easily define what we mean by "this cat"; we cannot so easily define what we mean by "cat."

Stop reading for a moment at this point and write down a brief definition of **cat.**

Let's consider for a minute how we can reasonably say that the symbol "cat" *points to* something in the world. With "this cat," we have no problem—we can actually point to the cat. What can we point to that corresponds to "cat"? Well, we could begin by pointing to this particular cat and saying that what we mean by "cat" is things that are like this one. But this specific cat happens to be a short-haired, gray, female, alley cat with one torn ear and two claws missing from its right rear paw. Surely a thing doesn't

Which of these things does a thing have to be before we'll call it a "cat"?

Does the meaning of the symbol "cat" include some cats that will never exist except in somebody's imagination?

Somebody has suggested that instead of using the concept "Map of the World" to refer to our perceptual process, that we think of it as a vast filing system in which each symbol is a file folder full of experiences that involve that category. Do you think this is a helpful metaphor?

have to be just like this cat to come under the symbol "cat." We'll have to define the meaning of our symbol some more.

We might say, as we actually do, that a cat is a thing that shares certain kinds of similarities with this particular cat. A cat, then, is an animal with certain structural and biological properties, with certain kinds of behaviors—it is a mammal, a feline, a house pet, has a tail, claws, fur. But examine these defining characteristics of "cat" for a moment. Which of them can you actually point to? Any of them? Certainly not. Once we leave the group of symbols that actually point to a specific example—this cat—we can no longer find anything to point to that really tells us what the symbol means. When a symbol seems to point to something and yet we can't find anything to point to that is its meaning, we call that symbol *abstract*.

Nearly every symbol is abstract. We really don't spend very much time talking about specific things in the world around us. The thing that makes it possible for us to have abstract symbols is our Map of the World. Our Map of the World allows us to generalize from a few examples of a thing to a symbol that includes every possible one of the things.

We can imagine that at the dawn of time a man saw one little wild, furry animal and then another one like it and another and another, and he invented the word, *cat,* to mean those four animals. When he saw a fifth cat, of course he included that one in the meaning of "cat." This went on as he saw thousands of cats. At some point, he began using the symbol "cat" to refer not only to the thousands of cats that he had seen, but to the untold millions of cats that he hadn't seen, and even to all cats that lived before his time and any cats that might live after him clear to the end of the world. "Cat" could even mean some imaginary beast that never existed and never will exist! Now "cat" no longer referred to something he actually saw around him; it referred to a category of things that existed only in his head—in his Map of the World.

An abstract symbol, then, is a symbol that refers to a category of things, and the category is one that you have set up in your Map of the World. The category is not something that exists independently of you; it exists only in your head. When you use symbols referring to these categories, or abstractions, in communication with someone else, of course he must share your set of categories. When somebody knows what you're referring to when you say, "cat," that means that he also has the abstraction, "cat," in his Map of the World. Before you and he can communicate effectively, your mental abstraction, "cat," and his mental abstraction, "cat," must be roughly similar.

It is these similarities between your abstractions and somebody else's abstractions that make a language. A language is first of all an enormous set of categories for classifying the world in our Maps, and of course it also consists of a set of symbols for referring to the categories. But if every speaker of English thought of the world in a different set of categories, the words of the English language would be nearly useless, wouldn't they? It is only because we all think in terms of the same sets of categories that the symbols can have meaning.

Levels of Abstraction.—When we say that every word that doesn't actually point to some specific thing in the world around us is abstract, we certainly don't mean to imply that all abstract words are equally abstract. Some symbols are more abstract than others. Certainly words like *democracy* and *brotherhood* are more abstract than words like *cat*. Words like "cat" come closer to actually pointing to something than words like "democracy."

In fact we can arrange groups of symbols in order of their abstraction, in order of how closely they come to being able to point to something specific. Look at this ordering of symbols:

> Events
> objects
> living things
> animals
> mammals
> felines
> cats
> female cats
> gray female alley cats
> this cat

If you've ever studied a foreign language, have you run into words that were very difficult to translate because English and that foreign language simply didn't share that category?

This list of symbols begins at the bottom with the least abstract symbols, and gets more and more abstract as it rises. The top symbol is the most abstract symbol we have, since we have defined Event to mean anything we can think about. Notice that each step on the scale of abstraction includes the things that are part of the meaning of the symbol below it, and it also includes some more things. "Female cats" includes all "gray female alley cats" and also all female cats that are not gray and all female cats who are not alley cats.

The reason that knowing about levels of abstraction is so important is this: When we make some statement about "this cat," it is fairly easy for our listener to verify whether the statement is true or not. He can look at "this cat" himself and see whether our statement is true or false. As soon as we begin to talk about symbols that are more abstract than "this cat," our listener can no longer easily verify the truth of what we're saying. Since "cats" only exists as a way of Mapping that we use inside our heads, how can our listener even begin to look at cats and see whether we're saying something true about cats? He can, of course, look at some examples of cats and see whether our statement is true

Is "Cats are independent beasts" a true statement? How do you know?

for those examples, but still it may be that he has chosen to look at some very unusual examples, and that these examples don't give a very good overall picture of what cats are.

Now nobody could possibly suggest that we throw out all abstractions from our conversation just because their meanings are of a difficult kind. But we can be aware that the problem exists, and we can make an honest effort to be careful when we're using abstractions. One way of being careful is to try to keep in mind that any abstraction is something *you've* done in your Map of the World and not necessarily something that really exists in the world. Try to preface each abstract statement, even if just mentally, with the note, "according to my Map," or, "in my Map." For instance, "(According to my Map) cats are uppity." (If you think "cats" is hard to define, try defining "uppity"!)

SYMBOLS AND THEIR EMOTIONAL MEANINGS

*What **is** the difference? "Point to" the difference.*

Most symbols not only tell you what we're talking about, what we're pointing to, but also how you should view that thing. They tell you whether it is a good thing or a bad thing, whether it is pleasant or unpleasant whether it is benevolent or threatening. What's the difference between a "discussion" and a "confrontation"? Between a "learner" and a "pupil"? Between a "preacher" and a "demagogue"? The difference is not that the person who uses these symbols is pointing to a different thing in the real world; it is that the person who is talking is *evaluating* the thing he's talking about. We call this evaluative meaning of symbols *connotative* meaning.

Nearly all words have some connotative meaning. When we refer to things by using symbols, we find it very difficult to name something without at the same time evaluating it. Even simple words like "cat" and "storm" have clear and evident connotative meanings, and we use the connotative meanings of these words when we refer to a "catty woman," or "a stormy marriage." When we say "a catty woman," we're certainly not saying that the woman appears to be a short, furry, four-legged animal that we keep around the house as a pet—we're saying that our emotional evaluation of the woman is similar to our emotional reaction to the cat.

The most common dimension of connotative meanings of symbols is the good-bad dimension. That is, most often the connotative meanings of words tell us whether the speaker thinks the thing he's talking about is good or bad. And the connotative meaning is quite separate from the denotative meaning. In fact, we can make ourselves a list of words that have very similar connotative meanings, and we'll find that the words "point to" a wide variety of things.

*What do these words mean? Now—what does **meaning** mean?*

Weakling	Tyrant
Rotten	Demogague
Polluted	Junk

114 / **Basics for Communication in the Church**

The way these words are related is that they all say to us "this is bad" even though their denotative meanings are very different.

Some words have such vivid connotative meanings that we use them in situations where denotatively they don't make sense. The denotative meaning of "a stupid car" is nearly nil—it doesn't refer to anything in the real world. But connotatively, the phrase is a powerful one in communicating the idea you have in your head. You use the word *stupid* for its connotative meaning rather than its denotative, or "pointing," meaning.

To discover the relationship between a symbol and its connotative meaning, you have to look inside the Map of the World in the Head of the person who is using the symbol. That is, connotative meanings are meanings about the speaker more than about the real world. Only after a speaker has evaluated an object and decided whether he thinks it is good or bad can he use a connotative meaning. And then the connotative meaning refers to something that has happened in his head much more than it refers to anything that happened outside his head.

The skillful teacher understands how the connotative meanings of words affect his learners and he is able to use the connotative meanings of symbols to increase communication. Symbols that have strong connotative meanings are powerful symbols. Because of it, they can communicate effectively when they are used consciously and intelligently. Since the church school teacher, for instance, is especially concerned with communicating about moral spiritual ideals with his learners, he need be especially sensitive to the connotative meanings of the symbols he uses. Likewise he should be especially sensitive to the connotative meanings of the symbols that his learners use when they're talking to him.

How can your sensitivity to the connotative meanings of words help you understand the things learners are communicating to you?

NONVERBAL SYMBOLS AND THEIR MEANINGS

Words and phrases certainly aren't the only symbols. They are the ones we use the most, but some other kinds of symbols are essential to the teacher in the teaching-learning situation. Let's examine some of them.

Expressions and Gestures as Symbols.—Facial expressions, gestures and tone of voice contribute important meanings to the communication process. Though these kinds of symbols are somewhat less clearly codified than verbal symbols are, they communicate just as clearly—sometimes even more clearly because the language of gestures and facial expressions transcends many verbal language barriers. A smile means very nearly the same thing anywhere in the world.

We can very easily illustrate the important contribution of facial expressions and tone of voice to the meaning of a sentence with some examples. Take the sentence, "I sure am glad to see you." Say it with a big smile first; then say it with a heavy scowl. The sentence changes meaning almost from one pole to the other be-

How many different things can you communicate to your best friend with facial expressions alone?

cause you've changed one symbol that is the key to interpreting it—your expression. Let's look at another sentence: "Sarah was very good in school today." Say the sentence over and over, each time emphasizing a different word. Do you notice how your tone of voice seems to change, and how the meaning of the sentence clearly changes? *"Sarah* was very good in school today" means that somebody else wasn't. "Sarah was very good *in school* today" means that Sarah must have misbehaved someplace else. And so on.

A change in expression is inherently interesting to people, and the teacher can use this fact to his advantage. Don't be afraid to show how you feel about the things you discuss in class. Plan your sessions so you can change your level of expression from time to time during the period. You may even find it useful to think ahead of time about what kinds of feeling you can show from time to time. Nothing is more dull than a long speech that has little change in emotion from beginning to end. Of course, your expression of feeling must be reasonably spontaneous, and it must be honest when it comes. But a little attention to changes in feeling during the hour can give you opportunities to communicate what are very real feelings. You teach through your feelings as well as your intellect.

Actions as Symbols.—All of us, looking back over our childhood, can remember situations in which somebody took a symbolic action —of honesty, of brotherhood, of love—that was so impressive that we remember it vividly years later. Actions can sometimes be powerful symbols, rich in meaning. As a teacher, you have a unique opportunity because of your continuing contact with your learners to make your actions speak to them.

> Which of your parents' actions do you remember most vividly?

To have real symbolic significance to learners, actions should be spontaneous and honest—a "real" reflection of the way you are. This is why many of our contrived actions have so little effect on children. Children can sense when we're "trying to tell them something," even through actions. But they can sense, too, when an action is the honest expression of our highest values and beliefs. The vivid memories you have of an action that an adult took, one that was symbolically very significant to you, may very well involve an action that the adult wouldn't begin to remember—one that seemed so normal to him that he took it for granted and forgot it immediately.

> Are you a good actor? Can you make a contrived action appear to be honest?

Life-Styles as Symbols.—We've all heard the old saw, "Do as I say, not as I do," and we react to it humorously because we all know that young people will never share the values we express if our whole lives are in contradiction to what we say. The way we pattern our lives is an important and powerful symbol to the young people we teach. And it's surprising how accurately they can "read" the symbolic meanings that are important in our lives.

If spiritual values are important to a person, then the young people around him are quick to recognize it and appreciate it. And if contradictions exist in our lives, even contradictions we're not aware of, young people can be quick to recognize those, too. Young people are idealistic. They haven't felt many of the pressures that push us to compromise with our own ideals. They don't realize, often, that every life represents one person's decision about which values are inviolate and which values must sometimes be compromised so that life can go on. And these are not things that can easily be explained verbally. They are things that must be demonstrated in the way we live.

In a certain sense, our lives are always "on trial" before our young people. They are searching for patterns, for examples. And as teachers we have a particular obligation to provide examples that we're proud of. Of course, we can't go around all the time thinking specifically about how this activity or that activity would appear to a young person, and we don't need to. Young people are much more understanding than we sometimes give them credit for. What we can do is to take seriously the fact that our lives serve as examples. Our very lives are probably the most powerful symbols that we can communicate with learners.

In what sense are our lives on trial before our learners?

CHAPTER 14

...Of Some Consequence

Every communication situation has some consequences. Every time we communicate, we cause some changes—changes in ourselves, changes in the people we communicate with, changes in the relationships between ourselves and the people we communicate with. The relationship between people who have communicated is never quite the same as it was before the communication.

Sometimes the consequences of a communication situation are enormous and earth-shaking, as when the leaders of several important nations hold an official conference. Sometimes the consequences are just as earth-shaking, but only for the individuals involved, as when a man asks the woman he loves to marry him. Or when a teacher is able to help a learner to a vivid image of God.

Most of the time, the consequences of a communication situation are small and difficult to see. They may be important, but they aren't very apparent. Just as every tiny pebble tossed into the ocean makes some ripples, even though they aren't very noticeable, every communication has some consequences.

CONSEQUENCES AND EFFECTS

Some of the changes that happen in communication situations are things we intended to happen and some are changes we had not

As a practical matter, what kinds of consequences do you expect from a one-hour church school session or other church meeting for education?

intended. We can never predict perfectly everything that will happen as a consequence of a communication, and so some of the things that happen in any communication situation are unexpected.

We call "everything that happens as a result of a communication situation, intended and unintended," the *consequences* of that communication. Among the consequences are (hopefully) some things that we intended to have happen—we call those things, *effects*. If we get the effects we wanted in the communication, if some of the consequences were ones we intended, then we have achieved our goal in the situation—we have been effective.

The point that we need to make clear by separating the idea of effects from the idea of consequences is that some of the things that happen as a result of a communication situation are unexpected things. We can never plan quite carefully enough to eliminate all of the unexpected consequences. So as we begin to evaluate the outcome of a communication, we must keep in mind the possibility of unexpected consequences and we must be watching for them. We may have secured the effects we wanted, but what consequences did we also get that we hadn't expected?

EVALUATING OUR COMMUNICATION EFFECTIVENESS

As we have discussed earlier, the goals that we set in various communication situations can be any of several kinds. Our goal in some situations often is simply to stimulate thought and to introduce the learners to some new ideas. In other situations, the goal of our message could be to make people laugh, to express humor. Occasionally our goal is just to demonstrate that we remain members of an important group that shares certain ideals, as for instance when we pledge allegiance to the United States flag together.

But three kinds of goals are consistently useful for the teacher to think about, even though we're aware that these three certainly don't cover every teaching-learning situation.

> Can you remember a situation in which you fully succeeded in communicating what you had to say, but in which an unexpected consequence of what you said ruined your effectiveness?

Guidance for Session 14
... OF SOME CONSEQUENCE

Aims for the Session

To consider ways of evaluating the teacher's communication effectiveness in teaching-learning with regard to the goals he has set. To discover ways of evaluating the teacher's effectiveness when changes in the learner's Map of the World are hidden. To begin thinking about ways of stimulating increased feedback from learners. To understand some special consequences that are possible in a series of teaching-learning situations.

Questions to Ponder

What are the various ways in which a teacher evaluates his work? What should be the place of his evaluation of communication effectiveness in his over-all self-evaluation? How can the teacher evaluate his communication effectiveness? How can the teacher use the feedback that he gets from learners in his self-evaluation? How can he get more feedback from learners? How can the teacher evaluate his success in communicating values and ideals rather than just isolated facts?

A Study Plan

I. Make a list. Think of some common situations in church school teaching-learning in which you could expect to be able to observe directly the changes in learners' behavior. Try to make some generalizations about the kinds of situations in which you can expect to be able to observe changes directly.

II. Do you think that learners' attitudes as reflected in the feedback you get really indicate how they will behave when the appropriate situation arises? If you're not convinced, then why worry about trying to evaluate your communication effectiveness by listening to feedback?

III. For the rest of this session, add this one ground rule to your communication structure: Before anybody says what he has to say, he must restate the comments of the preceeding speaker **to the satisfaction of the preceding speaker.** That

First, we may hope for *understanding*. That is, we may be aiming to bring an idea to the clear perception of the learner, even one that he may not be able to agree with. Second, we may hope to *convince* the learner that something is true. In other words, we may hope to lead him to change part of his Map of the World to agree with our Map. Third, we may hope to *persuade* him to change his behavior. That is, we may want him actually to act upon the change that he's made in his Map of the World.

When our goal has been to change the learner's way of behaving, that is, when we wanted to persuade him, then we can evaluate our effectiveness fairly easily. We can watch his behavior and see whether it has changed or not. In these cases, our effectiveness is relatively easy to evaluate.

But in many situations, our goal is not to get an immediate change in the learner's behavior. Sometimes we're simply trying to make some ideas clear to him; for instance, we may be explaining the Old Testament meaning of prophesy. And other times, we're trying to convince him that some ideas are right. This may be the case when we're discussing our understanding of the significance of the elements in Communion, for example. These changes in the learner's Map of the World may not lead to visible changes in his behavior.

In all of these situations, it simply isn't practical to depend upon our observations of changes in behavior to evaluate our communication effectiveness. We can't just watch and see whether we've communicated well.

Since we can't evaluate our effectiveness directly in these cases, we must use some indirect means of evaluation. We must make the assumption that the learner's attitudes—the meanings that he has in his Map—reflect the ways in which he will actually behave when the appropriate situation arises. We must assume, sometimes with some deserved skepticism, that the way he thinks he'll be-

> What are some situations in which you might be able to observe behavior changes directly?

> Why are we sometimes a bit skeptical that a person's attitudes really represent the way he'll behave when the situation arises? If we're skeptical, does that mean that what a person says he'll do is meaningless?

is, before you say your piece, feed back to the preceding speaker the things he said. At the end of the session, evaluate the effects of this tremendously increased feedback. Do you feel that the group communicated better during the session? How was it better?

IV. Discuss: How can the teacher in a church situation adapt the public school examination feedback for his church purposes? Share ideas and experiences with other teachers. Can you use written, ungraded exams in the church setting? Are there ways of having exam-like discussions that can give you high feedback?

V. To build your sensitivity to between the lines meanings of the things learners say, practice by watching a play on TV analytically. Try to "read" the attitudes behind as many of the things the actors say as you have time for. Then when the play is over, try to figure out the attitudes that underly the story—what must the author believe to write this story? Get as far below the surface as you can without straining your own incredulity. Were you able to predict the outcome of the story early in the hour by watching very carefully how the author structured the characters' attitudes?

VI. Compile some evidence from your own TV watching experience about the perspectives of TV programs in other areas than violence. Use the three points near the end of this chapter to organize your approach. You may get your thinking started by analyzing these examples:

A. (In situation comedies.) Husbands are silly idiots, entirely incompetent people whose lives must be managed by their wives.

B. (In situation comedies and most dramatic shows.) No matter how bad things may seem right now, everything will turn out all right in the end. (How realistic is this idea?)

C. (In variety shows and musical reviews.) Love between a young man and a young woman is the most important thing in life; if a man and a woman love each other, then nothing else matters.

. . . Of Some Consequence / 119

have, or the way he thinks he *should* behave, is the way he actually will behave. And rather than observing his actual behavior, we'll have to be content with looking at his *intentions*. If we can't look at his actual behavior, at least we can get some clues about his Map of the World.

FEEDBACK

Many of these clues are volunteered by learners in the feedback they give us right in the communication situation. The comments they make, the things they seem to be interested in, the expressions they have on their faces, all tell us things about our effectiveness if we're listening carefully. But we must be paying attention; we must be sensitive.

The feedback we get is usually subtle. We must be ready to "read" it carefully if we're going to make good use of it. It comes to us in the form of facial expressions, in the form of patterns of attention and inattention as we change the subject, in the form of the unspoken assumptions and attitudes behind the things the learner actually does say. Feedback is seldom clear and it is seldom easy to understand. Often the feedback we get represents feelings and attitudes that the learner himself only half understands. He sometimes isn't even aware of the attitudes that lead him to react the way he does.

Some of the best feedback comes through the connotative meanings of the symbols that learners use when they talk to us. Much of the feeling-tone in the things people say tell us things about them that they may not be aware of. And these may be very significant feelings toward the meanings we're trying to teach them. So if we can simply become more sensitive to the connotative meanings of symbols, then we'll be beginning to increase our skill at "reading" the feedback that's available.

And this can be the information that makes the difference between success and failure in our communication. If we're sensitive, if we're tuned in, if we're reading the signs fully, we can restructure what we have to say so that it fits in with the meanings the learner is applying. If we're insensitive, we can miss many opportunities to be effective in our teaching.

GETTING MORE FEEDBACK

One of the most common problems that people have in using feedback to evaluate their effectiveness in communication is that they don't get enough feedback. Especially in the teaching-learning situation, the teacher would nearly always like to have more feedback than he gets. He knows it would allow him to be more effective.

What kinds of ways does the church teacher have open to him to stimulate more feedback from his learners? How can he encourage his learners to talk back, to give him the kinds of informa-

The clinical psychologist is an expert at "reading" this kind of communication. How do you suppose he learned to be so good at it?

How much feedback is "enough"? How much would you need to have before you'd just as soon not get any more?

tion he needs to evaluate his effectiveness? Here are some ideas that may help to get you started in your thinking.

Examinations.—Public school teachers get an important kind of feedback from the examinations they give their students. A good teacher uses the examinations his students write as much to evaluate the job he's been doing as to evaluate the work the learners have been doing. The teacher can learn a lot about himself and his communication from students' exam papers.

Can we give examinations in the church school?

Of course, the public school teacher has some other purposes for giving examinations—purposes that the church teacher ordinarily doesn't share. The public school teacher must give formal grades to his students at the end of the year, and examinations are the accepted way of evaluating student's work. And many public school teachers feel that without the element of coercion that's present when students know they'll be examined, they wouldn't work very hard.

Many church group leaders feel that examinations, as such, are not likely to be workable in the church settings. Because of the way they're used in public school, examinations necessarily cause a certain amount of resentment between teacher and learner that might interfere with their relationship. But might we be able to use something similar to examinations that doesn't have the element of coercion and resentment? Some church school teachers have found that questionnaires are useful if the students know they won't be graded, and questionnaires could form the basis for some very interesting discussions. Others have held "summary and review" discussions at the end of a unit of work that give a lot of useful feedback. Use your own imagination!

Use the Discussion Form.—As we saw earlier, the discussion form provides the teacher much more feedback than the older form in which the teacher stood in front of the class and lectured for the whole class session. The discussion form encourages feedback—part of its very foundation is the continuous exchange of feedback between teacher and learners. It makes the teacher one of the learners, in fact; it gives the teacher a chance to learn as much as the students do.

Keep Communication Channels Open.—It makes some sense to assume that the longer you remain in communication with somebody, the more you're going to learn about them and about the best ways of communicating with them. This suggests that it might be worthwhile to try to communicate with your learners as often as you can outside the formal class situation. Learners can tell you things in informal surroundings that they wouldn't feel ready to say in a formal class. And the longer you keep the channels of communication open, the more information is likely to come through them—information that can help you communicate better.

What kinds of things can you do that will encourage communication between you and learners outside class sessions?

Keep in mind, however, that a channel is not entirely open if it is always filled with messages *from* you *to* the learner. If you're always talking, then the learner never has a chance to say the things you need to hear. Silence is an important tool of the teacher. Nothing will stimulate people to talk to you more than for you to be quiet. Communication abhors a vacuum; if you leave an occasional long pause, other people will rush to fill it, perhaps with information you'd really like to have. Learn to keep quiet part of the time.

Read Between the Lines.—Some of the best feedback a teacher gets is feedback that the learner isn't aware he's giving. But because he isn't intending to say what he's saying to you, he isn't being very clear about it. You have to read between the lines of what he intends to say to see the things he hasn't intended to say. The connotative meanings of the symbols he uses, his choice of things to talk about and things to ignore, the unspoken assumptions that lie behind the things he says—all of these meanings are there *for the teacher who is looking for them.*

> Can you remember a situation in which you discovered part of somebody's attitude toward you when he wasn't aware of what he was telling you?

Of course a young person's symbols are likely to be less formal than the ones you'd use, but are there also more significant attitudes behind the symbols he uses? Why did he jump on that idea to talk about rather than the dozen other ideas that came up in class today? What kinds of attitudes might lie behind that puzzling thing he said to you after class? What would a person have to believe to say that, or to say it that way? What attitudes is he telling you about?

> What effects will your own preceptions have upon the way you understand the feedback your learners make available to you?

Many experienced teachers have found that as soon as they became awake and sensitive to the feedback students were giving them, they were actually getting quite a lot of feedback. They just hadn't noticed it before. Once you begin to feel confident that you can stimulate the feedback you need if the flow of it begins to taper off, then you may begin to notice that you're not having to work very hard for it anymore. You're beginning to recognize the feedback that was always there just below the surface.

PERSPECTIVE IN A SERIES OF MESSAGES

It is certainly no surprise to the parent or to the teacher that the more one person communicates with another person, the more closely they share similar attitudes and values. Over years of marriage, husbands and wives find themselves agreeing more and more closely about the important ideals in life. And as children grow to maturity in a home, we expect them to share the attitudes of the family. The parent and the teacher realize intuitively that a long series of communications can lead to a sharing of ideals that no single message, no matter how effective, could bring. One communication situation can lead to a sharing of pieces of information; a whole series of communication situations can lead to a sharing of attitudes—of *perspective*.

> The more people communicate, the more they tend to agree. Why do you suppose that happens?

122 / **Basics for Communication in the Church**

Television advertisers have long since grasped the power of continued communication. They pay vast amounts of money to have an idea or an attitude placed continually in front of people, over and over and over and over again. They know that what one message cannot do, a lot of messages over a period of time can do. And the thing they can do is to communicate attitudes.

Every message has a point of view. That is, every message is based upon some underlying attitudes in the communicator. An individual message ordinarily communicates only on the surface; it doesn't result in sharing of the attitudes behind it. But a whole series of messages, each one based upon the same underlying attitude, can communicate the attitude itself. Even though the attitude never comes to be part of the explicit content of the message, the fact that it is consistently repeated over and over in a series of messages that appear to be "about" a number of things means that the perspective itself may be communicated.

What kinds of perspectives do TV advertisers communicate? Are the ads effective?

A perspective appears in a series of messages in three ways:

1. The messages consistently select some things to talk about and ignore other things.

2. The messages consistently label certain things as important and certain other things as unimportant.

3. The messages consistently look at the things they're about from a single point of view.

To illustrate how a perspective can appear in a whole series of messages without ever being explicitly discussed in any one of the messages, let's take an example that may not be immediately relevant to the church situation, but will be interesting to every parent and every teacher. Let's consider the perspective of American television programs toward violence. We'll simply take the three points above and apply them to the wide variety of television programs in which violence appears.

What do you think television's perspective on violence is?

1. "The messages consistently select some things to talk about and ignore others." There are a whole series of standard television formats that almost necessarily involve violence: western shows, detective shows, mystery shows, spy shows. In nearly every episode of every program in these categories, violence will be part of the show. Violence is consistently selected for attention.

2. "The messages consistently label certain things as important and certain other things as unimportant." One of the ways that an idea can be emphasized in a television program is by putting that idea at the climax of the program, at the place where the basic plot is resolved and the story gets ready to end. In a number of kinds of television shows—westerns, for instance—the climax of nearly every episode is violent. Another way of emphasizing an idea in a television program is by putting it at the beginning when everybody is paying attention. Nearly all detective shows and many standard western formats consistently begin with violence.

. . . Of Some Consequence / 123

3. "The messages consistently look at the things they're about from a single point of view." The most important violence in many standard television plots is the violence that occurs at the climax of the show. And what happens at the climax? The hero beats up the villain or kills the villain and saves the day. In other words, the hero accomplishes the good goal, the goal we all hope he reaches, by being violent. The violent good guys win out over the violent bad guys by being better at violence.

Is this a realistic portrayal of life?

Does this sound familiar to you? Do you recognize the pattern from countless television shows you've seen? How well do you suppose this perspective is being communicated to the young people who watch the cowboy shows and adventure shows on television?

PERSPECTIVE IN THE CHURCH SCHOOL

As a teacher you have continuing contact with young people. You communicate with them week in and week out, perhaps even for several years. You have a particularly good opportunity to communicate perspectives—attitudes—to them. You're in a position that a television sponsor would really envy.

What kinds of perspectives do you communicate to your learners?

And the delightful thing about perspectives in continuing communication is that we can communicate them almost effortlessly. We communicate them just by being ourselves, just by being Christian people who can talk about the world with young people from a Christian point of view. As long as there is some room in the teaching-learning situation for spontaneous conversation and discussion, the attitudes we hold will be communicated to our learners whether we like it or not. We may not be conscious of communicating them, in fact we probably are unaware of many of them and our learners may seldom be very conscious of them, but they are being communicated. Just as a dedicated Christian parent can bring a life of spiritual commitment to his children, a dedicated Christian teacher communicates a life of Christian love and spiritual values to his learners.

PART III

The Journey of Communicating and Learning

By Beverly Welton

CHAPTER 15

A Starting Place for the Journey

Exploring Communication in Teaching-Learning

We are always communicating. All that we hear, see, taste, smell, and feel we respond to in some way that communicates (or miscommunicates) what we perceive.

We are always learning from communicating. Because we are always communicating and learning, each of our lives is a journey of communicating and learning. Although we are all on the same journey, we are certainly not all taking the same routes. None of us knows what we will come upon around the next corner of our journey. Neither do we know with whom we will be traveling.

The Christian gospel speaks to all of life, if we are fortunate enough to see it, hear it, or feel it; and if we recognize it. Jesus said, "I am the way, and the truth, and the life," and many of us are committed to following his way. Also we have taken positions of leadership in the Christian community, and we sense an urgency about becoming good communicators of the faith with which we have been entrusted.

As a skill, communication has something in common with other skills—it can be learned. The ability to communicate effectively is not something with which we are born. Many churches are conducting workshops or training programs to improve the communication skills of their leaders—the kind of training you're probably involved in.

MAPPING THE JOURNEY

As with any planned journey, the Journey of Communicating and Learning which you are taking needs some mapping—some idea of destination, some possible routes that can be taken, some practical vehicles to carry you. It is possible to take an extended Journey in Communicating and Learning, spending considerable time exploring in depth all the areas along the way. Of course, some persons may pick up this text and discovering the journey in Part III, decide to fly over it—scanning the pages, landing here and there for an occasional stop-over.

When have you seen the gospel? heard it? felt it?

Could principles of advertising ever serve communicating in the church? Why or why not?

There are several kinds of journeys that could properly be called communicating and learning. Perhaps, we can begin to see our course better by looking at some of the journeys that we will not be taking.

Our journey does not take in the principles that are basic to advertising and selling. It is not aimed at learning to know how to break down the emotional defenses of persons so that they will "buy" what we have to "sell." It is not, in any sense, a study in manipulating persons.

Our journey does not include learning the skills of speaking and writing that one might expect to encounter in classes on speech or journalism. These communication skills are important and they will benefit the learning group when they are put into practice during the learning sessions.

How do persons contribute to the Truth?

Our journey covers important interpersonal and group communications as they are related to teaching and learning, specifically in the Christian community. This journey aims to build community. The learning groups may begin as congregates of individuals, but as persons continue the journey, they should begin to understand each other, to listen to each other, to care about each other, to allow diversity of opinion without estranging each other, and to assume responsibility for their communicating. The journey is a search for Truth; it recognizes that each person contributes to the Truth and is a vital part of the search.

This text offers plans for the journey, which communicate where others have gone. The plans are offered to learning groups because communicating and learning need to be lifted up to conscious levels. We know that learning and communicating are going on all

An Introduction to the Study of Part III

This section of Basics for Communication in the Church focuses on teaching-learning procedures as they relate to communication. Every activity should be a part of communicating. Chapter 15 emphasizes relating the leader roles to the communication model. The remaining chapters emphasize exploring communication—in group development, in new situations, in setting goals, in group planning, in individual study, in using media, in sensitivity to persons, in interacting, in enabling learners to learn, in relating the gospel with day-to-day concerns, and in dealing with our traditions.

Problems and barriers to teaching-learning should be approached through communication skills. Methods and media should be selected by the way they aid communication. Feedback should be obtained constantly, since communication is dependent upon it. Application to the age groups you teach should be made constantly.

The goal for Part III is to present resources and suggest opportunities through which a person can learn to communicate effectively so that persons can progress in their achievement of the objective for Christian education.

Guidance for Session 15
A STARTING PLACE FOR THE JOURNEY

Aims for the Session

To discover some of the resources each person brings to the Journey, to map where the Journey may go, and to learn five leader's guidelines which are derived from the communication model so that the group can better prepare for the following sessions.

Questions to Ponder

What do I teach without using words? What guidelines are controlling why, what, and how I teach? Do I communicate these guidelines to the learning group? Am I flexible enough to learn from my students? How can my understanding of the communications model serve me? Who or what teaches me? How can I communicate and teach more efficiently and effectively? How can I become a more accepting person? What are some of the barriers I face in being open? How can I overcome these?

A Study Plan

I. Simulate teaching-learning groups.

of the time, but we are aware, also, that much of it is misdirected. Teaching is communicating. You are invited to come on this journey and to learn that teaching and communicating are one and the same thing.

ASSIGNING TASKS FOR THE JOURNEY

If your group is setting out on our Journey of Communicating and Learning, you should probably know that it is not like a journey in the first-class compartment of a jet plane—where people are comfortably set apart, served, and entertained—where passengers have little involvement in flight operations, in the lives of other persons ticketed on the flight, or in helping stewardesses with their assignments. Our journey is more like a group of friends driving in a caravan—seeing as much as they can of the country, enjoying each other, depending upon each other to make camp, repair cars, buy groceries, care for children—and then around campfires talking about what they are feeling and thinking.

MEMBERS OF THE GROUP

In order to become the best possible communicators of the Christian faith, persons need to be accepting. Group members need each other to like them, to respect them, and to encourage them. Communication flourishes when acceptance is present. Persons are built up rather than diminished. When there is acceptance, defenses drop and both senders and receivers are free to explore new ideas together. Communicating takes a great deal of energy when what is being communicated is either a new idea or is not clearly stated. When everyone in a group listens to whatever any person says, each person knows that he will be listened to.

What can you do to help persons listen to each other with the purpose of understanding?

If your learning group is composed of fifteen or more persons, divide into two groups to simulate two teaching-learning sessions—one, an effective session and the other, an ineffective session, using whatever curriculum materials you choose. If your group is small, you will profit most by simulating an effective session. Your process should not be hurried. Consider carefully what elements should be included in the simulated class session that will demonstrate the use or misuse of communication. Engage in the simulation for at least fifteen minutes. If you are in two groups, you should observe each other's simulation. Ask the observers to list what elements they see in the teaching-learning simulation. Check to see if there were discrepancies between what you intended to portray and what the observers said that they perceived. Then discuss your feelings and understandings resulting from the simulations. Did the teacher use the guidelines presented in the text? If the guidelines were not adequately considered in the simulations, ask the two groups, How would you change your simulated class session to show your understanding of the guidelines?

II. Sharing. In pairs, share with each other what you would like to accomplish as a result of this study in communicating. After the pairs have shared, ask each partner to report his partner's desired learning to the total group. Partners should freely correct any miscommunication that may have taken place. A partner should continue to express what it is that his partner wishes to learn until the latter is satisfied that he has been understood. These desired learnings should be recorded on large pieces of paper cr chalkboard so that all persons can see them.

III. Looking ahead. A leader may print the aims for all of the sessions for the Journey on newsprint, so that the whole group can see each one at the same time. If the leader has done this, then the group may read these aims and make suggestions about other things that might be included that would bring about the desired learnings expressed in the sharing time. Or they may begin to make deletions, according to where the group is as they start the Journey. These suggestions for change should be recorded so that when the group is ready to decide on an aim for a particular session, the learners will have these suggestions with which to work.

A Starting Place for the Journey

When we listen attentively with the motivation to understand, we are respecting another person and his words.

If persons are to learn about communicating, there must be a lot of communicating taking place between persons in the learning group. Learning by doing is the surest learning method. If the learning group is communicating, it will be dealing with feelings as well as messages. So, it is most important that the members of the group be supportive of each other and totally accepting, especially when there is conflict.

Think of times when you have seen ideas shaped by a group and improved by the interplay of communicating.

The learning will be without too much tension if persons think of their learning as tentative rather than final. Group members can learn to play with ideas. When a person tosses out an idea, he should not keep too close to it. He should allow it to rise or to be shot down on its own merit and not be overly concerned because it was his idea. Ideas that can be bounced around take a group shape and frequently improve in the interplay.

Group members will need to risk failures in communication. The group can profit from these failures if everyone stays with the task and really tries. The best planning group I ever attended benefited by a request of two members to take a few minutes to become reconciled so that they would not hinder the progress of the whole group. They knew that they could not participate totally without a few minutes spent intently in coming to an understanding, and they trusted the entire group to support them.

It is important that the learning group sets its own goals. In the beginning of the study, the group may use the aims as they are stated in the session guidance in order to move them into their study. But, as the group proceeds, it will probably decide to modify the suggested aims. You can depend on curriculum resources to give you some possible directions by indicating aims, goals, possible learnings, intended outcomes, or something of a goal nature. By reading these, the group has a base for suggesting change, adaptation, or acceptance.

What causes a person to feel that others are depending on him? How is this feeling communicated?

During the journey, each person should be undergoing transformation. Through the learning activities, group members should learn much about themselves. Everyone is important to the group taking our journey, because each person is depended upon. If members come near their potential in communicating, they will have one of the greatest experiences in their lives by going on our journey.

LEADERS OF THE GROUP

Most learning that takes place after a person is ten years old is peer group learning. In order for persons to learn from each other, it is best not to have a group of over fifteen members and ten is a better number. There can be further subgrouping for some learning experiences.

The leadership for the group can be assumed by one person, or it can be passed around to persons in the learning group. It is not necessary for the leader to know more about communicating than the rest of the group.

The leader should be as receptive to the suggestions coming from the group as he is to those coming from the text or other resources. If a leader disagrees with an idea coming from someone in the group, he should ask others in the group to clarify the idea, perhaps by restating it or by giving an illustration or example. The decision either to move ahead with the suggestion or to dismiss it should be the result of a group consensus.

Persons on our Journey of Communicating and Learning should have the opportunity to experience communicating in the Christian community, not just discussing it. If you are a leader, be yourself. If you have never been a leader before, tell the group. Be open and trusting. Encourage and stimulate the members of the group to be open and trusting. Remember, they don't need you to tell them anything, but they do need you to lead.

For you, what is the difference between communicating and discussing how to communicate?

Five important guidelines for communication that a group leader or teacher should have are closely related to the Communication Model that was presented in Part II of this text.

1. *Communicating Requires Getting and Holding Attention.*— If the members (students) of a group are to perceive a particular event which is known, seen, or held only by the leader (teacher), the leader must get and hold the attention of the group if the event is to be communicated.

Only a novice teacher assumes that he has the students' attention simply because he is before the group and is talking or writing. Think of the times when you have missed the message while you were engaged in examining the teacher's tie, trying to recall who it is that the teacher reminds you of, or daydreaming about some other event that has gone before or perhaps is yet to come.

Students are most likely to be attentive if, within a series of events, the sequence of events is changed. If a teacher gets and holds attention, he will probably also get interest; but it is most unlikely that he will get interest without getting attention. Novelty or variations in teaching-learning methods usually increase attentiveness and decrease boredom. The more involved group members are in learning activities, the more likely communicating and learning will take place.

An event might be a sentence. Change the construction of the sentences in this paragraph into simple sentences. Are they less likely to get attention? More likely to get attention?

One evening a teacher, working with former high school dropouts, accidentally kicked a wastepaper basket during the class session. He was intrigued by the class reaction of attentiveness. Through the years, these students had developed bad listening habits. The teacher wondered if interruptive noises could serve learning. After experimenting awhile, he discovered many disruptive practices which helped his learners to be attentive.

A Starting Place for the Journey / 129

In another study, it was discovered that some learners accomplished more in a noisy atmosphere which required them to concentrate and to shut out distractions than they did in a quiet place where there were no distractions.

Young children are unlikely to remain interested for long if an adult talks full-face to them, because language problems are too severe for preschoolers. Expecting them to construct a mental image of a scene from a spoken description poses enormous difficulty for them. Interest can be maintained for a longer period with small children if a visual aid shows what the teacher is referring to.

New problems demand attention. When the Black Manifesto was proclaimed, a lot of persons were aroused who had never before been involved in the issues of black powerlessness. Intergenerational conflicts have generated nearly as much attention as man's first walk on the moon—perhaps more. Our culture—including the church—is barraged by new problems being created by technology, transformations of biomedical research, and big business. Attentiveness of youth and adults in how the gospel relates to these pressing concerns should not lag as long as appropriate media and methods are used to deal with them.

2. *Communicating Includes Interpreting Feedback.*—Recognizing that communication is not on a line from one person to another, but that it is circular and depends upon the addressee to react or respond, the leader uses feedback processes which enable him to gauge the effectiveness of his communication.

> Can you think of a group of persons to whom the Black Manifesto clearly communicated its intent? What were the barriers to communication in the writing? in the group?

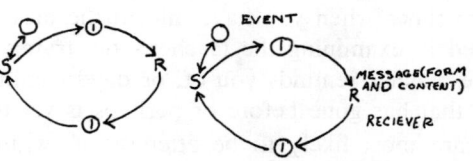

Not all communicating brings desired learning. Leaders find it helpful if they can get feedback which can be evaluated as to how nearly the learning goals were met. The teacher who is complimented by feedback such as, "My, that was a good lesson you prepared this morning," is not getting feedback on the learning that took place in relationship to the goals that were set. Teachers and students who find satisfaction and reward from learning will seek good tools for feedback. A group without clearcut goals and purposes may avoid feedback, rather than seek it. Effective teaching-learning calls for well-thought-through statements of goals and purposes which can be measured.

Leaders and teachers of small children cannot expect long verbal evaluations. They will need to devise different ways to discover if the communicating and learning have been meaningful. A teacher of a first grade group asked the children near the end of their session, "What kind of bell would you like to be, if you were a bell?" The answers of the children would help her to know if they had discovered significance and meaning in bells, particularly a New Year's bell.

"I would like to be a bell that the ice-cream man rings, and I would make all children happy," Mark volunteered.

The teacher, trying to stimulate the others to respond, asked, "What bells have you heard? How did they sound? What was their message? How did they help? What bell would you like to be?"

After a pause Jeff decided, "I would like to be a Christmas bell so that people would give some money to the poor."

"I want to be a school bell so that all the children will come back and play and I won't be lonely," said Marie.

"I want to be a bell to give people a new year and a clean calendar," mused Susie. Earlier the class had talked about the New Year's bells and the symbol A.D. for *anno Domini,* literally translated, "in the year of the Lord."

Typical feedback methods are question-and-answer and discussion, which when overused become uninteresting for most persons. Examples of many kinds of feedback tools will be presented in the following chapters of this text.

Feedback is especially important to a leader because it tells him how the group members have perceived the teaching-learning event—what was communicated.

3. *Communicating Improves When Needed Resources Are Provided.*—In order for a group member or student to respond adequately in some situations, he requires materials with which to work. A leader or teacher needs to anticipate these as well as he can.

One Saturday afternoon the youth in a seventh and eighth grade group created a display portraying, "Hurts in My City." These depictions were made in response to a trip they had made through the city. After their work was assembled, it was placed in the foyer of their church building to sensitize the church members to the needs of many persons in their city.

All of the materials needed for creating this display could have been secured by the youth—and much of it was—but the teacher greatly assisted this learning experience by arranging for transportation, contacting places to visit, and gathering together many basic supplies for constructing the display.

A learner's response to an event can be greatly limited or enhanced by how a leader uses available space, time, and resources.

> How does this question serve the teacher in discovering what was communicated?

> Write in this margin some other feedback methods which would serve to evaluate communication.

> Think of situations in your experience where communication was severely limited by lack of supplies.

A Starting Place for the Journey / 131

> How practical is memorization today when information has surpassed our ability to communicate it? What are alternative methods?

4. *Communicating Includes Managing Information.*—The content of Christian communicating is relating the gospel to all knowledge and experience. The sheer bulk of current knowledge causes a frightening communication task. The creation, diffusion, storage, and retrieval of knowledge is all a part of the phenomenon referred to as the knowledge explosion. Traditional methods of linear transmission cannot contain all the information that abounds in the persons who make up our learning groups. Each person helps the group when he communicates how a particular piece of information relates to his life. All knowledge is relative to our experience of it. Also, it is tentative, since our world is one of continuing creation. Teachers should receive meanings from students and help them in managing all available information so that learners can organize it and make sense out of life.

The content (message and medium) of teaching cannot be entirely internal either to a teacher or to a learner. In order to communicate a message, one uses publicly understood forms (media), such as language, symbols, and other representations. Although communication cannot be perfected so that we can completely understand each other, it must be sufficiently external to carry commonly understood meanings.

When a message sent in one medium produces fuzzy results, it is wise to try communicating the same message in another medium. In fact, to improve the presentation of information and greatly insure learning, it helps to use several media.

> Does your earliest memory of estrangement enable your understanding of the Garden of Eden experience? What was your Exodus experience? What do these experiences communicate?

A group of young adults were discussing the story of the expulsion of Adam and Eve from the Garden of Eden. Some of the group were having difficulty interpreting this event, when one person asked, "What is the earliest memory you have?" His question seemed distantly removed from the discussion, and several of the group were reluctant to allow it. But the questioner was more persistent than the reactors, and soon several persons had shared their earliest memories. Each of these memories was of an event in which they felt estranged—such as being laughed at, being shut away from a brother who was ill, being left with a stranger, being lost. Each person was awed by the discovery of his Garden of Eden experience—his first estrangement.

The crossing point concept in curriculum is dependent upon the organization and management of information. The crossing point is where the world with its many problems, issues, and values meets the gospel claims of faith, worship, and discipleship.

5. *Communicating Is to Bring About Change.*—All communicating has consequence-response-change-learning. Both leader-teacher and student-learner must change as a result of communicating. Without change, communicating is incomplete. To promote change efficiently, a teacher must find ways of communicating effectively.

CONSIDERING RESOURCES FOR THE JOURNEY

After mapping the journey and assigning tasks, we need to consider resources for our journey. The skills of group members should be made available to the group. If all the group members have an understanding of each person's abilities and limitations at the beginning of the journey, they will not be spending time trying to discern this for themselves nor will they be threatened by an unknown quantity in a co-traveler.

> What would be the best way of communicating to discover each person's abilities and limitations in a group?

The resources of the local community which apply to parts of our journey should be scouted out either by the leader or by someone appointed to this task.

USING THE TEXT

The text should serve as a second leader in describing and illustrating the journey. If the designated leader disagrees on matters of technique and judgment—well, all the better. Students should *not* be encouraged to accept with reverence every word they read in a text or hear from a leader. They should, instead, read and listen with minds wide open and critical faculties in full operation. Ultimately their judgments should be their own. If this text serves only to get students thinking critically about communicating interpersonally and in groups, it will have served a worthwhile function.

For many of us, the challenge is to create materials that will serve the most persons. This means that some persons reading the text will be reminded that they have already been on this path, while other persons will be taking this journey for the first time. We who prepare resources have no illusions about the difficulty of our task, and yet it is the only one open to us if we are to pursue excellence in depth study and honor the diversity of talents among our readers.

Vocabulary and methods related to curriculum are not defined because this text is one in a series of texts prepared for the setting, "Foundations for Teaching." If you need assistance with curriculum vocabulary or methods, you will find a great deal of help in the preceding texts or in *The Church's Educational Ministry: A Curriculum Plan* or *Tools of Curriculum Development for the Church's Educational Ministry*.

Marginal notes are intended disruptions to your reading of the text. They should enable attentive reading and cause you to bring your experience to the situation.

Communicating cannot be done alone. A person can read the text giving descriptions and illustrations of communicating, but this is not the same as communicating. For this reason, it would be best for learners, whenever possible, to take your journey with others. When you must go alone, talk with co-workers, friends, family—maybe, even strangers—as you go along. Communicating with someone will enhance the happenings along the way.

MODULAR PROGRAMMING

The communicating and learning concepts presented for our journey favor modular programming over the linear programs that we usually follow. One contradiction to this (and it may seem enormous to the reader who is not in a learning group using the guidance proposed in the following chapters) is the linear text. The text presentation is definitely linear—developed in a systematic "line" and logically ordered. If a leader were to use this text for lecturing about a path to Truth, expanding here and there on the author's ideas, he would not be in dialogue with the group members. The learners would have to go on the leader's journey, trying to catch glimpses of the truth through his telling. Such linear programming would tend to cause the group members to become passive spectators rather than participants—more jet plane riders than car caravan travelers.

In what situation would linear programing provide the best communicating procedures?

Modular programming has several connotations, so rather than defining its meaning, we shall look at the way it is used on our journey. The first evidence of breaking away from a strictly linear approach is the insertion of marginal notes. These call the attention of the reader away from the text and encourage him to insert some of his own thinking and creativity.

The other inclusion of modular programming is in the guidance material. Most of the guidance offers a wide variety of choices—at least for the group, if not always for the individual.

Modular programming moves away from the image of the teacher who has all the content and paces it out according to how he perceives the "average student" can handle it (linear programming). In the modular programming the teacher is a part of the learning group. He will learn as the others do—from resource materials and other persons, but he will perform some leader tasks.

Suggest ways in which a message can be communicated effectively by more than one medium.

Modular programming, as it is presented in the guidance, offers alternatives and gives greater freedom to the learners. It also permits them to learn in a way which best suits them, and it assumes personal responsibility for learning. By having modular programming in the guidance, it will be necessary for groups to select learning styles and to adapt the guidance to what can be done in available time. This selecting makes the Journey less on a predetermined line, because it allows the travelers to do many things, although probably no one can do them all.

I wish you farewell! I will not be with you all of the time, but I will be there to guide you when you choose. My best wishes go with you on our Journey of Communicating and Learning.

Exploring Communication in Group Development

CHAPTER 16

Reach Out for Someone

BELONGING[1]

I belong to myself.
  My thoughts are my very own.
  No one knows what I
    am thinking or why.
My feelings are my own.
  The things I feel are more
    a part of me than my
    right arm.
  To know the things I feel
    is to know me.
I belong to other people
  For when I share my
    thoughts and let them find my feelings,
  I have given them a part of myself
  They own a part of me.
  I belong to them. . . .
Lord, help me to give little pieces
of myself that I may belong to others.
But even more, help me to accept
pieces of others, that they, too, may
belong.

—Shari Castle, 16

---

[1]Edwin E. Hinshaw, *Adventuring with Youth* (Richmond: Friends United Press, 1969), p. XIII.

If I were to rank myself somewhere between 1 and 10 with 10 being completely open to others and 1 being completely withdrawn, what number would I assign to myself, generally? in **(name of a particular group)**?

Guidance for Session 16
REACH OUT FOR SOMEONE

An Aim for the Session

To understand some communication skills in encounter, assuming roles, and creating a learning environment so that persons can communicate more effectively in the areas of feelings, attitudes, and group development.

Questions to Ponder

What should my role be as a group leader in communication? What motivates me to be a leader? Is this motivation likely to cause me to assume positive roles or negative roles? What kind of impression do I make on students? Am I able to predict the consequences of communication? Do I have the nerve to fail? to ask assistance from the group? What needs of my group members is it really necessary to be aware of in order to communicate effectively? What qualities are necessary for honest and in-depth communication? Can I trust the group? How have I changed since I started the study of **Basics for Communication in the Church?**

A Study Plan

I. Share communication experiences. If the group is larger than eight, divide into subgroups for this sharing time. Provide large sheets of paper for each group. Consider the following:

A. Situations in which you did not understand a message and you did not inquire what the person was trying to communicate, but you later learned of the miscommunication. State the circumstances which caused you not to inquire, and list these on newsprint.

B. Situations in which you did not understand a message so that you inquired of the person what it was that he was trying to communicate. State the circumstances which caused you to be free in making this inquiry, and list these on newsprint.

C. Share the qualities of honest, in-depth sharing which students discovered under Encounter and Communication. Discuss how these affect communication.

D. Choose from marginal notes those you would like to use as resources for dialogue. The communication process in choosing the marginal notes may be recorded on a tape. What was your criteria for se-

Any group setting is packed with human relations needs which have to be met before persons can get on with mastering a subject. Besides physical needs, persons need to be loved, to belong, to have personal recognition, to feel secure, to change (learn). Also, we need to have a sense that what we are engaged in is meaningful, purposeful, and thus fulfilling. Human purposes and objectives are most important. When an adult tries to remember what made a difference to him in his church-related learning experiences, he is likely to recall either a teacher who knew him personally or a teacher who refused to consider his personal needs in order "to get on with the lesson."

What a person learns and what he becomes depends to a significant degree on how he feels about himself, about his group members, and about his teacher or leader. Human purposes for teaching-learning settings of the church have always been honored, yet, with the exception of a few educators who are so rare we never forget them, teachers have done little about attending to personal needs. Most educators agree that academic achievement is highly correlated with attitudes and feelings, and so today in education there is pressure to deal more directly with feelings, and this pressure comes not only from critics, but from students.

In order to deal satisfactorily in the area of feelings and attitudes, teachers are developing skills in communication. Some skills directly related to a group's developing in communication are encounter, role association, and creation of learning environment.

ENCOUNTER AND COMMUNICATION

Communication as people confront each other is a fascinating interplay of subtle (and sometimes not so subtle) assumptions and

---

Recall the times when your learning achievement was augmented by feelings of self-respect and worth. Were there any learning experiences in which you excelled but felt you were insignificant in the life of your teacher and/or classmates?

---

lection? At some point during this sharing period, a designated leader should stop the communicating (dialogue) and request the last three persons who spoke to state their reception of the foregoing message, their assumption about the message and the intent for their subsequent message. If a tape recorder has been recording the session you can play back that portion of the dialogue, if needed.

II. Role-play to discover how children communicate in a group process and how they work out group roles and discipline. Ask five or six persons to role-play a learning situation in which they are fourth graders making a frieze about the hardship Jesus faced during his last week. Supply the group with shelf paper and colored chalk. This is a project the children wanted and they are all eager to work on it. Knowing that this group of children can handle their project, the teacher is working with another group. Everybody is cooperating, until one in the group (designated) begins to mark on the section that "belongs" to another child. How will the fourth graders deal with this situation? (The teacher will give no help to them.)

If the group is large enough, ask one observer for each person to identify the group roles that person assumes and how they aid or hinder communication. Let each person in the role play express the feelings he or she had in identifying with fourth graders in this situation. How did they feel about the teacher's unwillingness to be involved in their human relations problems?

III. Identify group roles in the communication process of this learning group. How do other members view you as a group member? How do you view yourself? If your group is trusting enough, display in large letters on newsprint a list of group roles, leaving a large margin of space beside each word. On another sheet of paper, list the members of the group, putting an alphabet symbol before the name (A,B,C, etc.). Each group member should place the alphabet symbol for every person opposite a group role he or she has played during the study of this course. As many persons can work at this at one time as the space around the newsprint allows. Group members should be advised to have in mind specific occasions when a person performed a particular role, in case they are challenged.

meanings conveyed by verbal or nonverbal messages. Persons learn to deal with confrontations with varying degrees of effectiveness, but difficulties arise frequently when meanings are not clarified or assumptions are not checked.

There is a communication joke which involves two psychologists who meet in the lobby of a convention hotel on their way to breakfast. "Good morning," greets Dr. Lane. "I wonder what he meant by that," muses Dr. Rhoades.

Since Rhoades's query probably would not be provoked by the language of the greeting, we wonder, Was there something unusual in Lane's tone of voice or behavior? Was Rhoades making an unfounded assumption that a hidden meaning existed in the communication? If Rhoades thought there was hidden meaning, and if he was like most of us, he did not directly question Lane—although he may have asked a third person if he thought there was any dubious message in the communication he received. By not checking with Lane, Rhoades allows this statement to cloud further communication between the two men. If Rhoades thought Lane was mocking him, flattering him, or using him by greeting him, he might assume that he understood Lane's intentions without ever directly checking with him.

In a teaching-learning setting, there are many chances for similar miscommunication to occur, especially because other persons are present.

For instance, a miscommunication interchange might go like the following one when a group was considering family heritage.

Do you (a) never, (b) rarely, (c) sometimes, (d) frequently, or (e) always ask a person to clarify what he is trying to communicate, if there is some question in your mind?

Mr. Lewis (teacher thoughts):

1. (Reception) I want students to be open and honest, especially Pat. I feel good that he has spoken freely.
2. (Assumption) He likes and trusts me. He has a good sense of humor. He is familiar with Irish names and their Roman Catholic connotation.
3. (Intent) I'll make a joke to show him and the rest of the group that I'm not an old fuddy-duddy. This will bring us closer and encourage more class participation.
4. "With a good Irish Catholic name like Pat Kelly, I thought you'd be the first person in the class to accept the mystery of Jesus being the Son of God."

Pat (student thoughts):

1. (Assumption) The teacher appreciates honesty and openness in students. He said so in class.
2. (Intent) I'll try telling him what I really think about Jesus. Maybe he can help me understand how he is divine. (I'll also show the kids that I'm not a square.)
3. "Mr. Lewis, my Dad is a Jew and he believes that Jesus was not any different from any other famous religious leader; and sometimes I wonder if he's right."

The meaning that Pat attached to Mr. Lewis' jest and to the group response was not inherent in the event. Write an alternate "reception," "assumption," "intent," and "message." How does your alternate communication differ? Do you think the circumstances may have been altered?

Assuming that the verbal confrontation went as it is printed, what other "assumption" and "intent" might the teacher have which would have changed his message and reestablished communication and group interaction?

Reach Out for Someone / 137

From this encounter, would you have predicted that the last set of Pat's "reception, assumption, and intent" would have been any different than they were? What do you think Mr. Lewis' prediction of Pat's consequent behavior might have been?

How might Pat have worded his message to better convey his intent?

What was inappropriate about Mr. Lewis' response?

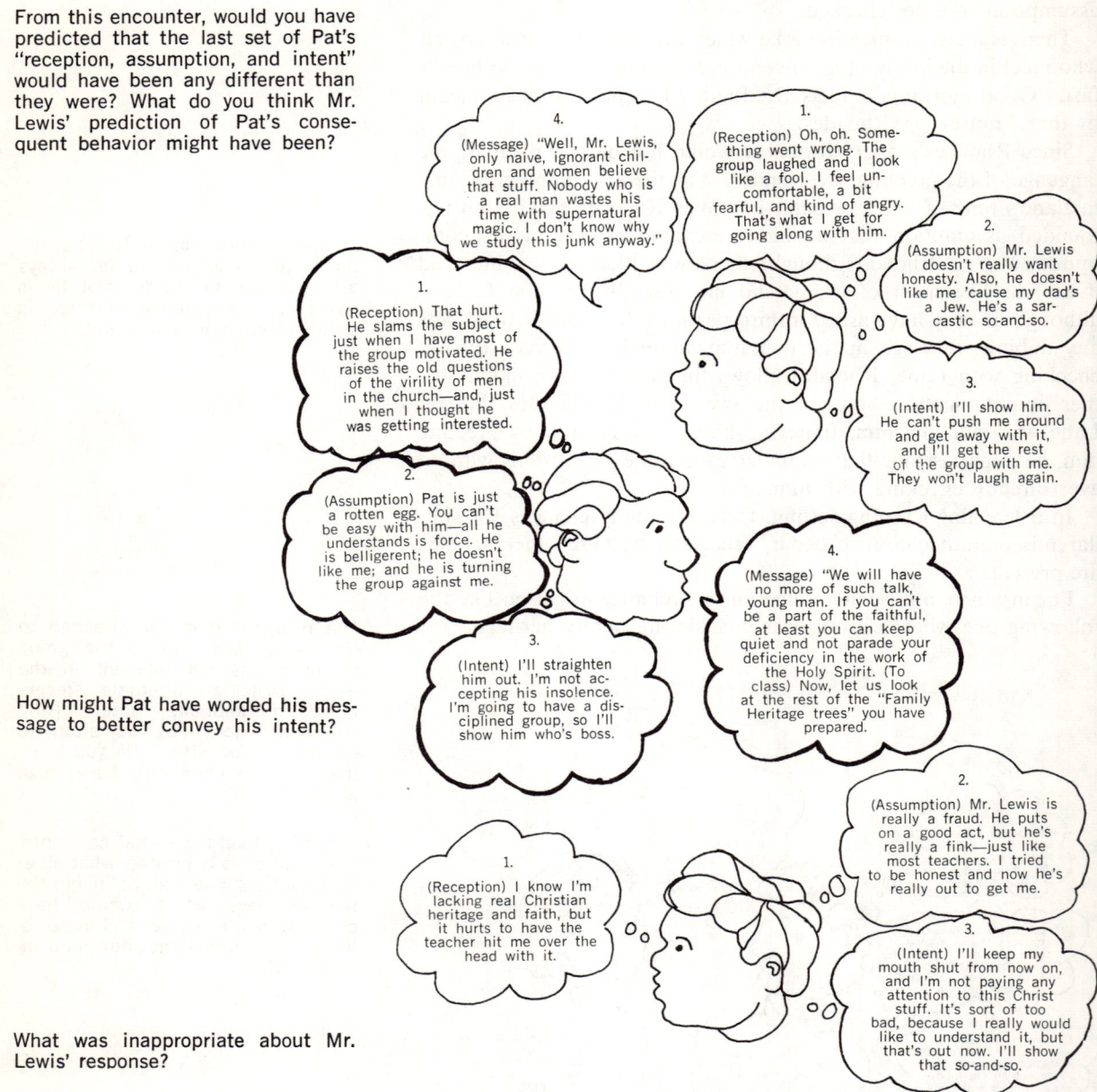

138 / Basics for Communication in the Church

Because of this blocked communication, the group was not able to interact. What followed was one-way actions, which resulted in cloudy communication.

Encounter includes feelings and perceptions in addition to messages. Communication occurs only when the receiver clarifies the messages and assumptions of the sender. Unfortunately, our cultural patterns discourage us from checking out assumptions, particularly if they are perceived as negative. Trying to avoid conflict, we often avoid encounter and communication.

The development of relationships is helpful to effective communication and, subsequently, to effective teaching-learning. As more meaningful relationships are formed by a learning group, the less need there is for clarification. With close friends we are not constantly on guard against misunderstanding because they tend to interpret our intent correctly even when our language is clumsy. In "understanding" each other they trust and mutually support each other. This kind of understanding is the context of love.

What are the qualities of honest, in-depth sharing? Can they be discovered and developed? Let's try.

1. Think of an experience you have had, which you are willing to tell anyone. Write it down.
2. Think of an experience you have had that you would tell only to a few close friends. Write it down.
3. Think of an experience you have had which you probably will not tell anyone and certainly not more than one, special person.

Is it true that it is easier to tell very personal experiences and problems to a stranger, rather than a friend? Why? Why not?

Now let us look at some qualities in listeners and differences in experiences. What are the qualities you would require of a person before you would tell experience No. 2? List these.

What are the qualities you would require of a person before you would tell experience No. 3? List these.

What are the differences in experiences Nos. 1, 2, and 3? List these.

Examine carefully the qualities of a person to whom you would tell experiences Nos. 2 and 3, remembering that students need someone to confide in and will often seek a teacher-listener. Recent research reveals that everyone can learn, provided he is given the opportunity to develop confidence and self-respect. Teachers significantly affect children's development of attitudes toward learning and communicating.

Can these qualities be developed? How?

When the possibilities of failure and negative responses are accepted by both teachers and students, *who know each other,* they can give mutual support and deal creatively with whatever is blocking communication. After all, friends often disagree, but they remain friends. When communication is blocked, people treat each other formally (ritualistic manner) or they avoid contact altogether.

Reach Out for Someone / 139

Thomas Edison is reported to have tried at least one thousand different substances in his attempt to find a filament for the first incandescent light bulb. An associate remarked that it was a pity that they wasted so much time on materials that had failed, to which Edison replied, "Nonsense, we didn't fail—instead we now know one thousand substances that won't work."

Do administrators of teaching-learning settings in the church have the nerve to risk and possibly to fail? Do teachers have the nerve to fail? Are teachers apprehensive of change or new situations because they do not have this nerve to fail? One attribute of a good leader is his ability to cope with failure, by making it a learning experience for everyone involved in the failure.

As a leader, could you be open enough with your group to try a new method, to fail in it, and to seek feedback from the group about why the method failed?

COMMUNICATION THROUGH ROLE ASSOCIATION

A group is more than a structure which can be adequately described by its composition, permanence, functions, interests, structures, cohesiveness, and sanctions—because it is a dynamic synthesis of social roles and communication is perpetually taking place.

In teaching-learning settings of a church there is no static group because each group is undergoing a dynamic process of transformation. New members come in, others leave; leaders come and go. Change is inevitable, yet a group is seldom consciously examined in light of what it is communicating. Each time a group undergoes changes of membership or leadership, it shifts and changes. More than that, each time a group meets, its members have changed because of their intervening experiences. All of these changes make it difficult for group members to know each other and to keep communication channels open. For this reason, one primary communication task of a teaching-learning group is to know each other.

Through the processes of getting to know each other, group members take responsibility. They talk to each other as well as to the teacher, and there is student participation expected in terms of planning, executing, and evaluating.

Do you agree that getting to know each other should continue to be a primary communication task of a church - related, teaching - learning group? Why? Why not?

Group Roles which can aid communication are:

Initiator	Energizer
Contributor	Tester
Information seeker	Procedural technician
Information giver	Recorder
Elaborator	Encourager
Clarifier	Harmonizer
Coordinator	Compromiser
Consensus taker	Expediter
Orienter	Standard setter
Evaluator	Group observer
Critic	Follower

Choose one of these group roles that aid communication and become a third person in the encounter between Mr. Lewis and Pat Kelly (see illustrated interchange under Encounter and Communication). How would you change the encounter?

Roles which may block communication are:

Aggressor	Self-confessor
Blocker	Dominator
Recognition seeker	Help seeker
Playboy	Special interest pleader

Sometimes a person can make a role which usually aids communication into a role that hinders. Watch for situations which illustrate reversal of group roles from aiding to hindering and vice versa.

Besides the group roles just listed, each group confronts perpetual changes in social roles incurred by its changing membership. Social roles also relate to facility or difficulty in communicating. The social roles of a student or a leader-teacher can be analyzed by using several components: (1) context—those persons or groups of persons who participate with him in the educational setting, and who share the same objective; (2) task—duties, or functions that a person is expected to perform; (3) status—rights, privileges, rewards, social standing, or occupation of a certain place in society; and (4) self—the attitudes of the person toward himself, toward others, and toward the reaction of others to him.

The components of the social roles of a student and a teacher-leader are compared in Diagram 1. The lists of components are

What components would you delete/add to the lists in diagram 1?

Diagram 1: Comparative Social Roles of Students and Leaders in Church-Related, Teaching-Learning Settings

CONTEXT	TASK	STATUS	SELF
Other students Leaders Family Church	Exploring, discovering meaning and experience Appropriating personally the meaning and value discovered in the field of relationships in light of the gospel Assuming personal and social responsibility	Member Communicator Good citizen Reputation of being church-related Respectable	Important Needed Honest Law abiding Compassionate Trustworthy Dependable

STUDENT

TEACHER-LEADER

Students Other leaders Administrators Parents Church	Providing and using resources Encouraging and supporting learners in group roles Developing and sharing in experiences Involving learners in questioning, problem solving, issues, goal setting, planning Evaluating, testing, experimenting	Honored position Credit to community Reputation Satisfactions Communicator Leader	Important Hard worker Surrogate parent Benefactor Confidant Example Dependable Knowledgeable
CONTEXT	TASK	STATUS	SELF

intended to be suggestive (rather than exhaustive) of what might be included in such an analysis of the social roles of members and leaders. These roles, as well as the group roles, affect communication within a teaching-learning situation.

One leader said that he thinks of his learning group as flowers, and remembers the caution, "Do not crush!" Group leaders need to "be someone" more than to "do something"—but to be someone involves allowing each other person to be someone in relationship and recognizing that each relationship is fragile, is growing, and is potentially beautiful. Leaders may find it difficult at times to resist *closing* a discussing by expressing a personal opinion, giving a little lecture, "typing up loose ends," or volunteering unasked-for advice. Each leader must be wary of this tendency and consciously invite further discussion, solicit other viewpoints, and suggest resource materials that might aid students in their learning. Persons need to struggle with the things that interest them and to use their capacities to the very limit, and a leader should give them that opportunity.

> Imagine a situation in which a group goes beyond the limitations and scope of its leader. What would it be like?

The aim of leadership is not to make carbon copies; rather, it is to create the environment in which persons may discover themselves and fulfill their potential. Because of this aim, good leaders constantly strive to broaden their scope, since a group usually will not attempt to go beyond the limitations and scope of a leader. To create situations in which a person or persons realize their potential is to risk disintegration or to cause a revolution, but the risk is heightened by not allowing the group to express itself.

A LEARNING ENVIRONMENT CONDUCIVE TO COMMUNICATION

What are the qualities we might wish for in a learning environment conducive to communication? We will begin the list as follows:

1. An environment that is accepting and forgiving.
2. One that takes a person out of self-interest and involves him in group activities.
3. One where the inducements to sociability are attractive and vivid.
4. One that makes definite and clearcut demands, yet lets the demands be flexible.
5. One that excludes formal punishment or long-lasting ostracism.
6. One in which there is hope of friendship and hope of praise.
7. One that displays the skills of communication that lead to greater pleasure, greater security.
8. One where rewards are immediate and directly related or coming from the activities.

9. One which allows a person to find his own identity by granting identity to others.
10. One which allows a person to become more fully a person by focusing concern on others.

Make your additions to this list.

Rarely are we surprised by one child's capability of having curative effects on another when their relationships are allowed to evolve naturally—while at play without adults involved. A child sees quite clearly that he must share, or the activity which he enjoys will cease; that he must honor his agreements, or the game will end; that he must show consideration for others, or he cannot have friends. The social necessity proves itself at all times and in thousands of ways, not because of our special efforts, but by sheer necessity. If a sense of decency and fair play has been taught in the home during the earliest years, it exerts itself when children are engaged in play with one another.

We are usually wise enough not to interfere unduly in children's relationships when they are in the backyard, but as soon as children are placed in educational settings, we suddenly act as if they had no capacity at all for practical sociability. We usually place all decisions in the hands of adults and proceed to prescribe everything for the children.

SUMMARY

In developing communication skills as a group, each person is involved in seeking both his personal identity and his group identity. Frequently this function is carried out through symbolization. The kindergarten child that pastes his attendance seal on a chart notes the symbolization of himself in relationship to his group. An attendance seal of a sheep or a flower petal may further identify the child with a flock of sheep which knows Jesus as its shepherd, or as a part of a beautiful flower, like real flowers which are created by God.

If it would improve a learning group to have the responsibility of group maintenance, how would you go about giving it to them, and what would your role be as a leader?

Music has a collective function which ties man to other men: groups. Songs may communicate a group's function, unite it, and stimulate its morale. Such music will quickly remind a person of his relationship to the group.

Communications training is capable, if properly employed, of producing substantial, educational change. It holds tremendous potential for improving education by dealing with its affective (emotional, social) components, reducing unnecessary friction between generations, reducing attitudinal blocks and group resistance to needed educational change, and creating a new day for groups within the church's educational settings. Effective communicating with others has been largely taken for granted, but as the abrasion of human existence increases in our crowded world, it cannot be ignored.

Have you allowed music to perform its collective function in your group? How might you more effectively use music as a communication tool?

CHAPTER 17

New World, New Wineskins

Do you agree that many people in the mid-sixties believed that there needed to be a change in church school education? Why do you agree or disagree?

Exploring Communication in New Situations

By the mid-sixties the need for change in church education was voiced by many people, including teachers, supervisors, parents, and ministers. Questions were raised about the adequacy of the education being offered to those who are enrolled in the educational organizations of the church. There was an anxiety that what was being taught was not relevant to the increasingly technical and complex society in which we were being thrust. Questions about educational practice and communication came out because of the sheer mass of information that was being developed at increasingly faster rates. Changes in the nature of knowledge, in child nurture, and in the technology of our society underlined the urgency to "tailor" programs to the needs of persons in today's world. Increasing world problems were challenging Christians to be a more effective leaven in society and consequently to call into question the church's ways of teaching.

To be sure, the church is called to be a place where we feel accepted and where we can depend upon having happy experiences, but it needs also be a place where we are helped to deal with significant issues in our physical and social world and how they are interrelated with the religious-spiritual world. A person has a right to expect his church's education program to enable him to grapple with ideas that are important and significant at the level where he can be helped to respond to them meaningfully.

UNREST IN THE CHURCH ENLARGES COMMUNICATION GAPS

What were the charges against education in the church during the 1960s? What changes are the seventies bringing about? What are the charges against the educational programs of the church? How should the many changes in our society alter my teaching? How can we overcome the divisive polarizations in our society? Do my students understand my language or am I "over their heads"? How can I "tailor" curriculum resources to fit my group? In what way does curriculum span the ages? How can I help my students to look at events from many perspectives? Am I dissatisfied with my present way of teaching? Why or why not?

A Study Plan

Several models for learning are suggested below in Nos. I through V. They are not exhaustive of all the possible ways of planning for study. Your group may create its own plan. If you choose to work with "A Study Plan" as it is printed, your meeting time may cause you to choose between models as a total group or to have subgroups working in different models.

Model I. Tailor curriculum. Work in task groups of two or three, but keep in mind communicating in one particular learning group within the educational program of your church. It would be helpful if one person in the task group teaches or serves as a leader of the learning group from one of the curriculum resources used in your church.

A. Identify the concepts which are to be communicated in the session you selected.

B. List the facts stated in the session which substantiate the concepts. Add any facts that you think will benefit the communication.

C. Find current material that

Guidance for Session 17
NEW WORLD, NEW WINESKINS

Aim for the Session

To understand that the charges against the church, the changes in society, and current polarizations need to be confronted with gospel concepts, communicated effectively with all ages and appropriated as a result of values teaching.

Questions to Ponder

Is the content of my teaching relevant to the lives of my students? Could it be more meaningful than it is? What can I do to predict more adequately what kind of teaching will reach the needs of my students? Do I feel sure that the gospel message, especially revealed in Jesus Christ, fits our world today? What do you predict will be the charges against the educational settings of the church during the decade of the seventies?

The following charges aimed at the church (from interviews) may give us insights into the kinds of communication gaps that unrest is causing.

"My church is out-of-date. It emphasizes past history too much and denies the present day. We must be living in the present if we are to reach into the future."

"The church I attend is out of touch. We don't deal with the real issues of today, and so it is boring. When we get bored, we get spiritually empty."

"Our church maintains a status quo that is out-of-date. We are last in race relations, in equality among the races and sexes, and in ministering for human welfare."

"Churches have a mania for constructing new buildings, but they do very little about a world on the edge of famine."

"In my church, all of the control is in the hands of people over fifty."

"Our adult education is mostly talk—mostly by the teacher, and people say, 'He has *talked to us* for years and we like to listen to him!' We seldom get into action. We talk a nice fight. We discuss, debate, even quarrel at times. I suggested to a large, men's class that they suspend Sunday meetings for six weeks and participate in such things as civic action, human rights, work with prisoners, work with mentally retarded patients. The response was interesting. One man said, 'I don't know who you are, nor who asked you to come. But I for one don't propose to do what you suggest, and I hope you aren't asked to come back!' "

Another indicator of a communication gap is uncovered by

Using the three questions following the subtitle, Unrest in Churches Enlarges Communication Gap, interview some persons in your church, neighborhood, school, or at work.

could be used to supplement the resource piece. Are there facts pertaining to the local community—to its income and expenditures, to its products and manufacturing plants, to its population trends, to its budgets for human welfare, to its growth or decline, to its entertainment—which would relate to the session and would be important to the communication? A newspaper is a slice of life. If you can't find anything in it that you want your students to understand, then you may not be teaching them to live in the world as it is today. A key word in education is change.

D. What is each learner's readiness for these concepts—his or her needs, interests, motivations, capacities, past experiences? How has the learner communicated his readiness?

E. Identify aids for values teaching printed in the resources. What else might be included in communicating values?

F. Isolate one concept and agree on a way of communicating the concept.

G. Then, move from the concept level to the values level and agree on ways of communicating the values related to that concept.

H. What changes do you predict as a result of your communication?

Model II. In a small group, share your learning which resulted from working wth marginal notes.

Model III. In a small group, apply the communications technique for problem solving—synectics—to a problem that your church is facing or a group within your church is facing.

Model IV. In a small group, write a sentence (which relates to a current issue in which there are three ambiguous words, such as "We wanted a perceptive eye not clouded with the hangover of memories." When the task groups are finished, ask one person (A from a group to read his sentence. When he finishes, ask a person (B) from another group to interpret A's sentence. (The communication model may be applied throughout.) A third person (C) will report what B said and make changes so that B agrees with the restatement; then C will give his interpretation and/or response. A fourth person (D) will tell what C said and make changes so that C agrees that he has been heard and understood; then D will give his interpretation/response. A fifth person (E) will tell what D said and make

Are you in the 58.5 percent or in the 36.7 percent?

a survey, conducted in the late 1960s by the National Opinion Research Center for the National Council of Christian Churches in The United States of America. It showed that 58.5 percent of those polled disapproved of the social and political involvement of the churches, and only 36.7 percent approved.

Several major denominations are threatened with schisms; members of the same congregation often cannot agree on what the role of the church should be in contemporary society. Ministers and laymen are often in sharp disagreement over what the message of religion should be in the modern world. Since the beginning of the church, it has been affected by polarization, which is described as variously—

$$\text{faith} \longleftrightarrow \text{works}$$
$$\text{reflection} \longleftrightarrow \text{action}$$
$$\text{personal religion} \longleftrightarrow \text{social action}$$
$$\text{conservative} \longleftrightarrow \text{liberal}$$

How can communication serve to keep polarizations in healthy tension?

The unrest in our churches could be greatly alleviated by persons who are skilled in communication. Many ministers who meet resistance from their congregation leave the active ministry because communication breaks down or there is no effort to communicate.

Some of the unrest in our churches comes from the unexamined changes in our world. We have not communicated about what these changes mean for the church.

Think about what our verbal and nonverbal responses to these changes communicate. In conversing with other persons about our understanding of these changes and the meaning we assign to them, what communication gaps are we likely to meet?

Many of these changes in our world present novel problems, which require answers and resolutions that differ radically from our preceding understanding. Synectics is a special communications technique for problem solving that can be applied to many situations. Briefly stated, it calls for making the strange familiar, and making the familiar strange. The ten basic principles of synectics are:

1. Proceed on the assumption that things are possible.
2. Isolate fixed ideas and overcome them.
3. Do not search for solutions, but for new ways to view the problem.

---

changes so that D agrees that he has been heard and understood. To practice communication, use this process with several of the ambiguous sentences written by the task groups.

Model V. For individual study, if you have a public library or public school library you may be able to get a child's picture book, "The Little House." What is communicated nonverbally about the process of change and its effect on space, time, interrelationships, equilibrium, and balance? What does the move of the little house communicate about coping with change? Is this way of coping with change always possible or desirable? What changes in your world are upsetting you and how are you communicating them both verbally and nonverbally? How can communication skill help you cope with them? If another group member uses this book for individual study, arrange to share your answers and to cooperate in problem-solving.

4. Recognize that new ideas (one's own as well as others') are fragile, and listen positively to them.
5. Seize on tentative, half-formed possibilities.
6. Entertain the apparently unthinkable.
7. Articulate the apparently unspeakable.
8. Defer conclusions until a number of variables have been floated.
9. Keep track (brief notations) of the process.
10. Enjoy your efforts in communication!

> Apply the synectics technique for problem solving to a problem which you are facing.

LANGUAGE POSES COMMUNICATION PROBLEMS

In each era of history new language emerges, bringing new meaning for old words and also creating new words. The compulsive clichés of the 1960s—"relevant" and "meaningful"—suggested a desperate search for identity. Will words such as "synectic or synthesis" and "wholeness" be the language of the seventies? These words would suggest putting the pieces together to create a whole, healing alienation, and humanizing a technological society. What words do you predict will symbolize the feelings of the seventies? Many of the major trends, visible and subterranean, that will shape man's life are present today. Can we identify these? Trying to determine the language and character of a decade at its beginning is a hazardous venture. Could anyone have foreseen the turmoil of the sixties? Some of the new words of the late sixties were acidhead, be-in, Charlie, dovish, earthscape, hawkish, holography, Lunar Module, inner city, laugh track, psychedelia, pulsar, soul brother, trips, up-tight, and voice-over.

Although word symbols are the most easily understood symbols for an event, there is still a great deal of room open to miscommunication because of the language problem. Few words in the English language are univocal—"having one voice," having only one meaning. Most words are ambiguous and their meanings are determined by their context—other words in the sentence, the event to which they relate, the personal understanding of the speaker or writer.

> I would avoid reporting that I was "on a trip." Whereas ten years ago the phrase would convey a singular message—that I was away from the city, today it could mean I had been taking drugs. Make a note of some phrases which could convey more than one meaning.

"You have to acknowledge man as a human being," says French futurist Bertrand De Jouvenel. "If you forget this, you lose everything." In the foregoing quote there are several ambiguous words. The statement is open to many interpretations. What do we do when we "acknowledge man"? In this context what connotation could be given to "human being"? "Everything" is all inclusive. Could there be some exceptions? Whenever we "bead" words together, either in speaking or writing, we are likely to miscommunicate. This is why a listener's response is so vital to communication.

> What do you think Dr. Jouvenel meant by his statement? Ask several other persons to interpret his statement. Does the statement communicate different concepts?

A teacher who feels that his words are unheard may be encouraged to hear later that they have entered the mind of a learner and worked to produce change—like a slow medicine. Sometimes understanding comes only when a person undertakes the telling. That is why the traditional lecturer-teacher receives more benefit from his teaching than his students do. When hearers become speakers, they enter and take their place in the chain of narrators, not simply echoing the words but responding to them.

Two persons seldom mean the same things by the words they use. There is, therefore, infrequently a pure reply. With every word in a conversation, understanding and misunderstanding are interwoven.

COMMUNICATION PRINCIPLE IN NEW CURRICULUM

The curriculum which was launched in the fall of 1969 is based in part on a teaching-learning principle made popular by Dr. Jerome Brunner—"that any subject can be taught effectively [communicated] in some intelligently honest form at any stage of development."

In order to put this communication principle into practice, educators needed to clarify the basic gospel messages which speak to man's persistent life issues. Then editorial teams, writers, and teachers would "tailor" each message according to (1) the readiness (basic needs, interests, motivations, capacities, developmental tasks) of a learner, (2) the way in which a persistent life issue confronts a learner (significance) at a particular age, (3) how it relates to a learner's past experience, (4) how it could be best communicated, and (5) what changes might be predicted as a result of the communication. These changes or learnings may be associated with skills, attitudes, motivations, perceptions (including understandings and appreciations).

What other definitions are given the word **gospel**?

The statements of learnings are formed by what the gospel has to say about persistent life issues. The word *gospel* is ambiguous, but when it is used in this curriculum it has been defined as God's whole continuous redemptive action toward man, known especially in Jesus Christ. (A discussion of persistent life issues and how the gospel relates to them may be found in "Change My Children," by Harold Johnson, Chapter 15 of *Basics for Teaching in the Church*.)

Designing a teaching-learning unit at any grade level requires more attention to how to communicate concepts than a dedication to how many facts can be conveyed. For a long period of time after the church school was established in the late 1700s the curriculum was primarily catechetical and totally content centered. During the first part of this century content was largely removed from the primary focus of the church school by prevalent misinterpretations of what developmental psychology required in teaching. Educators understood "child-adolescent-adult development" as an approach to their physical, social, and emotional growth. While conceptual growth was always added to the list, teachers' concerns for social and emotional growth were regarded as primary. Conceptual growth was an expected result but was considered to require little of a teacher's time in planning and programming. This emphasis was actually a most beneficial one, serving to balance the previous ignorance of the powerful effects of emotional stresses and problems upon a person's interest and ability to learn. It did, however, establish a new imbalance in which the need for conceptual content was frequently overlooked.

> Do you experience emotional stresses which interfere with your interest in learning and your ability to learn? What are they?

During the past few years there has been a growing interest in restoring balance to the curriculum by relating life's persistent issues to the gospel message. Fears that intellectual stimulation through deliberate content selection might be damaging to young children are contradicted by considerable psychological research and theory. Children require stimulation and regular opportunities for environmental exploration in order to experience learning satisfaction. To discover steps that come between a person's present experience and his richer maturity is a prime communication function of teachers at all levels—to help persons advance toward the acquisition of knowledge and efficient modes of thinking and to enable them to find meaning. This view regards a teacher as a mediator between a person's present stage of development and the communication of an organized body of knowledge which he can attain.

The "emerging" curriculum idea from the first half of the twentieth century, with its insistence that only those experiences which emerged from day-to-day-living would have meaning, is becoming increasingly difficult to defend. If children can deal with ideas and derive pleasure as well as learning from appropriate activities, there seems no sound reason to avoid planning specific content selection. The assumption of the old curriculum, that the child was the one who was best equipped to judge which ideas he could handle and to initiate his own learning, prevented teachers from selecting content and planning how it would best be communicated. It restricted the child's learning opportunities to his own immature perception and understanding of the realities of the world.

> What is the difference between the new curriculum and the "emerging" curriculum of the first half of the twentieth century?

The new curriculum resources present basic gospel messages which are communicated to all ages. For an example, the learning "We are created in God's image, interdependent yet free," is restated in the following ways:[1]

Kindergarten: God made human beings different from animals and other things, and this difference is something wonderful, for which we are glad.

Grades 1-2: God gives me my life: I'm glad I'm alive.

---

[1]The following statements are excerpts from Christian Life and Ventures in Christian Living Curriculum, Perspective 1, Second Semester.

Grades 3-4: God created me in his image: We can't explain everything that happens, but we can trust God.

Grades 5-6: God created the universe so that each part is dependent upon every other part. Man is unlike animals in that he has intelligence to make long-range plans, to invent, and to make complicated discoveries. Man also has the freedom to choose.

Grades 7-8: Man is not simply a biological entity, but he is destined to be a spiritual being having freedom and responsibility in relationship to a loving God.

Grades 9-10: Man is a being whose meaning derives from God. God created man with great potential for heights of creativity or depths of depravity. To achieve his most fulfilling potential, man must find a balance between thinking too highly of himself or having too low an opinion of himself.

Grades 11-12: Man is a living and complete person who reflects in his own personality the nature of God. Man is the object of God's love in spite of all the weaknesses man often displays.

Adult: When we seek to understand ourselves as human beings, we discover that we are a bundle of conflicting forces and that our behavior is often contradictory. Because of this paradox in our nature, many of us live in constant tension with ourselves, between what we believe we are meant to be and what we know we are. This frustration frequently involves a sense of guilt, which biblical doctrine attributes to man's sinful nature.

TEACHING WHICH COMMUNICATES ON THREE LEVELS

Experience teaches us that there is nothing permanent, except change; history teaches us that the solid supports of yesterday become the rubble of today. Standards, values, and principles have varied greatly from age to age and from society to society; indeed they have varied greatly from one generation to another within the same society.

Within the last twenty years, the impact of television and the increasing number of nursery schools have altered the influence of home and church in the shaping of values. Now the educational settings of the church are serious about values teaching. For a fuller treatment of values, review pp. 65-70 in *Basics for Teaching in the Church,* the first course in Foundations for Teaching.

Choose another gospel message from a curriculum resource for one semester in the new curriculum. Search through the resources in each grading (of that semester) and note the way this gospel message is "tailored" for each grading.

Can you illustrate the statements in this paragraph?

Dr. Sidney B. Simon identifies three levels of teaching in an ascending order of importance: (1) fact level; (2) concept level; and (3) values level.[2]

Examples of the three levels of teaching are given below, using the learning, "We are created in God's image, interdependent yet free," which was just illustrated for the various ages. These examples are for youth and adults.

1. Fact level teaching:

    Who created all kinds of living creatures, such as cattle, fish, birds, and every living thing?
    Who are the greatest of God's creatures?
    In how many days did God create the world?
    From what did God make man?
    In what ways is your freedom limited?
    What is the experience which Paul describes in Romans 7:14-25?

2. Concept level teaching:

    What is the meaning of no two persons looking alike?
    What do you think it means to be created in the image of God?
    If God cares for us, why do we get hurt?
    Why did God make the world?
    What did God plan for man?
    What is the relationship God intends man to have with animals?
    Compare God and man. How are they alike? different?
    What do you think would happen if you tried to be completely independent?
    What do you think the Psalm means when it says man has been given dominion over the "works of thy hands"?
    Does belief concerning human nature affect the way a principal runs a school?

> How does the concept level differ from the fact level?

3. Values level teaching:

    Can anybody take your place in God's heart?
    Some people are starving to death. If you were God, would you let this happen? How would you stop it?
    If you were God and had made the world, how would you feel? When do you feel proud about something you make?
    How do you feel about being created by God?
    Is there anything you can do about your destiny?
    Do you ever try to "play God"? What do you do?

---

[2] Sidney B. Simon, "Three Ways to Teach Church School," in *Colloquy*, (January 1970). Division of Publication—Periodical Department, United Church Board for Homeland Ministries, Philadelphia.

New World, New Wineskins / 151

How does the values level differ from the concept level?

Why should people try to help each other? If you had a million dollars, would you share it with the poor? If you had no money for food for the next two weeks, would you steal money? food?

Is it not a kind of sickness of the mind, one which peculiarly afflicts Christians, to begin a study of man with a focus on the meaning of guilt? Is there not something essentially morbid and unhealthy about such an approach? Do you ever feel guilty? When?

Would you say that there is something fundamentally good in human nature? If not, would you hold that the youth of our land who respond to the challenge of the Peace Corps are actually motivated by self-centered love of adventure, curiosity about distant lands, or a desire to escape from home? Do you do anything which you think stems from fundamental goodness?

Do you feel guilty for the wrong you do? In what way does your conscience motivate you to nobler living? Can you be patriotic and not hate a nation your country is at war with?

How might this learning be revisited at the high school level? How might it be stated? What method of teaching would you choose?

All three levels of learning are important. Facts are necessary. We can't build concepts without them. Facts should be plentiful and accurate. We can't make valid value judgments without considering all of the facts which impinge on an alternative. Teaching at the fact level stops short of helping learners see what the facts add up to in terms of concepts which provide a framework for understanding and dealing with the social and physical world. We need to go beyond facts to understandings and generalizations, which logically link facts together.

A basic concept—a group of persons can produce more by working together, each performing one small task, than if each person tries to produce a whole product by himself—is a concept which teachers try to communicate to all ages. Kindergarten children usually receive it with suspect. A vivid experience of this concept at the kindergarten level would provide a good base for further learning and revisiting of the idea at higher grade levels.

The week before Easter a children's activity was to make simple paper baskets with handles. There are many concepts and values which can be taught through this activity. One teacher chose to communicate the concept that working together on a product could be more productive than working alone. The teacher demonstrated how to make the basket. Each child made one of these, admired the work of other children and put his basket aside to be filled with candy later.

The class was informed that there would be a race to see whether the children who continued to work alone could produce more baskets than children who would work together as a team. Asked to predict who would produce more baskets, the children overwhelmingly voted in favor of those working alone.

Since it had taken about fifteen minutes to make individual baskets, it was decided to limit the race to a fifteen-minute period. This time, the group was divided into three teams of six children each, with one child in each group appointed as the group supervisor, to keep his team supplied with paper, paste, and scissors.

Two groups were to work individually as before while one group would divide the total task among the members of the team so that two children would cut handle strips, another two would cut slits to make corners, while another two would paste on decorative flowers. Ellen, who was supervisor for the table where group cooperation was being demonstrated, became aware of a bottleneck at her table. She noticed that handles took longer to paste than corners, and so she helped to redistribute the tasks at her table for more efficient cooperation.

The children enjoyed the race and all worked earnestly. Several children remarked that every one was supposed to work just as carefully during the race as he had when he was making his very own basket. The children agreed that sloppy work would not be acceptable.

Notice how the children maintain their group roles and social roles throughout this demonstration. Apply the communication model to Ellen and Jimmy. (Someone perceives an event and reacts in a situation to make available materials in some form conveying content of some significance.)

When time was called the children were assembled and the three supervisors were asked to report on results. Steve reported that his group of six children, working individually, made six baskets. Barbara's report was the same. Ellen reported that her group worked as a team, dividing the tasks, and that this group of six children produced twelve baskets.

It was pointed out that the paper-basket-making race did not turn out as the children expected. The children were asked to state what the experiment showed. "Children who work together and help each other make the most baskets," Jimmy announced.

Notice how Jimmy states the basic concept, "That a group of persons can produce more by working together, each performing one small task, than if each person tried to produce the whole product himself." How did Jimmy "tailor" it?

The readiness and need for young children to organize and see relationships among their observations of the world around them points to concept development as an important teaching level. The urgency of the need of all persons for a conceptual framework for dealing with the world underlines the significance of teaching concepts such as increased productivity through cooperation.

If the teacher, however, had presented a choice between communicating the concept of cooperation and the value of expressing one's creativity, the group may have chosen the latter. Then an entirely different teaching model would have been used to communicate value.

We need more values teaching, which confronts students where they live. Too frequently we stop at the concept level. The more we work at the values level, the more adequate, practicable, and relevant our teaching will be. Values teaching is an attempt to bridge the gulf between living and learning. One "no-no" in values

> Using the gospel message you chose as directed, write teaching questions for each teaching level—fact level, concept level, and values level.

teaching is the leading question designed to draw a "correct answer." The teacher-leader is not a dominating authority, and students learn that there are no set answers. Values teaching helps persons to look at everything from many different angles. Students soon learn to be more open because they know there is little chance that they will be batted down for not feeding back what the leader tells them.

SUMMARY

Experiences are different in each society and at different times in history, which causes communication gaps. The church's educational settings should communicate with the person as he is today, helping him to cope with the world as it is and as it seems likely to become.

The content of Christ's message deals more with attitudes, values, life-styles, and human relationships than verbal dogmas, definitions, or formulas. It is in the process of making free choices and in the living out of personal decisions that "religious content" is discovered and communicated. Verbal statements or dogmatic formulas remain unreal and external without being rooted in and validated by human experience. "Content" (fact) hasn't really "gone" anywhere; it is just linked together logically and communicated as concepts. In order for it to be understood in a "flesh and blood" context, it must also be communicated as values. For a new world, we are preparing new wineskins.

CHAPTER 18

A Vision of Tomorrow

Exploring Communication in Setting Goals

The word *communicate* comes from a Latin word which means "to make common, make known." If a group is working at the same task with a desired outcome in mind, it probably has a shared goal, something which is held in common which is communicated and communicable. When we look at communication, therefore, we view it as a sharing process, as a process by which students and leaders grow, as a process from which we exclude no one.

We communicate best when we participate as equals. Learning is facilitated when everyone in the group feels, We are all in this together. Communication in the process of setting goals is crucial to the whole teaching procedure, yet so frequently taken for granted. While studying this chapter and any related resources used by a study group, a person should come to a better understanding of the necessity for good communication taking place while goals are being set.

EXCLUDE NO ONE IN COMMUNICATION

A climate favorable to open discussion and mutual acceptance is most conducive to communication. By sharing the wisdom of his experience—knowledge, understanding, and insight—a group member will enable his group to set realistic goals. The degree of participation in forming goals will vary according to age. Irrespective of age, each person in a learning group wants to be recognized as important, to be accepted, and to be treated with respect. If he is a part of a democratic group, he is free to express his views.

A teacher can often accurately assess where each of his students is in his learning, but to allow each student to summarize what he thinks and feels about a subject provides the student an opportunity to assess his own growth and for his group members to accept, reject, or question their fellow learner. In this manner a class gains solidarity and identity. It can then say quite accurately, "This is where *we* are."

Most learning groups in the educational settings of the church are homogeneous, so that common goals are not difficult to reach. However, there may be some group where members are sufficiently different that the time alloted to find out "where we are" will need to be considerably extended. The early life histories of children living within a few blocks of each other can be as remote from one another as is the island Madagascar from Manhattan.

Teachers of children need to listen to where children are, because getting older makes a difference in one's experience. Sometimes a junior high or high school helper can "hear" a child more quickly and more accurately than an adult can.

There is also an experience barrier between boys and girls and between men and women. Often this barrier to communication is heightened by different social expectations of the two sexes.

Other barriers to communication and setting goals are stratifications which separate persons, such as status, race, background

> How would communication in goal setting differ between an elementary group and an adult group? What are your basic assumptions about the ability of these two groups to communicate goals?

Guidance for Session 18
A VISION OF TOMORROW

Aim for the Session

To learn to formulate effective group goals as a result of practicing good communication principles, of recognizing and overcoming barriers to communicating in setting goals, and of building personal confidence in using new learnings about goals and communication.

Questions to Ponder

Should unattainable goals ever be set? Should goals always be group goals, or might there be some individual goals? Should the teacher's goals be any different from student goals? Should goals always be known? What are the functions of unit, cluster, and session goals? Should there always be session goals stated? Should goals be set that will require working on them outside the scheduled times for meeting? Should the class participate in setting goals? Could there be occasions when time for group maintenance and process goals would exceed the amount of time set for content goals? What are barriers to setting goals? What kinds of goals should be set for the group? In what ways can I motivate the group to set goals?

A Study Plan

I. Engage in communicating and goal setting for Session 18.

A. Discuss the suggested aim for this session, using such questions as:

1. What does the statement communicate about the anticipated needs of a study group?

2. Do all of these needs exist in our group? Which needs apply to our group?

3. What other needs do our group members have that are related to communicating goals and setting goals?

A Vision of Tomorrow / 155

Think of groups you have been a part of which have had some of these communication barriers to overcome. How did they overcome the barriers? If they were not successful, think of ways in which they might have overcome the barriers.

(geographic, economic, cultural, educational, occupational), native ability and language patterns.

When goals are not set by the total group but by a committee, a team of teachers, or one teacher, the goals should be clearly communicated and the teacher ought to be especially alert to hearing feedback of how the group is understanding. If the teacher (or subgroup) fails to communicate a goal, it is not likely that the group will accept or attain the goal.

When the goal of a teacher or subgroup is presented, the group will have to interpret it and perhaps restate it in order to make it theirs (appropriate it). It is necessary that this step be done if the group is to be committed to the goal. In other words, the group must "buy" it, and the teacher must "sell" it.

Recall an experience of being in a group that was uneasy because its members were not sure what it was they were supposed to be doing. How was this resolved?

A group is usually very uneasy if it doesn't know what its purpose is. The annoyance with unclear purposes is frequently expressed: "What are we supposed to be doing?" "Do you know why we are here?" "What's supposed to happen?" Some nonverbal responses to the lack of a common goal are to leave the group or to stay but not to participate in whatever is going on.

A leader may not be clear about a goal; or he may believe that his goal would be rejected although it is important to him. A leader may believe that he has an acceptable goal but he may desire his students to "discover" it. When a student asks such a leader what he is supposed to be doing, the leader may suggest that there is to be a surprise ending. If the leader is actually insecure in his goal, he may defensively respond to a direct question about purpose. Perhaps he would react by saying, "You'll find out soon enough."

If a teacher keeps his goals for the class to himself, some students will "psych out" the teacher, which is a way of figuring out what *he* (the teacher) wants.

Often a stated goal suffers from COIC fallacy—Clear Only If Clarified. Groups governed by unclarified goals may be working

B. After the above questions are answered, ask the class to state a purpose for their session. Write a proposed statement of goal on paper or chalkboard, and ask the group to suggest revisions. Make the changes as a result of group consensus.

C. In which of the five categories of goals (see under Students and Teachers Grow . . .) does your goal for this session fit? Does the goal statement suggest that a person does something (such as develop, apply, summarize, interpret, investigate) so that the person will change (learn)? The "so that" part of a goal is a test of how well the first part of the goal has been communicated.

D. Discuss how setting goals relates to the "crossing point" concept in curriculum. As you are discussing this, test frequently to see if your group members are communicating or if there is a need for clarifying statements.

II. Practice communication through verbalizing goals.

A. As a total group, decide on one unit from a teacher's or leader's guide for which you will write learning goals.

B. Divide into groups of three and write one goal for each of the five categories.

1. Develop a summarizing or interpretative understanding.

2. Develop or apply a generalization
3. Develop an insight into a concept
4. Develop an attitude or a value
5. Apply a skill of inquiry

C. Use the communications model (below, right) to practice communicating goals to a group. Repeat the process until group members communicate that they are developing skill and confidence in both goal formulations and goal communications.

1. One person from each group will assume the role of teacher.

1. Someone

on as many assumptions as there are persons in the group. A group may go along with unclarified goals for many reasons such as no real expectation of learning, a resistance to learning, a dependency upon the teacher, a trust in the group, a feeling that what the group is doing is irrelevant and won't make any difference anyway, a feeling of fulfilling an obligation in attending sessions without feeling responsible for learning.

What other reasons might there be?

A stated goal may be open-ended, and in fact it usually is to some degree. What is to be learned may not be stated, but areas to be explored may be set; time limits may be determined; procedures for using data may be described.

A COMMUNICATION PROCESS FOR SETTING GOALS

Goal striving is descriptive of personality: purpose is what makes the striving intelligent. Since purposes are so basic to goals, it is essential that teachers and students communicate when they are setting goals. Testing communication and clarifying it whenever it becomes necessary aids goal achievement. Understanding and accepting goals allows persons to satisfy their needs, to move with confidence, and to give maximum help to each other. Aimless group activity is rarely productive.

Dean Smith was teaching thirteen students in a combined fifth and sixth grade class in the church school. The curriculum resource that he was using suggested that the class deal with the concept, "You Can't Be Human Alone," for two sessions. It also suggested that the approach to this concept should be "to provide opportunities for the learners to explore the person-to-person relationship as a part of God's plan for man to experience the meaning of humanness."

One day as the children came into the classroom, Dean suggested to each arriving student that he cut out two kinds of pictures (from the many magazines on a corner stand): (1) persons alone, and (2) persons in groups. Then when nearly everyone was there,

---

2. He selects one of the goals which his group has formulated.	2. perceives an event	7. so that the group will understand it and accept it as their own.	7. of some consequence.	4. as a group member fulfilling an assignment during the class session,	4. in a situation
3. He presents it	3. and reacts				
4. to another group of three persons	4. in a situation	III. As a group, formulate your group goal for your next session, using the communication model.		5. and print, or write, or illustrate	5. to make available in some form
5. in a way which he chooses, (spoken, written on newsprint, picture, symbols, etc.)	5. to make available materials in some form	1. Each member of the group	1. Someone	6. what you think should be a goal for next week's session,	6. conveying content
		2. think about what should be a goal for next week's session.	2. perceives an event	7. so that other persons in the group can understand your projected goal and be able to respond to it.	7. of some consequence.
6. conveying the content of the goal	6. conveying content	3. Go to the chalkboard or newsprint stand,	3. and reacts		

Dean instructed the children to tack the pictures to the bulletin board and to put the magazines and scissors away.

"What things can human beings do together that they can't do alone?" Dean asked the class, while he chalked at the top of a board the words "Alone" and "Together" and drew a vertical line from top to bottom to separate the two.

Quickly the children came to the board and wrote their ideas. In haste, some things were repeated, which endowed them with special emphasis.

> Why would it be valuable to the communication process to have the children write their ideas on the board, rather than having the teacher record them?

"Do you think that God created man in such a way that it is necessary for all men to care about each other? Think deeply about that question while I put it on the board," advised Dean.

"Well, not all men—just the ones you are around," said Nancy.

"Just people who do things for you," figured Dorothy.

"Well, our parents do for us 'most everything we need," Jeff contended, "but someday we won't need them to do things for us."

(Quite a few agreed with Jeff.)

"God told us to love others, but I don't see how you can love somebody you don't even know." Jan was a bit puzzled.

"Do you think, if a tornado was coming toward the school, that God would make the tornado skip over the school?" Shirley hurried on: "I think so, but my girl friend doesn't."

"What was there about this question (pointing at the board) which made you ask yours?" Dean wondered.

Shirley was decidedly flustered. "Well, it wasn't your question," she confessed, looking at her purse and opening and closing the catch. "I asked my mother, and she said to ask Mr. Smith next Sunday."

"What did Shirley do just now?" Dean inquired of the group.

Susan said openly, "I don't know. I wasn't looking at her."

"When she spoke, what did she do?" probed Dean.

"She wanted to know . . ."

"No, what did she *do?*"

"She asked you a question," Mike stated, with a bit of disgust.

Note: If the class is not prepared to work on a goal for the next session, you may discuss this assignment and schedule it for the next session.

IV. Build confidence in each person's ability to communicate.

The leader of this learning group is as eager as any other teacher-leader to see ideas take action. Action is not easy because persons frequently communicate rationalizations for their feelings, such as these—

Rationalization
"It's a complicated idea and won't work.
"It's not a bad idea, but people aren't ready for it."
"The idea is okay, but it would never work with my group."

"I've always been in favor of the whole group being behind the goal."

Feeling
I am comfortable and don't want to change.
I'm afraid people wouldn't go along with me and I'd look silly. Failure is hard for me to take, and my class is rigid and doesn't want change.
Let someone else do it this way and I'll go my own way, if that's okay.

Action is a part of learning. It may be reacting differently from your usual style. Communicate with each other about how this session has been meaningful to you and what you are thinking about doing to reenforce your learning about communicating and setting goals. Communicate doubts you may have, and discuss how these may be overcome. Check frequently to see if what you are saying is being perceived accurately. Create some "in-group" feelings to support persons to change after they leave the training session, as a result of their learning.

"Mike, how does her act of *asking a question* relate or have anything to do with the question on the board?"

"I dunno." (Long pause) "Well, maybe it's because she needed you to answer her question, since her mom and dad couldn't."

The group agreed that her question did have that in common with the question on the board. The list on the board under the question looked like this—

>Ones you are around
>People who do things for you
>Parents (for now)
>Not people you don't know
>People you need, like . . .
>Teachers.

"Shirley, we'll take some time at the end of class to talk about your question." To the class, Dean addressed another question. "What other people do you need?"

"Doctors and lawyers," Glen glibly added.

"Merchants and chiefs," snickered Dolly.

Jeff denounced them. "You're just being silly."

Dean waited a moment and then said, "Jeff suggested that we might not need parents when we get older."

"They won't even be around then," Glen jeered.

"But when we get old, we'll need care," Dolly declared—a bit surprised by her own insight.

"Do you think this is a very important question?" Dean inquired. "Think carefully before you speak," he warned. "I'll give you each five minutes to think quietly about it. You can jot down a word to remind you of each idea that you have."

In what other ways might the teacher have handled the interrupting question?

After the allotted time, the children gave their reasons for deciding that it was an important question. Dean asked them if they wanted to work at finding answers to the question, and he said that he would help them. The group agreed, and on the board, Dean made the following change—

What do you think Dean Smith's purpose was for declaring a five-minute quiet time?

> *Goal: To explore whether God created man in such a way that it is necessary for all men to care about each other.*

The formulation of the goal had reached the third stage. The first stage was the text formulation of an approach as follows:

>To provide opportunities for the learners to explore the person-to-person relationship as a part of God's plan for man to experience the meaning of humanness.

The second stage was in Dean's study notes where he had penned the following:

>To understand that being human means depending upon each other: all men are interdependent.

The third stage came when the question on the board was changed to read as the following goal:

> To explore whether God created man in such a way that it is necessary for all men to care about each other.

Before going on to planning, the goal needed to go through a fourth stage of being restated by a member of the class. Helen, a quiet but articulate sixth grader, stated the meaning of the goal as follows:

> We are going to find out if we have to care about everybody or just the people we want to, and I suppose we'll want to know what would happen if we decided not to care about everyone.

How do the four goal formulations differ? How are they alike? Apply the communication formula to Helen, (someone perceives, etc.).

Without going through the fourth stage—the goal written in the language of the age group—and checking the reception of the class, the goal would not have been communicated, "held in common." Goals must be phrased so that students understand them and recognize them as relevant to their own day-to-day concerns.

Sometimes a group goal can be reached by communicating the products of our imaginations. Mental images can be highly motivating. I have heard it said that anything the human mind can imagine, it can, in time, do. I don't know whether that is true, but I am reminded of a letter written by Wilbur Wright to Octave Chanute on May 3, 1900: "For some years I have been afflicted with the belief that flight is possible to man. My disease has increased in severity and I feel that it will soon cost me an increased amount of money, if not my life."

Do you think it is true?

Imagining is realizing creativity; it is another way of saying, "Let's get on with the possibilities." For example, if you were to teach a cluster of sessions through which you desired first and second graders to grow in awareness of Jesus' life and teachings, you could have them communicate imaginative answers to the question, Whatever could have been the reasons Jesus came? Groups of children might even act out some of their ideas, and ask the rest of the children to guess their thoughts.

STUDENTS AND TEACHERS GROW THROUGH COMMUNICATION RELATED TO SETTING GOALS

Fundamental goals, such as stated in the Objective for education in the church's ministry, are all-inclusive goals, and directly striving after them is often self-defeating. Attainment of the Objective is a continuing experience and can never be thought of as finally achieved.

Give another example of how imagining can enable goal setting.

As persons communicate specific goals and attain them, new horizons open up before them. Goals are suggested at each level—sessions, clusters, units, semesters, perspectives—interrelated, supportive, and moving from specific (session) to general (objective).

Goals may also be expressed as "aims," "approaches," "purposes," or "What This Session Is All About."

160 / **Basics for Communication in the Church**

Goals for sessions, clusters, and units should be, to some degree, measurable. After a cluster goal has been communicated and the group has a commitment to it, the session may include both content goals and process goals.

For instance, a cluster goal might be as follows:

> *To relate the events of Jesus' death and resurrection to the concept that God loves every man.*

And the session goals supporting it might be as follows:

> *To understand that because Jesus trusted in and depended on God's love and care for him—even in the most difficult times. . . . We can trust in and depend on God, too.*

> *To believe in God's continuing love and concern for each person and to find appropriate ways to celebrate the joy of Jesus' resurrection. To affirm each other as persons.*

> *To gain the insight that, following Jesus' death and resurrection, the persons who believed in God's continuing love and concern revealed it. To affirm each other as followers of Jesus.*

> *To find ways in which we can reveal God's love to others.*

> *To evaluate group roles and social roles in order to maintain in our group an environment of love and concern.*

In what ways are the four session goals measurable?

Goals, as they are suggested in curriculum resources, are by necessity general enough to communicate to most groups. Therefore, they are seldom specific enough to apply to a particular teaching-learning group.

Teachers, in their preparation, should apply the printed goals to their own group by restating them to relate to the needs of the group. The supporting structure of learnings is concepts as they mesh and interweave. Goals may be sharpened for communication by limiting them to one of the categories below. A statement of aim or goal should include meaning—relationship to another understanding, generalization, concept, value/attitude, or skill.

What is lacking in each of the illustrations following "not:"? Why (in each case) is the second statement better?

1. Develop a summarizing or interpretive understanding.
   Not: To understand that forgiveness is a powerful, Christian concept and is an important part of the way of love taught by Jesus.
   But: To understand that forgiveness is restoring relationships that have been broken and that forgiveness is a part of the love Jesus taught and we are to follow. (An understanding related to a skill.)

2. Develop or apply a generalization.
   Not: God reveals himself through people who show his love.
   But: To discover that God reveals himself through people who show love and that when you show love you reveal God to others. (A generalization related to a concept.)

A Vision of Tomorrow / 161

3. Develop an insight into a concept.
   Not: To become aware of what the church is.
   But: To become aware that persons reveal God to other persons as you do and that persons who do this are known as the church or the loving community of faith. (A concept related to a concept.)
4. Develop an attitude or a value.
   Not: To state what a religious attitude is.
   But: For each person to gain insight into his life-style and to change any value previously held which no longer serves him. (A value related to a skill.)
5. Apply a skill of inquiry.
   Not: To list ways science can contribute to Christian theology.
   But: To investigate and test some scientific methods or principles, which seem to conflict with Christian views of God, man, and the world. (A skill related to some implied understandings.)

In setting goals, consider the time you will have to work at achieving them. As one person aptly said, "No one would decide to drive from San Francisco to New York in one day, yet many persons are just as unrealistic in setting goals for a meeting."

Monika Hellwig writes, "It is the question rather than the answer that educates, and the question is meaningful only to those who personally and willingly ask it as their own. This means that the educator cannot share [communicate] with students a question that is not genuinely and fully his own. Usually we are afraid to share questions that are genuinely our own; we keep thinking that we ought to be prepared with the answers before we can risk the questions to which we have no answers. At this point we are really vulnerable, but it is at this level of vulnerability that genuine education takes place."[1]

SUMMARY

Goals are communicated and set to give direction and purpose to planning and to learning. They should be stated as clearly as possible, communicating the needs and desires of a group. They must be goals which the group members can communicate, accept, and act upon. Goals help in the selection of activities and resources and in their logical arrangement. Goals must be attainable, to some degree, so that the learners can have a sense of accomplishment and achievement. Goals provide a basis for evaluation, because without goals, a group would not know if its task had been achieved nor if there was any accomplishment. The communication feedback in setting goals will be noticeable in planned evaluations and in behavior.

[1] Monika Hellwig, "The Christian Revolution and the Christian Educator," *The Christian Century* (August 20, 1969), p. 1089.

When time will not allow a group to achieve a goal, why not allow the group to decide in what way they will compromise? Keep goal setting realistic!

CHAPTER 19

Bridges to Tomorrow

Exploring Communication in Planning

For your journey in learning, you would probably not hitch your wagon to a team of "Communicating" and "Planning," because "Planning" keeps pulling this way and that way, and it makes "Communicating" jumpy.

Communicating is important to planning, but it is difficult to tie the two together. In planning, a person juggles a lot of ideas in his "mapping system." He comes out with half an idea here and half an idea there, and he is not sure that they go together. If he tries to share them he sometimes cannot even make complete sentences. In the planning stage, a person may choose to remain noncommunicative because he doesn't want someone to label his tender, underdeveloped idea, "half-baked." If a person should decide to act on the basis of such an untested idea, we might say that he went off half-cocked.

Generally the statement of a learning goal does not communicate the steps it takes to reach the goal; usually it doesn't even give hints. So, in the first stages of planning, the mind figuratively tries on different ways of moving toward the goal. It predicts what would be the likely outcome of a particular act. It selects the steps which it considers to be most efficient or perhaps most pleasant—depending somewhat on the goal requirement. One of the hazards at this stage of planning is not being able to predict with 100 percent accuracy. Another hazard is prejudging a step without even mentally running through it to ascertain if there might be some possibility in it that one has never thought of before.

What partial planning do you have in mind just now? What must you do with this thinking before you can make it an operative plan? Do you need more information? Do you need to test some idea?

Guidance for Session 19
BRIDGES TO TOMORROW

Aim for the Session

To work at the task of planning as it relates to communicating or to work at the communication skills of clarifying, disagreeing, adding, applying, sensitivity, census taking, summarizing, and recording so that communicating and planning skills are recognized as coordinate skills.

Questions to Ponder

Should regular class time be used to develop skills in communication and planning? Can planning for learning enable the learning process? If so, how? What makes communicating while working on a plan so difficult? What are the tools for planning? How can we predict a learner's response to a plan? Is planning really necessary? Why or why not? What is the purpose of planning? Who should do the planning? What problems are encountered when one group does planning for another group? Should the teacher have some goals in addition to group goals? Should other group members have goals in addition to group goals? What steps are there in planning? What materials are needed? How can I learn what motivates each group member to attend? How do we show that we care and accept others? How should we use curriculum resources in planning?

A Study Plan

In this Study Plan there are five suggested ways of working toward the goal, "Aim for the Session." Your learning group should set their goal and select which ways they will work toward accomplishing their goal.

I. Create a study plan for session 19. The group should observe their communicating process as they set their goal. By planning the steps they will take to achieve their goal, they will be testing the goal's communication. If someone suggests an idea which seems way off target, he may be receiving a different communication from the goal than others have. When the Study Plan is completed they may work through it to evaluate it in terms of its implications about "what communication is and how it affects planning."

II. Test communication through feedback on talks. Ask several persons to give short talks (three to five minutes for each), with each talk based on one of the following questions: Why should Christian education change? Why is the product of group planning infinitely superior to individual planning? Why are persons needed in an educational setting of the church even though they attend irregularly or come late and disrupt the class?

Divide the learning group so that there are one or more persons assigned to the following four tasks: clarify, disagree, add, apply. While the speakers are giving their short talks everyone in the learning group should be listening with their assignment in mind.

Bridges to Tomorrow / 163

Planning is the step that follows setting a goal. It asks the question, *How do we get started?* Some questions which stimulate communicating for developing a plan are as follows:

> What do we need to know?
> What do we already know?
> What needs to be done?
> What does this mean to a Christian?
> What is being done?
> What could we do?
> What problems are there?
> How can we get involved?
> Who (or what) will help us?
> What effect would the results of our planning have?
> What different ways can we look at such things as needs, problems, programs?

What questions would you add to this list? Would you remove any of the questions? Why? or Why not?

There may be times when a group has not done the first step—that is, set a goal. When we have no vision of tomorrow, there is no need to build a bridge to it. If a leader falsely assumes responsibility for setting a goal but is so frustrated in it that he has not set a goal, then he may fill the time allotted for the session with activities that cause the least amount of friction and the most good feelings. This may let the leader and group "get by," but it will not develop the kind of Christian concepts and values in persons that our world so desperately needs.

Why should Christian education change?

As Christian education changes—in part from the momentum

After each speaker has given his talk, (a) persons assigned to "clarify" should ask questions of the speaker whose answers would serve to clarify something he said that was not clearly understood; (b) persons assigned to "disagree" should make their points; (c) persons assigned to "add" should give additional thoughts about the question assigned to the speaker; then (d) persons assigned to "apply" should give examples, illustrations, cases, or projections of what happens (or would happen) if things were done as the speaker suggested.

III. Check assumptions which influence communication. Supply each person with paper and pencil. Each person finds a partner and writes (a) the name of his partner, (b) how he thinks the person became a part of the group, and (c) what he thinks his partner's motivations are for being a part of the group. Ask partners to discuss how accurate their perceptions were, using such questions as, What did I do or say that caused you to think that is why I originally came into the group or why I am now attending?

Change partners, selecting someone you do not know well, and write as you did before (a, b, and c). Discuss your perceptions with each other.

As a total group, list (and record) the things which shaped your perceptions—such as degree of participation, questions asked, special interests, past experiences with partners, intensity of responses.

IV. Choosing criteria for the communication roles in a group. In small groups (3-5 persons) discuss the questions, What would be the criteria for a good census taker? a good summarizer? and a good recorder? Have one person record these criteria on a piece of newsprint so that what is recorded can be seen by each person in the group. Ask one person to communicate this criteria to the whole group either at this session or the next session.

V. Evaluating criteria for communication roles. This procedure (V) may come after all of the group or some of the group have worked through.

VI. Or the group may bypass IV (working in small groups) and work together in choosing and evaluating criteria for a good census taker, a good summarizer, and a good recorder. Be sure to have an appointed census taker, summarizer, and recorder for this group discussion and decision-making process.

When the group agrees by consensus that they have completed their twofold task—setting criteria and evaluating it for three communication roles, then ask the appointed persons filling these roles for this session to communicate (1) what their role was, (2) what they did, and (3) how they saw their roles in relation to the criteria determined by the group.

Allow the group discussion to continue until everyone feels he has communicated (has been heard and understood).

164 / Basics for Communication in the Church

of the forces around it, and in part by our will to change—how do we plan for its future?

The purpose of planning is to communicate those conditions that are concrete and cannot be wished away or avoided. We plan with our ideals in view, and implicit in every statement of an ideal there is a statement of what we do not want. An architect's plan is so complete and detailed that it directs the work of carpenters, plumbers, electricians, painters, and everyone who contracts to build whatever the plan calls for. The architect's plan communicates with almost perfect prediction of the end result (feedback).

What makes the plans of Christian educators different from those of an architect?

COMMUNICATION BENEFITS GROUP PLANNING

To say that planning for the way a group will reach its learning goal must be done by the group may seem unduly repetitious. For who else but the group can plan for it? (The designated leader or teacher is an important person in the group.) Even if the group's decision should be that each person should engage in individual study, it is essential that the decision was made by the group.

Sometimes group planning is quite slow, but in most cases the end product of group planning means more and accomplishes more than individual planning.

Do you agree with this statement? Why? or Why not?

A teacher is quite likely to hand out, tack up, or dictate a full-blown plan when she fears that boredom in the planning process may dampen a group's enthusiasm. Take this chance; persons are surprisingly self-sufficient, and we too often curb communication processes. It is difficult to know whether a group is aimlessly playing with ideas or is creatively playing with them. Ideas, expressions, and responses don't always occur when we want them to—why would they?

The benefits which the group members derive from learning procedures may depend largely on the degree to which they are a part of the planning. After the group has stated a learning goal in its own language, each person can be encouraged to communicate a personal or more specific goal which would be related to the group goal.

Give an illustration of this.

After the group has answered all the questions listed near the beginning of the chapter, members should agree on who will take particular assignments in carrying out the learning activities. This includes such things as getting resources for the study, choosing procedures and techniques for group sessions, and assigning responsibilities for leadership functions. They should also decide the time when the activities should be completed.

Perhaps the most important thing to keep in mind while planning is the group. The completed plan should have structure, but it should not be so rigid that it could not be changed in light of the needs of the group. All age groups communicate many outside influences which they bring into each meeting. The plan should remain flexible enough to deal with questions as they arise.

What are some "outside influences" which affect a group?

Bridges to Tomorrow / 165

The author is putting a lot of stress on group planning as opposed to teacher planning. What benefits do you see in group planning? What problems do you foresee in having your group do its planning?

Think of a group that you are in or of a class that you teach. Write the names of the members in one vertical column. In a second vertical column, write how you think the person came to be a part of the group. In a third column, write what you perceive his motivations are. Use communication skills to test your perception.

Sometimes a teacher or a committee may make plans for the total group. Whenever this is done, it is a *must* that the plans are communicated. The total group needs enough time to react to the plans and to change them in any way they feel is necessary (in light of the goal they set previously). There may be times when several plans for small groups will be suggested, then each member should be allowed to choose the group with which he wishes to work. He will quite naturally, through participation in the activity, shape the plan.

THE GROUP THAT PLANS TOGETHER COMMUNICATES

There may be many reasons why the persons in a particular group have come together. Whatever the reasons are, they are important and will influence the group communication. Some persons may come as a fulfillment of a duty; others because they enjoy the fellowship; some because they are visiting a member of the group. Some are seeking group life in a new community. Some come at the invitation of a leader or group member. Whatever the reason may be for persons coming together, the important thing is that they *are* together.

The reasons why persons come together are communicated in many verbal and nonverbal ways. Individual motivations for being a part of a group might be security, new experience, recognition, finding values, or desiring to respond. That which attracts a person to becoming a part of a group may be a special activity, a possibility for service or status, personal gain, the desire to maintain tradition, to be a part of the fellowship, or to find new friends. Those things which limit a person's communication may be fears of rejection, ridicule, group expectation, not knowing the goals of the group or the subject matter, lacking time, not sharing the same values, or pursuing vested interests.

In order that the persons present may form a group that can set goals and form plans, it will require work on the part of everyone. Group living results from effort. It requires the development of communication skills and the willingness to work for the group even when it may mean not doing exactly as one desires.

Some individuals find it difficult to be a part of group life. A person might feel a pressure to conform, when his own deepest feelings tell him it is not best. If such a person can work alone toward the goal set by the group, he may have some very meaningful input at a later time. The group will need to be considerate of his particular needs and for each person's needs.

What additional reasons might there be that some persons cannot work well in groups?

Perhaps a person is fearful that his creativity will be destroyed in so-called "democratic" action. And, if he is truly an artist, his fears may be not only real but substantiated. An artist often communicates best by using media rather than by participating in dialogue.

A person may communicate that he is not mature enough to

accept the chastening and correcting of a group. Such a person should be carefully watched yet not overprotected, for he must gain his maturity and ability to work within a group.

Group experiences are most important; it is through human relationships that we discover who we are, who God is, and how he works.

The kind of group that plans well together is one in which each child and adult feels wanted and accepted. Feeling free to express negative feelings is a good sign that there is an accepting fellowship. Such a group considers each person's contribution as significant.

The irregular attender, the latecomer, and the newcomer pose communicating problems for a group engaged in planning. Since attendance at the educational settings of the church is not compulsory, we need to deal with these persons in a way that makes them feel genuinely wanted and needed and in a way which will benefit the planning group.

Why would the author suggest that although persons attend irregularly or come late and disrupt the class, they are still needed?

A most necessary group role, especially in planning is the consensus taker and summarizer. This role can be disturbing to a group (even though helpful) when it is not considered necessary. The late arrival, newcomer, or absentee who enters the group sometime after the planning has started gives the person who acts as summarizer and consensus taker a legitimate reason for performing his role. The consensus affirms where the group is. The summary statement should be tested immediately to see whether the feedback refutes the statement or authorizes it (to see if communication has occurred).

When the communication skills of consensus taking and summarizing are done well, it greatly assists a recorder. What would the criteria be for a good census taker? a good summarizer?

Summarizer	Someone
perceives what has been planned	perceives an event
and reports it to the total group,	and reacts
especially for the benefit of a late arrival,	in a situation
by summarizing the plans, pointing out their positions on the newsprint,	to make available in some form
about how the group will get started toward reaching their goal, giving some steps they will take,	conveying content
so that the late arrival can get "on board."	of some consequence.

CURRICULUM RESOURCES SERVE COMMUNICATORS

Those of us who are responsible for communicating to other persons about particular subjects are constantly looking for resources that also communicate the same kinds of ideas or which

Bridges to Tomorrow / 167

will help us in our communicating. Most printed curriculum materials contain too many options for one planning group to use them all. This must be so in order to provide as much help to as many groups as possible. Some materials even contain too much content.

One teacher was quite unhappy with a course that had too much content in it, and one day it was possible for the teacher to attend a meeting where the author was the guest speaker. After the meeting, the teacher confronted the villain with the words, "Your material dealing with Moses is very exciting, but your sessions on Paul are dull."

"Yes, I know," responded the author. "I had to include too much material in each of the sessions. What have you done about it?" he inquired.

"Nothing," the teacher said.

"Why not?" enjoined the author.

The teacher reported that suddenly he realized what was expected of him as a teacher—to help a group select from the resource that which would best serve them.

When a group is involved in planning skills and communication skills essential to good planning, the planners may deal more with process than content. *Content* is a selected portion of meanings and experiences to be learned. *Process* refers to the ways understanding, concepts, and values are created and utilized. When stress is put upon process, greater importance is attached to the methods of acquiring and utilizing content than upon learning the content. This may sound a bit technical or complicated, but one fisherman communicates the same information by saying, "Knowledge keeps no better than fish." If we stress content learning, we really prepare ourselves and our students for unlearning. For example, a multitude of learners *knew* that the earth was flat; that the atom was indivisible; that infants thrive best on arbitrarily regulated feeding schedules;

From the history of Christian education, add a "fact" or concept that is no longer accepted.

SUMMARY

Communicating is important for planning, but the two do not go together easily. In our work, we set goals and then we do the planning. But if the group we are working with is not brought along on the process through sound communication involving the teachers and the learners with each other, the whole procedure loses a great deal of its effectiveness. It is very desirable for the group to plan together, and the curriculum resources that undergird such a process are the most helpful tools. For real learning to take place, the planning work itself may well deal more with process than with content.

As we build our bridges to tomorrow, may they be so carefully constructed that traffic will flow easily and repair jobs will be infrequent.

Exploring Communication in Individual Study

Within the subtitle of this chapter the words *communication* and *individual study* are related, and yet they seem to be in apparent contradiction. Our learning tells us that communication is not a line, but it is a loop—going from S (sender) to R (receiver) with feedback to S (sender).

Inner Resources for the Journey

CHAPTER 20

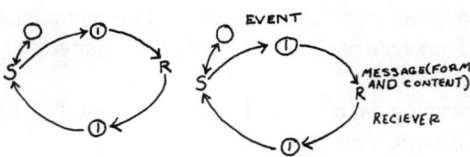

Recalling our experiences with the word *individual* we have images of being alone, separate, isolated, apart from, or thinking of one thing as distinguishable from all other things.

When we think of individual as it is related to study we may recognize it as a time when one person is in preparation for a later confrontation with another person or persons. This is one way of relating individual study to communicating—anticipating an interpersonal exchange following the study.

Another way to see communication as it is related to individual study is to think of a person in communication with another person or persons, *in absentia,* (perhaps even post mortem) using a particular medium, such as reading a book. Great artists in all fields continue to speak to us through print, recording tapes and disks, films, and artifacts. In the case of a contemporary artist, a student might be able to tune in on a TV talk program when an artist is being interviewed. Another kind of third-person communication with an artist comes through the writings of critics, reviewers, translators, and interpreters.

Persons engaged in mass communications have a number of sources for feedback, such as letters, opinion polls, telephone calls, gallery walks, open houses, personal appearances.

As we consider the person in individual study, we will consider him sometimes as a receiver and sometimes as a sender. We shall be dealing with skill in communicating as it relates to learning, such as thinking and listening, including skills subordinate to these; skill in communicating is basic to teaching for discovery.

COMMUNICATION AND THE DISCOVERY METHOD

Persons who learn the skills of inquiry, self-direction, self-selection, and discovery are forming habits of disciplined learning which are necessary for communication. The teaching-learning setting which promotes discovery is fun. It's not so much learning what

Add to this list what would prompt you to write to an editor of a curriculum resource (a) to request clarification of a concept, (b) to suggest revisions before another printing, (c) to report on how the piece is being used, (d) to _____.

Write a critical reivew of a television program, a film, a book, or a magazine. What assumptions did the script writer, producer, or editor make about you? What were the clues that suggested these assumptions?

you like as it is liking what you learn. The freedom of a learning environment which allows individual study is very productive. Often the communication of a fellow student stimulates learning more than communicating with a teacher.

If persons are accustomed to being told what they should know and if very little opportunity is allowed for feedback, they are not likely to be or to become logical, reasoning adults, and they are quite likely to harbor some erroneous concepts because communication has not taken place. When persons are "told" something and no feedback is allowed, the chances for miscommunication are high.

Paraphrasing is often a helpful way of rearranging a message and discovering new meaning.

Select a portion of scripture and paraphrase it.

"The Hound of Heaven"

There really isn't any hiding place, Lord. I can put you off; pretend you don't exist, push you out into the wide, blue yonder; laugh about a computer that cares; but you're still there and you don't go away.

O Lord, you have looked through me, and now you know what I am. You know every move I make. Even from a distance, you know my thoughts. You know the way that I am going to go and I guess you know the ways that I have already been. Lord, I haven't said one word that you haven't known about. You have been in back of me and in front of me and you've had your hand on my shoulder all the time. This is kind of hard to understand!

Now where could I go if I wanted to get away from your Spirit? Where would I have to go to get out of your sight? If I went up to the observatory and looked at the stars, well, I know you'd be there. And I suppose if I should go down into that dreary, library basement, I'd find you there, too. Now if I thought the night would

---

Guidance for Session 20
INNER RESOURCES FOR THE JOURNEY

Aim for the Session

To understand and to employ effectively the basic communication skills of thinking and listening, which are necessary for discovery and learning.

Questions to Ponder

Do I "jump to conclusions"—basing judgments on unfounded evidence?—interpreting with insufficient facts?—deciding and valuing without considering all of the alternatives? Do I hold an opinion as a result of my own thinking or because a respected teacher states it? Do I seek sources of information other than those provided by a class or a teacher? Do I concentrate on what other persons say? Do I think about what I have to say while another person is talking? Does my mind wander to unrelated subjects so that I miss what is happening in a session? Am I able to respect my own thinking? Can I be open-minded? Do other persons frequently tell me that I have missed the meaning of a statement? a story? a scripture? a film? Am I a good summarizer? Do I frequently relate a new learning to another understanding that I already have? Do I listen critically? Do I take opportunities to compare my observations with another person's observations? When I am not sure of what another person means, do I ask questions for clarification?

A Study Plan

The following study plan for this session (and possibly for additional sessions between session 20 and session 21) is based on concepts presented in the text about individual study and the discovery method as these relate to communication and learning. Learners may be given a choice of five different learning activities as outlined below, or the group (after setting its goal) may decide on another Study Plan that will serve them better.

I. Reading. The learners may select printed resources which are related to the Aim for the Session. During this session, the learners will read from these printed resources and prepare a brief report on what they

cover me, I bet I'd find that the night is as bright as the day. I mean, for you, there's no difference is there—between night and day?

O God, test me and search through my heart; look at every one of my thoughts. Find things in me that are dead, and lead me out of them, Lord. Lead me on the way to life.

—Psalm 139
(Paraphrased by Mary I. Hales[1])

Learning through discovery has inner reward, and lessens a person's need for some other person to communicate to him his personal worth or reward for learning. Some of the inner rewards are delight of coping with problems, elegance of relationships, sensory excitement of manipulation, satisfying the expression of inner states of experience, surprise at creativity, and relaxation after resolving a tension.

Discovery also makes a learning more accessible to memory and future communication. Discovery is an individual process and it enjoys a hunch that is practical, or resolving tensions which arise from the imagination and which are generated by emotion.

In a learning group using the discovery method, communication is at all levels. When entering the room of a group involved in individual study and discovery, a person might wonder if there was any learning taking place. The sights and sounds of communication are everywhere apparent.

A generous supply of equipment and materials is a great aid to teaching-learning, but, contrary to common belief, it does not make the teacher's job easier. When materials are in short supply, class control can be with the teacher. For example, all learners see the

Teaching for discovery assumes good problems. Add to this list of things to look for in finding problems: (a) incompleteness, (b) trouble, (c) contradictions, (d) inconsistency, (e) injustice, (f) unresolved tensions, (g) _____.

[1]*Power,* Ecumenical Youth Readings, January-February-March, 1969, Christian Youth Publications. Used by permission.

have read. These resources can be found in curriculum materials, church libraries, public city libraries, public school libraries, and personal libraries. They may be books, journals, or magazines.

II. Research. The learners may select some aspect of the Aim for the Session and gather all the related material they can find from media such as books, magazines, journals, TV, radio, film, interviews; and write a research paper. Such topics as "Language Enables Us to Understand Each Other," "Sympathetic Listening," "The Speaker's Goal: Securing Cooperation in Thinking," "Characteristics of an Observing Person," "Hostility Blocks Good Listening," "Suggestions for Outlining Speeches," may challenge students to think for themselves about the implications of basic communication skills such as thinking, reading, writing, speaking, and listening.

III. Creative Activity. Students may compose poetry, construct mobiles, draw cartoons, make posters or a collage, decorate the bulletin board, write a short story, write a TV script, prepare a tape recording, make a film, communicating some insight, concept, or attitude related to the Aim for the Session.

IV. Listening. Students may listen to tapes, records, radio, or group interview and discuss what they heard. The students' short outlines of what took place during the sessions should be compared and discussed in order to learn about thinking, listening, and skill in communicating.

V. Seeing. Students may view films, television, photo essays, or go on a field trip and discuss what they saw. Compare and discuss short outlines which each student has written to describe what took place during the sessions. This should help them learn about thinking, listening, and skill in communicating.

In order for students to carry out their chosen activity, it is important that they understand the Aim for the Session, that they read all of chapters 20 and 21 in the text, and that they understand the learning activity of their choice. An assigned leader for this session should take whatever time is necessary to help each student as he gets started on his assignment.

Inner Resources for the Journey / 171

same demonstration; all react at the same time; all are simultaneously exposed to the same teacher questions. When materials are plentiful, class control is with the learners. Each student sees the results of his own exploration. He is free to react differently, that is, according to his individual ability. Responses are not simultaneous nor in unison. The noise level is greater. There is excitement in learning.

It would be foolish to assume that Christianity has suddenly changed from whatever it was to a discovery or inquiry kind of activity and that because of this change we teachers must present a new Christianity in a new form it has now assumed. The basic message has not changed nor have the basic teaching-learning procedures (methods). Individual discovery and inquiry have always been the way a person learns, and it is encouraging that now we teachers are trying to enable that learning process. The intention of learning to be a skillful communicator is to stir up students—not tie them up.

The teacher's greatest significance in the discovery process is bringing students together in events through which they can test and revalidate their old conceptions and commitments. Through discovery they can become aware of new understanding or insights, or commit themselves to greater loyalties. They can communicate their doubts and sharpen their questions or reorder some facts into acceptable concepts.

Learning through discovery has only the limitations of imagination. Discovery may come at any time. Undoubtedly, random learnings occur during the time that a teaching-learning group is together, and these can be completely unrelated to group or social roles, set goals, or learning skills. The discovery method, however, proposes to undergird intentional learnings related to such conceptual goals as follows:

Illustrate this from your own experience.

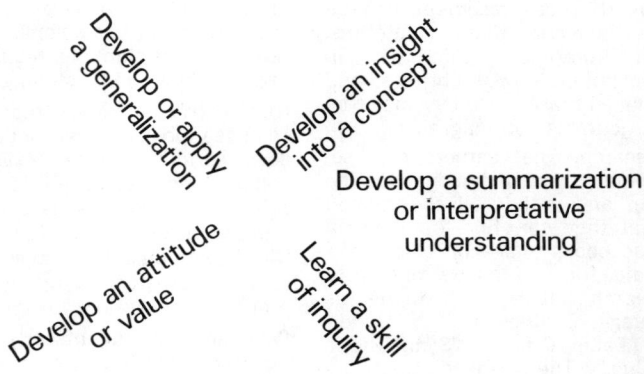

All of these goals assume teaching on the concept level or the values level, being careful to ascertain that sufficient facts are communicated to support the concepts.

Any of us who have been "telling" our classes for years may be uneasy with a student's learning being dependent upon discovery. We would see some hazards like the question of authenticity—"What will happen if he learns the wrong things?" Of guidance—"Isn't discovery leaving too much up to chance?" Of imbalance—"In a student's freedom of selectivity, what would I do if he completely ignored the Scriptures?" All of these concerns are real. What a teacher who relies on "telling" does not always recognize is that the same questions apply to the "telling" method. Telling is not synonymous with communication because it is only one half the loop: Telling goes from Sender to Receiver and stops there.

> How do these questions apply to the "telling" method?

THINKING SKILLS RELATE TO COMMUNICATION

Thinking is an active process and can be learned only by doing it, and it takes time and repeated performance to master the skills that are a part of it. Many of these skills require skill in communicating.

In his introduction to the book *Teaching for Thinking*,[2] Louis E. Raths suggests that many examples of behavior communicate both thought and lack of thought. To illustrate the latter they name eight behavioral syndromes as follows: (1) Impulsiveness, (2) overdependence upon the teacher, (3) inability to concentrate, (4) rigidity and inflexibility, (5) dogmatic, assertive behavior, (6) extreme lack of confidence, (7) missing the meaning, and (8) resistance to thinking.

> An illustration of impulsiveness appears in the story of Jimmy. Cite situations from your experience which illustrate other behavioral patterns which indicate lack of thought.

Thinking includes such procedures as comparing, summarizing, observing, classifying, interpreting, criticizing, looking for assumptions, imagining, collecting, and organizing data, hypothesizing, applying facts and principles in new situations, decision-making, and designing projects or investigations.

SUMMARIZING

In the last chapter a marginal note and an item in the Study Plan called for a listing of characteristics of a good summarizer. Did you include the following things?

1. Includes all of the important points.
2. Recollects the time sequence accurately.
   (what came first, second, third)
3. Identifies points of view with person who contributed them.
4. Communicates clearly, briefly and concisely.
5. Emphasizes the important ideas.
6. Omits irrelevant ideas.

> Think of a good summary to which one or more of these characteristics would not apply. Why not?

---

[2]Louis E. Raths, Selma Wasserman, Arthur Jonas, and Arnold M. Rothstein, *Teaching for Thinking, Theory and Application* (Columbus, Ohio: Charles E. Merrill Books, Inc., 1967).

COMPARING

In comparing two things, we consider their differences and similarities. When the purpose is real and the motivation is high, the quest proves to be stimulating to both students and leaders.

After listening to a recording of James Weldon Johnson's poem, "The Creation," third and fourth graders might be asked, How is the recording like the Genesis story of creation? How does it differ? The insights the children get into the nature of God may give them a sense of security in the created order in which they live.

Junior high youth might list the differences between a Christian and a non-Christian. In an ecumenical study setting, these students might compare some differences in the beliefs of several faiths.

An adult might compare the story of creation as recorded in Genesis 1:1-2:4 with his understanding of the world which is based on scientific investigation.

Regardless of the age of a group, persons can engage in the thinking processes of comparison either in group communication or in individual communication, such as writing, diagramming, mapping, film making.

OBSERVING

Looking is merely the mindless act of the eye, whereas observing draws upon reason, feeling, experiences—the human context. Observing gathers introspective qualities as well as sensory data. When we compare objects, we engage in observing. But the word, *observing* communicates more than the word, *comparison*. The sharpening and maturing of the skills of observation lead to the ability to analyze and then to symbolize, which are necessary for communicating.

1. Observation may be focused upon any event such as a mass demonstration, a piece of sculpture, a mother bathing her child.

2. Observation is the way one sees an event—perceives it.

3. It is more than seeing, for it includes hearing, feeling, smelling, and tasting.

4. Through perceiving an event one may in turn communicate meaningfully to the world.

5. Persons traveling together rarely observe things in the same way.

How is communication dependent upon what is observed?

Observing is closely related to skill in communicating, because what is communicated is dependent upon that which is observed. No one expects a deaf child to communicate the event of a loud noise because persons know that the noise has not been observed by the child and is therefore not an event in his life.

ORGANIZING

Organizing generally follows planning. It is finding ways to put the plan into effect, marshaling the forces. One definition of learning is, "Learning is the correct organization of facts." That definition falls short of many definitions, especially the description of learning tasks of the church's educational settings, but it stresses the high priority in learning that organizing has.

Organizing is an inclusive term. Within it may be gathering data and classifying it. Persons are constantly gathering information. The more perceptive the person, the more items and details he receives through communication and the more he notes and remembers.

Kindergartners keep busy with the task of classifying data. One of their games is to imagine what it would be like if creation were not consistent.

"Did you ever see a baby kitten grow up to be a dog?"

"Did you ever know a bunny to grow up to be a donkey?" Children gleefully add to the absurd collection, until they say, But this is how it really is—

> baby kittens grow to be cats
> baby puppies grow to be dogs
> baby bunnies grow to be rabbits . . .
> God planned it that way.

A youth might write an opinionnaire on sin, which he could use in gathering data. One way of testing his questionnaire would be to see if he could classify the statements into categories; he could look for assumptions which underlie the statements; he could inquire of several persons to see if they think the questionnaire communicates what he intended.

An adult group exploring major issues involved in our human situation might list problems facing humans. Subgroups might classify these according to some organizing principle. When the subgroups reported their classifications they could test the classifications by discovering if they communicate to the members of other subgroups. That is, Can members of other subgroups identify their organizing principle?

Using ten to twelve pieces of note paper, write one problem involved in communicating news via television on each slip of paper. Group the slips which have problems that are closely related. Identify this relationship by labeling the classifications. What was your organizing principle?

LISTENING IS A COMMUNICATION TASK

If you have had the experience of talking to someone in an adjoining room and then discovered that the person had left the room while you were talking, you know how disconcerting it is to talk when there is no one listening. One thing that is more upsetting is talking to a group of students when there is no one listening. We know from our experience that a student will be selective in his listening, so the importance of criteria for selective listening needs to be stressed.

*As a student, what criteria do you use for selective listening? What causes you to listen? What causes you **not** to listen?*

Listening is also a language art, which uses the thinking procedures—comparing, summarizing, observing, organizing, classifying, interpreting, criticizing, looking for assumptions, imagining, collecting and organizing data, hypothesizing, applying facts and

Why would the author classify thinking, listening, and reading as language arts?

Inner Resources for the Journey / 175

principles in new situations, decision-making, and designing projects or investigations. Listening (as well as reading) is related to readiness factors necessary for successful communication, such as a student's experience with language, the size of his speaking and hearing vocabulary, his ability to follow a short sequence of ideas, his interest in language, his familiarity with some of the concepts in the content.

Much classroom listening must be placed in the voluntary category, if we are accurately assessing what happens within a learner. Listening to facts, stories, poems, tapes, records, comments by the teacher or other students seems to require a strong element of voluntary choosing. Requiring students to listen to everything, whether they wish to or not, only cultivates nonlistening habits. Thus communication breaks down. A student's listening skills may improve dramatically when he has a voice in selecting or planning the material to be heard.

Skills in listening are fundamental to learning—knowing, understanding, and valuing. The curriculum of the church's educational programs usually will not include a goal of learning a skill of inquiry, such as the skill of listening. Teachers, however, should be alert to indications that a student's difficulty in learning and communicating may be due to poor habits in listening. Such a fundamental skill of inquiry should be learned in a student's secular school experience, but occasionally a person will not learn to be a good listener. A church school teacher who recognizes a listening problem in a student may be able to help him.

A teacher will have many opportunities to discover problems that students have with skills of inquiry closely related to communication, such as listening, reading, logical thinking, perceiving, symbolizing, problem-solving, problem-finding. Most teachers will need to evaluate their activities in terms of the importance they are placing on these skills as opposed to the importance they are attributing to "right answers." How a student arrives at a concept, an understanding, a generalization, or an attitude is most important.

How does a teacher's expectations affect teaching for discovery?

Let's look in on a fifth-grade teaching-learning group, whose teacher has just finished reading a story about Bonhoeffer in order to illustrate the concept "freedom."

"Who did Bonhoeffer think was responsible for helping men to be free?" asked Mrs. Andrews.

Jimmy was waving his hand before the question was finished. "Okay, Jimmy, who do you think it was?"

Impulsively Jimmy exclaimed, "His friends who plotted a way for him to escape."

"Do we all agree with Jimmy?" inquired Mrs. Andrews.

Would the restatement of Mrs. Andrews' inquiry from the way it is stated in the text to "How many of you agree with Jimmy?" change the communication? In what way?

The facial expressions on most of the students was puzzlement. Some were undoubtedly reasoning that Jimmy must be wrong because Mrs. Andrews was checking on group agreement.

176 / Basics for Communication in the Church

"Barbara," Mrs. Andrews directed her question to a student who was usually very perceptive. "Who do you think was responsible for helping men to be free?"

"I think it was Hitler," Barbara responded.

Mrs. Andrews was emotionally upset with Barbara's answer, because her husband had been shot down over Germany during World War II. "Of course, it wasn't *Hitler*. It was *Christ* who gave man his freedom." She emphasized the names. Mrs. Andrews' frustration, owing to the responses which she had not anticipated, blocked her ability to think about what had happened to cause the misunderstanding, why it had happened, or how to work through it.

Mrs. Bonner, the other member of the teaching team, calmly began to reconstruct the situation. Quietly and with affection, Mrs. Bonner said, "Barbara, I would like to know more about your answer. There were many people who thought Hitler was going to bring the people the freedom they wanted. What do you recall that he said or did to give people hope?"

Barbara recalled, "He told them that they were great people; that they would have the good life; that they would have jobs; and that they could rule the world."

"Yes, he promised all of that. Did he come through with these promises? Do the German people rule the world today?" continued Mrs. Bonner.

"No," replied Barbara.

"Barbara, you remember that part of the story very well. Do you remember the part especially about Bonhoeffer?"

"No, I don't remember," Barbara said.

Evidently, Barbara's mind had wandered during the last part of the story telling. What distracted her? thought Mrs. Bonner. She knew that any further discussion about Bonhoeffer would be meaningless to Barbara.

Jimmy had listened, evidently, yet his impulsive response indicated a lack of thinking.

Mrs. Andrews had emotionally told the desired answer to her question. How would the group deal with that?

Mrs. Bonner asked Mrs. Andrews to write on the chalkboard her question and her answer:

Question: Who did Bonhoeffer think was responsible for helping men to be free?

Answer: It was Christ who gave him his freedom.

"How many of you think you can discover for yourself the answer that Mrs. Andrews gave?" asked Mrs. Bonner. "Everyone. Okay. What are you going to do to find this answer?"

"Listen to the story again," one boy said.

"Read the story silently, so that I can look at all the words," replied Barbara.

Can we accept Mrs. Andrews' emotional response or are we still bound by the image of the "perfect teacher"?

Imagine and write a possible conclusion to this teaching-learning situation.

Mrs. Andrews indicated that Barbara was usually very perceptive, but after this performance the teacher might check occasionally to see if Barbara is having a problem with inability to concentrate.

The purpose for relating the roles of the two teachers is not to compare them, but to show how team teachers can relieve each other.

At this point, both teachers could criticize the curriculum resource for including the question, but perhaps another class would not have any trouble with it. Curriculum resources need to be "tailored" to fit the needs of a group.

> What other communication problems can you find in this situation? What other communication problems are raised by the imagined ending which you wrote?

"Look in the Encyclopedia to find out when Bonhoeffer was in prison and where Christ was at that time," decided a third student.

It was obvious to both teachers that the concept was very difficult for a fifth-grader to understand. One sentence in a story giving an answer is not sufficient to carry the whole concept of Christ making men free. While the students pursued their inquiry, the teachers were finding ways to get feedback after the students had "discovered" the answer for themselves. The teachers agreed to add a question to the chalkboard from the curriculum resource, as follows: "Would you say that there is a sense in which Bonhoeffer was free and his guards were not? Give a reason for your answer."

For those students who finished quickly, Mrs. Bonner invited them to ask their questions about freedom, freedom in Christ, freedom in prison, lack of freedom.

In this situation there were many problems which affected communication. Problems not referred to were the crowded room in which the group meets, distractions in the room, and inability to group students for individual study. In spite of the problems, the communication skills were excellent—the give-and-take between team teachers, the affirming a student when her answer was rejected, the freedom of expressing feelings, the adjusting of pre-planning when an unanticipated learning need became obvious.

A student may be unable to learn if his perceptual abilities are impaired or his home life is stultifying. Culturally deprived children need desperately to develop language and to learn thinking procedures and communication skills, because they know in their bones no one is listening to them.

Many activities which employ the skill of listening are related to interpersonal relationships in communication, which will be discussed in chapters 22 and 23. A great deal of listening is involved, however, in individual study, especially if a wide variety of listening environments are created, using records, taped reports, dramatic readings, filmstrips, movies, radio, television, and field trips.

SUMMARY

Inner resources of skills in thinking and listening greatly benefit a student's learning. In individual study he is a receiver of many communications and his task is to select and arrange the data so that it serves his understanding. Communication can be checked by feedback which reveals accuracy of ideas, integration of messages, interpreting, imagining, applying information, efficient decision-making, and creative designing. Listening is an important part of communication and it too can be checked by feedback and by purposeful action.

CHAPTER 21

Media Resources for the Journey

Exploring Communication in Using Media

Visual communication is international: it has no language limitations and can be perceived by persons who can neither read nor write. Obviously, it would have some problems stemming from such things as cultural differences, various amounts of experiences, knowledge of the visual arts. Visuals can reinforce a verbal concept with imagery. If a child in the Congo had never experienced snow, neither words nor pictures would effectively communicate what snow is. Visual communication—printed, projected, electronic, linear, modular, or three-dimensional—can interpret new understandings of the physical world and of social events. In so doing this, it involves the beholder's participation in a process of organization.

Media are not ends in themselves, but they may be employed by students according to their abilities. Skill in using communication media will greatly benefit learning and teaching. Meanings, values, and other infinitely variable and robustly human characteristics are not too amenable to objective verbal probing. They lend themselves to indirect, visual communication.

Skill in communication is acquired through repetition, evaluation, change, or experimentation. An ancient Chinese proverb speaks to teachers—

> I hear, and . . . I forget
> I see, and . . . I remember
> I do, and . . . I understand

GRAPHICS

Among the most widely used of all media to communicate in teaching-learning settings are graphic representations: pictures, posters, charts, graphs, maps, displays, and other visual and symbolic carriers of ideas.

Describe a meaning or value which you think would be better communicated by visual media rather than verbal media.

Guidance for Session 21
MEDIA RESOURCES FOR THE JOURNEY

Aim for the Session

To understand and to employ effectively the basic communication skills of thinking and listening, which are necessary for discovery and learning by evaluating the learning and learning activities used in session 20.

Questions to Ponder

Did I consider or adequately predict the learners' responses to choosing a learning activity in session 20? Did I try to predict which learning activity each student would choose? How accurate was I in my prediction? What positive or negative feelings were there in response to the learning activities in session 20? How did these feelings emerge? Were there behavior problems? Conflicts in motivation? blocks to learning? Is there a change in attitude toward the learning activities between the beginning of session 20 and the end of session 21? Is there freedom in this learning situation for expressing frankly what an individual feels or believes? In what way can evaluating the learning and learning activities of session 20 add to reaching the aim for that session? Could evaluating detract from the learning experience? What are the purposes of feedback? of evaluation? What is the difference between feedback and evaluation? To what extent was the aim for session 20 attained?

A Study Plan

If your learning group is larger than twelve, divide into two groups to carry out the session plan.

I. Listen to reports by persons who selected the learning activity of "Reading" in session 20. Listeners should be prepared to summarize what the speaker said and to respond to it. A First Responder will summarize the report and ask the speaker if he agrees with the summary. The First Responder must adjust his summary until the speaker agrees that it is accurate. Then, the First Responder will make his statement about the content of the report.

Find graphics which effectively compress information, display dynamic balance, and communicate through color.

Look at the colors in the classrooms in your church. What changes would you make?

One of the attributes of effective graphics is the compression of information. Because they suggest or refer to things other than themselves, graphics are said to have referents.

Another attribute of effective graphics is balance. Perfect symmetry does not seem interesting to the multitude of sophisticated viewers of today. Dynamic balance is more in keeping with modern life-styles.

A third attribute of effective graphics is communicative color. Ancient people used color as a language. Although colors have lost their symbolic meaning for a language, they stir our emotions. An excellent example of this is *Red Is No Longer a Color*, by Myra Scovel, published by Friendship Press. Regardless of race or nationality, children respond best to pink, red, yellow, and orange. Children relax better in gaily colored environments (as do most adults). We have just about abandoned the notion of subduing persons with drab, cool colors, except in some of our schools and other institutions.

In our times, graphics are "in," yet research shows that the indiscriminate use of graphics shows no purposeful end and may even work against learning. Planned, multimedia events are composed to cause persons to sensate, to "groove," to feel and, therefore, to know. One research report, however, suggests that pictures are inferior to words when the desired outcome is to evoke a sensory response to quality, rather than to the form of a thing. The age and sex of the children in this study did not affect the outcome in any known way. Many graphics lack the indefinite feeling of words and therefore do not call for imagination. The papering of walls with pictures, charts, displays, and posters will serve no instructional end, unless the teacher or student knows what response he is trying to elicit.

A Second Responder must summarize the First Responder's statement about the content, checking with the First Responder until the First Responder feels he is understood. Then, the Second Responder will make his statement about the content of the report.

A Third Responder will follow through the same procedure of the First and Second Responder.

II. Listen to the research papers read by those who chose the learning activity, "Research," in session 20. Assign persons the tasks of listening in order to (1) ask questions for clarification, (2) disagree with content (if they honestly disagree), (3) add thoughts about the subject of the research, and (4) give illustrations of the concepts, values, or skills discussed in the research.

III. In light of the learning experiences in session 20, discuss Marshall McLuhan's statement (**Look** magazine, February 21, 1967), "The notion that free-roving students would loose chaos on a school comes only from thinking of education in the present mode—as teaching rather than learning—and from thinking of learning as something that goes on mostly in classrooms."

"A Study Plan" for session 20 represents modular programming rather than the more common linear programming which follows a strict and systematic line of development. Modular programming is singled out for discussion here because of the immediate advantage it offers for those persons teaching in the church. The inflexibility of linear programming sometimes conditions students to become mere recipients of religious concepts rather than active pursuers of Christian truth and insights.

IV. Divide into groups of two or three and write a modular study plan for a unit of study which a particular class might use. What learning activities might you suggest from which the learner may select? Use six major categories of activities: READING, RESEARCHING, CREATIVE ACTIVITY, LISTENING, SEEING, and DISCUSSING.

V. Fill in Opinion Blank. What points impressed you most about today's session?

Graphics are often more efficient than words, however. How many words would it take to describe the picture, "The Live Storm," by John Steuart Curry?

All age groups may greatly benefit by immersing themselves in graphics, for the sheer joy of experiencing all of God's creation insofar as possible—attending art exhibits, photo displays, using the picture files at the public library, looking through picture magazines, studying books about the graphic arts, poring over graphics in books which portray styles of living in other centuries. Graphics which "speak" to us reveal some things about us as receivers.

SOUND MEDIA

An attentive stroll through a series of educational settings of a church will reward us with a maze of sounds—singing, laughing, crying, piano playing, typing, whirring film projector, recorded music, clattering money, talking, splashing fountains, ringing bells, crashing blocks, and on special days in the kindergarten we might hear a bird singing, a puppy barking, a kitten meowing, a squirrel chattering—these are the many sounds of teaching and learning. Each communicates a message; each message holds a meaning for the listener.

The ability to listen is, of course, closely related to using sound media. David K. Berlo in his book, *The Process of Communication*[1] states that the average American spends about seventy percent of his waking hours in listening, speaking, reading, and writing—in that order. Although we know that persons with hearing difficulties experience problems in learning, there is no assurance that a good hearer will be a good listener. Good listeners (even those who are hard of hearing) become interested in practically anything. It is difficult to bore them.

Less competent students prefer listening to reading and they learn more in the process. Listening arts seem to be less difficult to master than reading arts. Almost anything which helps students to focus attention on messages seems to work: repeating directions; noting emotional words which block objective listening; listing distractions in the environment; and any other commonsense activity. One factor which allows distractions to creep in is that persons can listen to much more than the normal speaking rate of between 125 to 200 words a minute. One university professor taped an hour lecture and played it back to his students in thirty minutes. The students had no unusual problems of understanding and actually seemed to concentrate better during the shorter version.

Perhaps we teachers could do some research for our benefit. Are there certain times when students seem to listen better than

Describe some teaching-learning situation in which graphic illustrations would not be as effective as words.

Look at some graphics which "speak" to you in order to discover something about yourself that you may not have known before.

All of your students hear you; however, some do not listen to you. What is the difference?

Reading, writing, and arithmetic have been traditionally accepted as fundamental educational skills. Should listening, thinking, and problem-finding be included? Give reasons for your answers.

Write the results of your research.

---

[1]David K. Berlo, *The Process of Communication* (New York: Holt, Rhinehart and Winston, 1960), p. 1.

other times? Do certain environments help or hinder? Do certain topics generate better listening? We can learn a lot about our teaching by tape recording our teaching-learning sessions. The simplicity, economy, and versatility of many tape recorders make them a most useful piece of equipment.

Using professionally taped recordings or disc recordings can bring a touch of realism to enliven an otherwise routine session. Encourage students to tape the sounds that they feel are relevant to the work of the group or to their individual study. Tapes give many opportunities for teaching-learning activities: Interviews can be recorded and edited for class presentation; sound tracks can be made for short films, filmstrips, or slide projections. A speaking track can be made as an overlay to a song like that of Simon and Garfunkel's, "7 O'Clock News," read over the carol, "Silent Night, Holy Night."

Group interviews by telephone can be exciting communication and the cost is no longer prohibitive to some educational settings of the church. These interviews can either be live and amplified or they can be taped.

SIGHT AND SOUND MEDIA

When we combine sight and sound, we have a different set of conditions and a new class of problems which are not encountered in media that are totally sight or totally sound. Sight and sound modify and qualify each other, and their combined effects will usually be greater than either effect alone.

It is difficult to think of a world without film. We point our cameras at events in our lives and in seconds the images of persons and happenings are recorded on film. Still images in one form or another are common communication tools in today's educational settings.

THE FILMSTRIP

The main instructional value of the filmstrip is its flexibility. It serves communication when the analysis of pictorial information is important, because it can be stopped at any frame and held as long as necessary. If sequential pictorialization is desirable but motion is not relevant, the filmstrip is an effective medium. (Filmstrips do not convey the concept of motion accurately.)

A few years ago filmstrips were losing their popularity because they were too passive. They did not communicate well because they did not involve the student. The real problem, however, was not the media, but the filmstrip maker. The first filmstrips were just an extension of the old teaching concept of "show-and-tell." The current filmstrips fit into the new curriculum designs and they ask more than they tell and mean more than they show. Some filmstrips present unfinished stories; dilemmas encountered every day are explored and students are faced with ethical decision-making which communicates their social awareness and personal bearing.

If possible, view some filmstrips made ten years ago and some late publications and compare them.

THE 35mm SLIDE

The value of slides is that they are not damaged or destroyed by shuffling and reshuffling, that is, if they are protectively covered. Slides made by professionals may bring knowledge of a thing to a student that gives him insight. There are two communication elements in a slide: the photographer's view, his insight, his meaning; secondly, what the slide evokes in the viewer. The sequence of a group of slides is provocative: the way a person puts together slides may communicate his ideas or values.

Slides may be shown in silence or with a musical background. If a musical background is used, a person should select the music with his purpose in mind so that the slides and music complement each other in communication.

An exciting and interesting learning project for a student is taking 35mm slides of scenes which portray a concept that he is building. As the student tries to film whatever will communicate his thinking—such as his insight into an understanding, his conceptual relating of life's realities, his application of a generalization—he will gain new insights. As he chooses readings or music to go with his slides, he will take a firmer grasp on his idea, and his idea will grow from a tender, fragile whisper to a strong, conceptualized conviction that can be communicated.

Shoot some 35mm film for slides which would be helpful in teaching a skill of inquiry. What scenes would you include? What sequence would you put the images in? Tape explanatory material. Decide whether or not a musical background would help the instructional value.

THE PHOTOGRAPH

The economy of reproducing quality photos makes this a popular, pictorial communication medium. Many magazines include photos as a part of their messages, and some magazines are mostly pictorial. Beautiful, four-color pictures of the Holy Land shrink this reality, without loss of important detail, to a few square inches of film and creates armchair travelers of us all. Teachers and/or department heads frequently keep picture files for ready reference. Pictures that are unusual and particularly relevant to communication may be mounted and covered with plastic in order to give them an extra long life.

From back issues of leading magazines, find photos and graphics prepared by the Bell Telephone Company which convey concepts about communication.

An individual study project which could further a student's inquiry into the Christian meaning of God's love is making a visual book, using current media (magazines, newspapers, photographs by students) to represent scriptural meanings of love—such as those found in Philippians 2:5-11; Matthew 25:31-40; 1 Corinthians 13:1ff; Matthew 25:26-29; 1 John 4:7-21; John 15:9-12 and 17:20-23; 2 Corinthians 5:14-21; Ephesians 4:11-16; Romans 8:35-39; Hebrews 13:20, 21.

Make this project your own.

Field trips, plays, projects, student work, and other events worth remembering should be recorded on film and displayed effectively.

OVERHEAD TRANSPARENCY

A most useful communication tool is the overhead projector which projects from a transparency. It is easy to use and can be used in normal light, which allows eye contact to be maintained during communication. The overhead projector is popular with public school teachers because it allows them quickly to visualize a concept (perhaps by using overlays) without turning away from the students. Also the transparent pens and pencils come in colors which add more communication possibilities. These projectors, while they may be considered expensive, are very useful tools.

THE MOVING IMAGE

The combination of filmed motion and recorded sound may form a logical, expressive, and appealing medium for communicating ideas. Film making is a language comparable to speaking. Composing and sequencing frames is like selecting and ordering words. Dramatic close-ups and dynamic angles qualify and modify visual subjects just as adjectives modify nouns. The movement in a film is like the verb in a sentence. To understand and use the moving image, persons need to become familiar with its language. An immature, naive viewer focuses on the plot in a film.

Does the church's educational budget include an allowance for film? Would you recommend this?

The sound motion picture communicates through channels like these: spoken words; printed words and symbols on film; sounds other than words; actions and gestures of actors; the tones of voice, inflections, and moods; embellishment and elaboration of printed words or symbols. In order to understand the intended message of a motion picture, decode the information we receive from each of the channels.

What would a mature viewer look for?

Since we cannot view everything that has been filmed, teachers and students may select films according to criteria that might include such things as (*a*) getting our time's worth, (*b*) suitability of the medium for reaching our stated goal, (*c*) keeping the communication uncomplicated.

Note some other criteria.

Teachers in the educational settings of the church may find that the movies made by their students in secular learning situations can be used effectively. Also, teachers and administrators should be informed about films available through lending libraries of city and state public libraries and from some denominational offices.

Write for catalogues and ask to be put on mailing lists.

In discussing a film, each person should be free to share his honest perceptions, responses, and opinions, feeling assured that they will be respected. Each person should expect to see something differently than other persons because of the different experiences he has had. Each person should be encouraged to help others see what he saw. Each person should be invited to analyze his understanding of the medium: What did the film maker do to make us see that? Why did we notice particular images, sounds, gestures, words, symbols, moods, facts?

Apply these questions to a film you have seen.

Film can cut across time, space, customs, language, and ideas. Good experiences in viewing and discussing films can help to bridge generation gaps, cultural gaps, racial gaps, social gaps, educational gaps, and other barriers separating and alienating persons. Its implications for all of us who deal in handling, storing, retrieving, and disseminating information is nothing short of revelation. Photography is already moving out of an era that most teachers have yet to enter. Tomorrow's technology into which some communicators are now moving is called *holography* and the resulting many-dimensional picture is called a hologram.

How can films bridge these gaps?

TELEVISION

The modern world is one which not only has available instant coffee and instant cereal, but it has instant civilization—largely due to television. The history of TV is fascinating reading about a medium which has developed haphazardly with few controls. Commercial television is determined by what advertisers are willing to sponsor and this in turn is determined by what people are willing to watch.

Educational television is struggling with promotion for sufficient funding and competing with commercial television for prime time viewing. Some educational television series can supplement curriculum resources for educational settings of the church.

What educational television has helped you?

The dawn of the day of cassette television heralds a whole new era in communication.

The primary influence of television on teaching-learning groups in the church is the way it is shaping the lives of students. It is possible that we teachers are watching very little commercial television, but this is not true of most of our students. If we want to know what is reinforcing and changing their beliefs and attitudes and creating the needs and interests they bring into our teaching-learning groups, we will watch television—whether we like it or not.

Watch as many different television programs as you can, particularly those you would not ordinarily choose and note the values they promote.

PRINTED WORDS

How the student uses the printed word is more significant to learning than what is printed. Because this publication is a part of a curriculum plan, it is referred to as a curriculum resource. The way in which each curriculum resource is used is more important than the printed piece. Curriculum resources are created to provide information, inspiration, direction, and guidance for learners, anticipating their goal setting as efficiently as possible.

A child's strongest motivation for reading comes because he observes adults obtaining information and enjoyment from the printed page. The less motivation of this kind there is in the home, the greater the need is for stimulating it in the church's school. Teachers can supplement the printed material provided by the church through borrowing books from a public library, a school

How could secular magazines and newspapers be used in an educational setting of the church?

library, or by asking students to share their books. Church budgets should provide at least a minimum number of Bibles, dictionaries, encyclopedias, and other reference books.

Other printed materials which can be used include:

1. Magazines and newspapers.
2. Posters focusing on ideas or concepts.
3. Maps, pictures, photographs, atlas, and almanac.

If a teacher discovers that his students do not own books, he may find inexpensive but good books to display in a book fair and make it possible somehow—perhaps through a joint penny fund—for each child to have a book of his own. This often encourages good habits in handling books.

How has television influenced the print medium?

For a time, some persons were predicting the end of the printed word, yet we are conspicuously dependent upon printed words and are somewhat aware of values associated with them.

Many curriculum resources provide excellent bibliographies of additional printed materials, as well as suggested films and other media. Teaching-learning groups are encouraged to supplement the curriculum resources. Some questions to be considered in selecting additional media are as follows:

1. How closely is it related to the learning goals?
2. Does the group perceive that it has value in relation to the learning goals?
3. Are there other resources which would serve better?
4. Does it provide additional information?

What other questions might be considered?

5. Is it likely to evoke feelings, insights, or understandings not otherwise touched?
6. Will it aid in clarifying or applying abstract or difficult ideas?
7. Does it provide a way(s) that would involve a student(s) who would not otherwise be involved?
8. Is it helpful to the creation of a desirable learning environment?

SUMMARY

In this chapter we have presented descriptions of media resources for the journey of communicating and learning. Although the media are frequently used in groups they lend themselves to individual study. We are constantly engaged in communication and any attempt to analyze it is to presume to stand apart from communication as an onlooker which one can never really be.

CHAPTER 22

Awareness of Fellow Travelers

Exploring Communication Through Sensitivity

Interaction is a process of communication between two or more persons when feelings, perceptions, and meanings are clarified whenever clarification seems necessary. Communication includes feelings and perceptions in addition to messages, and it occurs only when messages and assumptions are clarified. Real interaction is rare in our American culture because we do not expect our assumptions to be checked by others nor do we feel free to ask another person to clarify his assumptions. Effective communication by teachers depends upon persons developing keen sensitivity to the needs of themselves and others.

COMMUNICATING FEELINGS

The process of communication—using any media, including words—is generally vague and often confusing because we understand other people's symbols in terms of our own development of meanings and values, as well as the experiences we have had. The communication has to transcend the raw data, the merely sensuous; it has to generate a value transformation into individual symbolic expression or perceptive appreciation. We tend to trust direct verbal communication more than indirect, esthetic, or nonverbal communication.

It's all right to share our thinking about our ideas, but not our feelings—this is what most of us grow up believing. The expression of true feelings is stifled at home, at school, at church (except, perhaps, on the sidewalks following business meetings—but better there, than never!). The danger in repressing our feelings is that it makes us distrust the feelings of others as well as our own. So, why are we taught this? It seems we are taught to squelch our personal feelings because they may be wrong—or bad—or at best, only momentary.

FEELINGS ARE FACTS

It's beside the point to classify feelings as right or wrong.

Following a role play by an adult group, the leader asked a

What recent experience have you had when you were confused by some indirect or nonverbal communication? Did you feel free to ask the communicator to clarify his meaning? Why? or why not?

What feelings have you had in a particular situation which hindered your ability to function to your fullest capacity?

Guidance for Session 22
AWARENESS OF FELLOW TRAVELERS

Aim for the Session
To value feelings as an authentic and legitimate part of communication and to understand the aims, methods, and feedback of interaction so that the students can employ their learnings in other teaching-learning situations.

Questions to Ponder
Are emotional processes ever predictable? What threatens students and leaders in teaching-learning situations? In what ways can we minimize fear in teaching-learning? What educational climate is needed for a person to recognize and change self-defeating attitudes—to test out and adopt more innovative and constructive behavior? What methods make group members feel that they are accepted? What are some ways that leaders reject students? Why is communicating feelings important in Christian education? What are some creative ways to express feelings? How can leaders enable students to see problems from the viewpoint of another person?

A Study Plan
I. Appoint one or two observers for this session who will report at the next session (session 23), using the Guides for the Observer at the end of this Study Plan.

II. Divide into groups of two. First, each person will make a What Wheel for his partner by writing, in the spokes of a wheel, descriptive adjectives that characterize the partner.

group of students, who were assigned to watch the action of a person who played to the role of a thief, "What feelings did you have about this person whom you watched?"

"I felt that he was a menace to society and should be put away," John replied.

"He didn't have any good reason for stealing," Sara said, "because he never indicated that he was poor. . . ."

"And, he didn't steal anything that is essential for life," added Jane.

"People just don't have any respect for the law any more," Arnold concluded.

The leader turned to the person who played the role of the thief and asked, "What instructions did I give to you?"

"You said I should take anything I wanted; that I shouldn't consider it wrong; and that I should act like the kind of person who thinks having a lot of things is important," responded Bill.

The leader did not correct Bill's statement because he recognized that *whatever Bill heard were the instructions he followed*. What he heard was the *fact* upon which he acted out his role. Another *fact* was that Bill felt that he understood the leader's instructions.

The instructions which the leader gave to Bill were as follows: Play the role of a thief whose philosophy is that (1) a man should take anything he can get; (2) there is no moral structure in the universe; (3) life is made valuable by the possessions a man can get.

The leader further inquired of the player, "How did you feel about the thief?"

Bill spoke slowly but surely: "Since I was in the role of this thief and I wasn't supposed to think that there was anything wrong with stealing, I was eager to get as many color TV's as I could, without getting caught. I really felt pretty satisfied about getting four of them. That was quite a haul."

"Now that you are out of the role and once again yourself, Bill, what do you *feel* about the thief?"

Exchange wheels and each person choose one adjective describing himself that he wants to explore further with his partner. Then each person will make a Why Wheel, writing in the spokes the reasons why he described his partner with a particular adjective.

The next step is to make How Wheels, writing in the spokes a range of actions which would either increase or decrease the trait.

III. Discuss the question, What is the value of role play in communication? At some point in the discussion, tape record consecutively three persons' statements. Stop the discussion, and ask the participants to reveal their perceptions of what they were feeling and assuming was the experiences of the other persons. What thoughts went through their minds that were not voiced? Were any of these thoughts revealed nonverbally?

IV. Choose a human relationship problem situation for several persons to role-play. Assign a coach to each role-player. After the role play has been going for seven minutes, stop the role play so that each coach can help the person he is assigned to. Continue the role play for five more mintues. Stop the role play and, if the persons were not playing themselves in this imagined situation, ask them to derole, telling what kind of person they were portraying and the reasons for their responses. Discuss the role play until each person feels satisfied with their understanding of what took place and until the problem situation is dealt with acceptably.

V. Each person fill in an opinion blank asking how it went today and recording a response to leaders and group members.

"Well, I think he's kind of dumb, really naive to put so much value on things and to think that it was really okay to take whatever he could, and I think he felt pretty sure he wouldn't ever get caught. I didn't really dislike the guy, but I thought he was being very foolish."

"How did you feel, then, when the observers said how they felt toward the role you were in?"

"Well, I thought that their feelings were exaggerated. I mean, the guy wasn't a murderer or really all that bad."

"But how did you *feel* when they made these statements?" the leader prompted.

"Well, not too good," laughed Bill.

"How would you describe your feelings? Were you hostile?"

"I felt they were being too harsh, and so I was a little resentful. I felt misunderstood: I wouldn't hurt any of them, but I felt that they were ready to hurt me. I felt guilty because, although I was playing a role in which I was to think it was all right to steal, I really couldn't feel that it was right. I think I felt just a little bit skeptical about how Christian this group would be if I really did get into trouble."

As the group continued the process of "de-roling," they grew open about their own feelings, very sensitive to the feelings of others and somewhat able to emphathize—"to walk in another person's shoes." Even then, I believe the group was not yet able to give honest opinions about the performances of fellow students. The usual excuses given for begging off of giving constructive criticism was that they didn't want to hurt anyone's feelings. Underneath that concern lies a deeper one—persons are afraid that their popularity rating will drop if they say what they think. After all, these students had been hiding their feelings since kindergarten (or before). To achieve any kind of personal growth and practical goals, students must be daring enough to express honest feelings about themselves and their fellow students—and, yes, their leaders/teachers, too.

The best group work is not a preparation for life, but a part of life itself. A teacher in a ninth grade class discovered that his students were hesitant in expressing honest opinions when they seemed to be an evaluation of each other's thinking. When they did voice conflicting opinions, they directed their communication to the teacher. The teacher decided to employ a technique that would enable the students to express and analyze their habitual reactions to situations and persons around them and, also, to develop new responses. First, the group would get into pairs to work on "What Wheels" for each other.

"Draw a circle about six inches in diameter, then draw intersecting lines across the wheel—like spokes of a wheel. About six or eight spokes. Fill in the spaces between the spokes with words

How can role play help a student to understand the important role that feelings have in communication?

Think of (1) a situation in which you begged off giving constructive criticism and (2) a situation in which you resisted receiving constructive criticism. What were the complicating factors in the situations? How might you have better handled them?

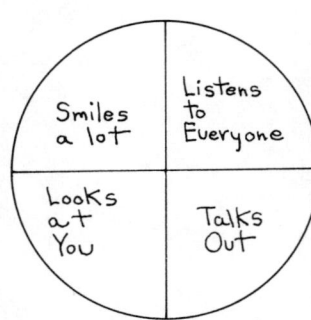

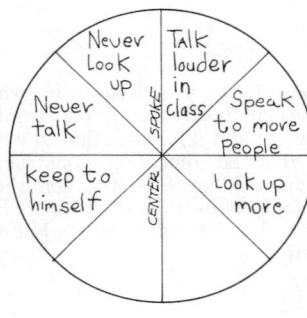

Do you agree with this statement? Why or why not?

and/or phrases that describe your impression of your partner," instructed Mr. Mohr.

John quickly drew his wheel and then said, "But, Mr. Mohr, I don't know what to write."

In response to John's comment, Mr. Mohr asked him, "As you look at Bill, what adjectives come to your mind to describe him?"

"Afro, short, quiet," John responded.

Bill just looked down.

"You have the idea," Mr. Mohr assured him. "Now continue filling in the rest of the spaces."

John's What Wheel about Bill

The partners exchanged their wheels so that they could "see" how their partners saw them. Then each person drew another wheel, which would be called a "Why Wheel." Each person chose an adjective that was used to describe him and then asked his partner to write his reasons for why he put the adjective in his What Wheel.

Bill smiled and asked, "Well, why'd you say 'Doesn't feel inferior'?"

John's Why Wheel about Bill

Bill was greatly pleased by the way John saw him. In a previous class session, Mr. Mohr had asked each person to write down what he saw when he looked into a mirror. Bill had written two things on his paper—"no good, too short."

Each person kept his partner and drew a third wheel—a "How Wheel." One spoke was labeled, "center spoke." On the right side of the center spoke, each person would write down how one of the traits taken from his What Wheel could be increased. On the left side of the center spoke, he would write the ways that trait could be decreased. John wrote in his How Wheel about Bill the ways that Bill would act if he felt less inferior and how he might act if he felt more inferior.

John's How Wheel for Bill

The class ended in a hubbub of sharing, conversation, and good feelings.

COMMUNICATING FEELING THROUGH THE ARTS

Communication of feelings is difficult. In communication we legitimize feelings, clarify them, and find a variety of behaviors we can use to express them. The fine arts express many feelings and persons can change through observing creative expressions of feelings—particularly in drama.

When we desire to have our students communicate the fullness of such abstract words as faith, love, revelation, God, and evil, we may suggest that they use metaphors:

"Love's no sideshow. It's the big tent that takes in everything. In fact, it's the sky that covers the whole midway and all the tents, the little tents and the big tents, the wagons and the trailers—everywhere people live and work and perform."[1]

Or perhaps we would suggest that they select music which they associate with their feelings; or perhaps that they would use finger paints, selecting colors that vibrate with feelings which they associate with abstract words like faith; or perhaps they could pattern body movements which would help them to communicate. We often use these forms of expression in children's groups, but we deny adults the sheer joy of communicating abstractions by using all of the senses.

A kindergarten child may learn about the dependability of God as he thinks, hears, feels, and acts out the seasons of the year. For example, let us look at some winter season activities. He may learn the song, "The Soft, White Snow"; or he may listen to some winter sounds that have been taped and he might create ways to make the sounds of winter. He might make a soap-flake painting of a snow scene, or cut out snowflakes, or make a wintry picture with cotton. He might plan a rhythm that suggests to him the rhythm of a snowflake. Or he might pantomime, "Having Fun in the Snow," such as walking, shoveling, making snowballs, making snowmen, making pictures of butterflies on the snow, playing fox and geese, skating, skiing.

A youth may communicate his understanding of God by singing, "He's Got the Whole World in His Hands," or by listening to one of several recorded versions of the spiritual. He might cut pictures and words from magazines and newspapers and put them together in a way that suggests how he understands God's relationship to his world. He might join with others in painting a mural. He might write a ballad. He might help to produce a play. He might read aloud from the Book of Psalms; he might write a drama which would confront an audience with the problems persons have in understanding what God is like.

Make a magazine/newspaper, (or use other materials) collage depicting the way you feel God is at work in the world.

When persons express themselves through the language of music, rhythm, and art they will be evaluating their feelings and they will be learning. Art is a direct channel for self-awareness. It can help a person develop a sense of personal and unique worthwhileness. All experience is fit for art, its only requirement being its genuineness and its need of realization. Intellectual and emotional, intuitive and logical elements all enter into the learning that may occur through art experiences.

Adult study groups may greatly benefit by immersing themselves with experiences that communicate through sensory channels. In addition to talking about other religions, they can visit the holy places of other religious groups, worship with them. Adult groups can attend plays together and afterwards share some of the mean-

Enlist a group to visit a television station—one of the most active communication centers of our day—and interview the programmer about the problems related to communicating feelings to the TV audience.

---

[1] Barton Hunter, "The Message of Love: Universality," *POWER*, Youth Meditations (January-March, 1968), p. 40. Used by permission.

ings they have been impressed with. They can visit in the homes of persons of other races and identify and empathize with those persons. They can attend concerts of sacred music, and some of them can sing in choirs. The more involved a person becomes in his study, the more he will learn.

Children's groups are frequently not as mobile as adult groups, and it becomes necessary for a teacher to bring unfamiliar items to the class to share. This is particularly true of inner city children, who have never experienced many of the tactile sensations that most students take for granted. Some suburban church groups are helping to make "touch books" for these children. The pictures in these books are covered with materials, so that children can learn about parts of their environments that have been previously inaccessible. The sense of touch can be a powerful aid to learning.

What do you understand better because you have the sense of touch than if you were deprived of it?

PERCEPTIVE COMMUNICATING

Persons who are perceptive are sensitive to themselves and to others. They do not jump to conclusions. Rather, they look at events from many possible vantage points and they test assumptions and intentions with careful consideration.

What we see and hear is determined greatly by what we are conditioned to see and hear or what we are prepared to see and hear. Oftentimes our perception is inaccurate or incomplete.

Communication is filled with emotions. In fact, emotions frequently shape communication and alter a message. The emotions of the message sender can cause him to misrepresent himself. The emotions of the receiver can either block communication or cause miscommunication. Sometimes our words are completely misinterpreted by someone who is trying to "second guess" our intent.

If we keep aware of the probability of miscommunication, we can check to see if our messages are perceived accurately. If we assume that speaking (or any media) automatically communicates our intent, we will frequently discover (usually, much later) that we have been misunderstood. Some quiet persons have become withdrawn simply because for them the risk of speaking is too great for them to overcome.

Can you think of a time when you perceived that the risk in your speaking was too great for you to overcome?

SUMMARY

Good communication requires not only an honest sender but a perceptive receiver. Feelings need to be communicated because they are a part of the facts—the raw data—of life. Feelings are probably best expressed nonverbally, particularly through the arts. Adults, as well as children, need to learn how to positively express emotions. Miscommunication thrives in our culture, since we have not been taught to deal openly with emotions. So, they creep into our messages and perceptions breaking down communication. Being in communication has a transforming quality of bringing two or more persons into a unity, producing community and communion.

CHAPTER 23

Interaction with Fellow Travelers

Exploring Communication Through Interaction

The more open a group is—knowing, trusting, and feeling for each other—the more assured each student will be that he will be in communication. This will encourage him to work up to his individual level of competence. Such a group is happy and self-directing. Being in communication is essential to interaction.

AIMS OF INTERACTION

True interaction produces a cohesive group in which teachers and students share responsibility for defining (setting goals included), carrying out, and evaluating the learning experience. In such a group, students unite with the teacher to get the job done, which is much more satisfying than the situation where the teacher tries to do the whole thing all by himself. The "let's-get-down-to-business" and "quiet-down-so-we-can-get-our-work-done" teacher is putting a great deal of value on learning the subject matter. He might increase his effectiveness if he asked, What is the value of learning subject matter if students do not increase in their ability to be satisfied, effective human beings?

Some statement of aims might be as follows:
If a group is using the processes of interaction, then—

Compare groups in which you are a part. Does the first paragraph apply to them? Why or why not?

How do you answer this question?

This would happen	*Not this*
1. Teacher would be one of the members of the group.	1. Teacher would be over and above the students.
2. Group would set structure of discipline and observe it.	2. Teacher would be authority and would determine punishment.
3. Group members would talk with each other.	3. Conversation would be mostly between teacher and students.
4. Mostly open-ended questions with no judgment on a student's thinking.	4. Mostly recall questions with "right" or "wrong" feedback.

Guidance for Session 23
INTERACTION WITH FELLOW TRAVELERS

Aim for the Session

To evaluate the experiences of group members in their learning experience (session 22) in communicating feelings and interactions so that the students may value feedback as an important part of the communicating and learning processes.

Questions to Ponder

How open and honest has our teaching-learning group become during our study? Did the last session help us discernibly? Are feelings of warmth, joy, and closeness frequent? Do we wish to influence behavior by dealing directly with feelings? How free am I from the fear of being judged by others? On what do I base my feelings of personal worth? Is this group one which I can trust? How can I express emotions so that they will be constructive rather than destructive? How can I learn how others feel toward me? Do other people have the same kinds of problems that I have? Can I trust evaluation?

A Study Plan

I. In groups of three to five persons (1) pantomime how God is at work in the world. (2) express through some art form their concept of the dependability of God.
II. Use the Agree-Disagree Exercise as it is explained in the text. End with group consensus.
III. Discuss the recorded consensus of the total group of the Agree-Disagree exercise. Did it communicate the consensus of the small group?
IV. Examine the reports of the observers of the last session—one on leader roles, the other on group roles. Were the perceptions accurate? Did the observers receive the intended messages?
V. Using the eighteen statements of aims for interaction in the text, ask each member to rate the group from 0 to 10 (10 for **this** would happen; 0 for **not this**). Each student should add his score and write it on the board. If there is a great variation, ask those who rated the group highest and those who rated it lowest to interpret their scoring. Try to com-

Interaction with Fellow Travelers / 193

Which of these "statements of aims" are already in practice in a group you know? How have these aims been achieved?

5. Teacher enabling students in skills of inquiry.
6. Acceptance of mistakes and learning from them.
7. Goals are clearly defined by the group.
8. Students feel secure and free to express themselves.
9. Balance between common tasks and individual responsibility.
10. Learning is self-learning and each person is responsible for his own learning.
11. Stress on perception and feelings as well as message.
12. Spontaneous participation of all students.
13. Sensitivity to needs of each other.
14. Openness and clarifying of assumptions.
15. High level of participation; experiences valued because they have meaning.
16. Warm feelings toward others in the group and mutual trust.
17. Confidence in expressing feelings.
18. View teacher as human being, with feelings, with whom a person can be open.

5. Destructive criticism by teachers.
6. Emphasis on not failing.
7. Goals are the "property" of the teacher and are hidden.
8. Students are psyching out their teachers to win a reward.
9. Group moves forward at a pace determined by the teacher.
10. Teacher assumes responsibility for student behavior and learning.
11. Stress only on content of message.
12. Formal recitation of a few students.
13. Insensitive of needs.
14. Guarded, hidden feelings and unchecked assumptions.
15. Neutral feelings toward the learning experience.
16. Neutral feelings toward the group.
17. Fear of speaking in the group.
18. View teacher as nonhuman object.

municate until you come to a group consensus on scoring.

VI. Ask each person in the group to think of one word which best communicates his meaning of life and self at this moment. When the group is ready, one person at a time should stand up and say the word with as much dramatic feeling as possible. Then persons, with freedom and without structure, sitting next to each other will interpret what they heard in the word itself and in the way it was said. Try to work through to common understandings.

VII. Discussion questions. What methods promote personal freedom in a church group? What questions do our students ask of us? Do they want the final word? or do they ask help in forming their ability to make judgments? Does man need community—must he coexist to exist? To touch reality, must he reach out to the "other"? Why is it so difficult to put ourselves in the shoes of others, sharing experience—making it common?

VIII. Using the following instrument, rate others in the group.

Who Are These People?

Read each description below and write the name of the student(s) it describes in the space to the right. It is possible that some names will not appear in any of these descriptions.

Who is very quiet but seems to be involved? _____
Who is a strong leader and has many good ideas? _____
Who is most willing to listen to the ideas of others? _____
Who can explain best the ideas or instructions that some persons do not understand? _____
Who's serious about the group work but not a fanatic? _____
Who likes to tell others what to do?
Who likes to be told what to do? ___
Who would you pick to see that a job got done? _____
Who would you pick to make sure that the group enjoyed itself? _____

Share the responses in small groups for about twenty minutes. Then, on a large sheet of newsprint, collate all of the individual sheets.

Perhaps you are feeling, as a reader, that these aims are lofty, noble, and desired, but that they are too idealistic—that in reality these aims cannot be achieved. A group composed of students and teachers will, of course, never be perfect, but these aims are achievable to a large extent.

METHODS OF INTERACTION

Sometimes the process of interaction requires great amounts of honest and patient negotiation, especially when an issue has the potential of separating persons. In the process of interacting, all persons are expected to be willing to change if it will make a more creative situation and if it can be done with integrity.

Many persons have not been in a group that probes below surface levels, nor have they felt the trusting support of such a community. The church should be constituted of such groups. In a teacher-dominated learning situation, the teacher serves as a switchboard linking messages between students. Shifting from this pattern of communication causes a great deal of hesitancy in students, who are not accustomed to being deeply involved. Groups who are confronting this new way of being together—a cohesive unit, rather than an aggregate of individuals—will need to be constantly reassured that what the group is doing in removing the teacher from a power position is truly what the teacher desires.

ROLE PLAY

A student is involved emotionally as well as intellectually in communication when he is in a role. Through acting out a role, a person can gain some insights into interpersonal situations. In some role plays, a group of students have a problem assigned to them and they play themselves. In other role plays, a group has an assigned problem and character descriptions of the role they are to play. On other occasions the students are allowed to choose their problem situation and to work out their solution as the rest of the group observes.

Role play is probably most effective when the students act out situations which are realistic and relevant to their experience. One group of ten- and eleven-year-old children, however, when they chose problems to illustrate the generation gap, selected problems that teen-agers face, and they imaginatively projected themselves into those roles. Two girls from this group chose to role-play a scene where an unmarried girl reported to her mother that she was going to have a baby. The girls acted out the roles convincingly, but as soon as the scene was over, the girl playing the role of the pregnant girl said quickly, "I wouldn't have done it the way she did. My mother would never kick me out of the house."

The mother role-player wouldn't change because she felt she had played the scene in the way her mother would have reacted to

In what ways, other than verbal assurance, can a teacher encourage students to assume leader roles?

List some problem situation that you think would benefit the students in a Communications Class to role-play.

such news. The girls agreed to change roles and to work out the problem differently. At the conclusion of the role play, many of the students were not sure just how this problem would be worked out in their homes and they agreed that it would be helpful to them to talk this over with their parents. The role play illustrated that the generation gap is frequently a communication gap, also.

Role play in a Communications Class would probably be most useful if the persons played themselves confronting a probable situation in which there would be interpersonal problems that would allow them to gain skills in communication and human relations.

If a coaching group is assigned, these persons should say things that are specific and helpful when they are conferring with the role-players. It should be emphasized that the coaches are learning how to be *helpful*. Each coach should put his comments in such a way that the receiver can accept them. This is practicing good communication.

AGREE-DISAGREE EXERCISE

This exercise is a method of interaction which requires good communication and can be used by a group in several ways. One way is to explore meanings in a particular area of content.

The exercise consists of a set of written statements. A copy is given to each person; he reads it through and indicates his agreement or disagreement with each item. If ten statements are written, five of them should favor one point of view and five should favor an opposite point of view.

Read each of the items below carefully and indicate your agreement or disagreement by placing a check mark (√) on the appropriate line to the left.

Agree Disagree

Do you agree that five of the statements in this sample Agree-Disagree Exercise favor one point of view and that the remaining five favor another point of view?

____ ____ 1. The adjectives "good" and "bad" should not be used to describe persons.

____ ____ 2. The genocide committed by the Nazi Gestapo was bad.

____ ____ 3. Air pollution is bad for people—and all other living things.

____ ____ 4. Adolph Eichmann was bad because he carried out orders to murder Jews.

____ ____ 5. It is bad for countries to be at war.

____ ____ 6. Peacemakers are good people.

____ ____ 7. Being good or bad is a personal matter; groups are not good or bad.

____ ____ 8. Good is a word to describe the quality of a thing.

____ ____ 9. A person is good who obeys the laws.

____ ____ 10. The United States has had some good presidents and some bad presidents.

In using the Agree-Disagree Exercise, allow the students time to read and to react to the statements, then divide the total group into subgroups of five persons. The leader will then instruct these groups to arrive at a consensus concerning their agreement or disagreement with each item. They may change the wording in any way that will help them in making these decisions.

Each subgroup should be informed that they will report their conclusions to the total group, including their changes in the wording of the items and their reasons for making them. If the total group is not too large, they may all work together at reaching a consensus. Whether the entire group reaches a consensus or not, the procedure brings out clearly the thinking of the students concerning the main issues raised.

The contribution this method makes to interaction is its insistence upon communicating. A group of persons that has become cohesive or is interested in the best possible interaction will be genuinely concerned about how each person feels about the content of a course, how it is being taught, how it might be improved to meet the needs.

BUZZ GROUPS

When the entire group of students is divided into a number of small buzz groups, each student is most likely to participate in the communication. Students will feel more free to talk in small buzz groups consisting of four to six persons. Buzz groups are valuable following lectures, audio-visuals, field trips or other presentations. Written questions for the buzz groups may help them to get started. About ten minutes is a productive period of time for most buzz groups. It is not necessary for buzz groups to come to any conclusions, for they really serve as "warm ups" to the total group discussion.

An excellent way for groups to get started is to have students, of their own choice, form buzz groups to warm up for the total group experience of communicating. If students know before the session starts what their goals are and what they are likely to be working on during a certain period of time, they can begin by involving each other in small buzz groups. A definite sign of a group which is not cohesive—not interacting at the most significant level—is one that waits each time they gather to have a teacher or leader call the group to order.

THREE-STEP DESIGN

When buzz groups disband, it is difficult to maintain the openness and spontaneity of input in a discussion involving a large number of persons. The success of this transition depends to a great extent on the group's cohesiveness and maturity and the skill of the leader. The last thirty minutes of a session could proceed on the first two steps of the Three Step Design, holding over the third step to start the next session.

Is consensus important in a teaching-learning group? Why or why not?

If a buzz group does not have as its goal "reaching a conclusion," what might its aim be? By what criteria would it be judged a beneficial method for interraction?

Is good interaction in the learning group necessary for learning the content of the Christian gospel? Why or why not?

Interaction with Fellow Travelers / 197

The three steps are as follows:
1) For ten minutes buzz groups (four to six persons) respond to an issue.
2) The next twenty minutes buzz groups find a partner buzz group. Then the larger groups will continue to discuss the issue and to summarize, until everyone is satisfied. Group summarizations should be recorded on newsprint. Copies of all summaries should be made available, if possible, to each person at the next session.
3) At the beginning of the following session in a group using the three-step design, the buzz groups (as formed in the first step) reconvene to discuss for ten minutes what all of the written summaries communicate.

Students are occupied in the Three Step Design on the content level, but they are also interacting and developing interpersonal relationships. Until the group becomes very sensitized and increasingly conscious of developing skills in group roles that aid communication, the leader will need occasionally to remind students about these roles. Awareness of the process of communication and related skills does not occur automatically. (Group roles and social roles are discussed in Chapter 16.)

BRAINSTORMING

In what teaching-learning situations would brainstorming aid the communication process?

This communication method works well in groups of about twelve members who are involved in solving a problem which is clearly defined and which could be resolved in a number of alternative ways.

Some of the basic rules are as follows:
1. Persons suggest possible steps to be taken.
2. List these ideas in rapid succession.
3. Criticism of ideas is not permitted.
4. Even wild ideas are accepted without evaluation.
5. All ideas are recorded with no effort to organize them into logical sequence.
6. Participants are free to build on the ideas expressed by others or to combine any number of previous ideas. This is referred to as "piggybacking" or "hitchhiking."
7. No idea should be missed.
8. Some groups may choose to set a quota of ideas.
9. Some groups allot a designated amount of time.

Brainstorming emphasizes maintaining group roles that aid communication by not allowing critical comments and by reinforcing a person through accepting all of his ideas.

The follow-up methods of using the data from the brainstorming will need to show respect for the ideas proposed. For example the input from brainstorming may form an agenda for committee work. There needs to be conscious and recognizable use of the data received through brainstorming, or persons will feel that communicating by that method is not worthwhile and the experience will not be satisfying.

ANALYSIS OF A PROBLEM SITUATION

A scene from life's experiences—written by a student, a professional playwright, a novelist, or a script writer—which gives an account of a problem faced by one or more persons can be an outside communication which becomes an inside communication when students begin to identify with the characters and bring their own personal feelings into the situation. First, the students analyze the emotional forces involved in the written scene; next, they isolate the problems or conflicts; then, they evaluate the personalities of those persons involved in the problem situation. Then the students begin to interact by talking about themselves—When have they felt similar *emotions?* What have they done about them? Did they ever face similar *problems?* How did they resolve them?

In the problem situation analysis, students test out, develop, and evaluate their abilities in communicating and interacting. The teacher listens and asks questions, but he does not demonstrate his ability to handle material.

Recall novels, plays, short stories, or feature stories which have given you insight into your own problems or those of others near to you.

SIMULATION GAMES

In building a cohesive group, teachers do not encourage competition, except in games. A simulation game represents the dynamic forces of a social situation and causes the players to deal with them. The game empowers them in an area outside their usual environs. The object of a simulation game is to involve students in the types of situations which conventional methods cannot clarify. In these games students are constantly engaged in communicating and negotiating. Although a game does not reproduce reality, it can give students realistic insights into forces which produce the situation.

Through simulation games, students become involved in the dynamic forces of the events. Simulation games from history frequently allow players to finish a game quite differently from the actual ending of the event in history. Then the students can compare the use of power, the possibilities of chance, and perhaps our Christian claim through faith that God acted in and through these events. For instance, we can and do proclaim in faith that God used Caesar Augustus to decree that there be a census taken in such a manner that Mary and Joseph would be required to go to Bethlehem and that Jesus would be born there to fulfill the prophecy and the Scriptures.

What makes dramatic play or simulated games modular rather than linear?

Many situations within history and the present life of Christianity could be communicated more dynamically through simulation games than in conventional, logical-sequence presentations. In learning about many events, we conventionally pattern our teaching-learning by (*a*) discovering what events happened, when, and where; (*b*) finding out about the personalities involved and their backgrounds; (*c*) looking for events in other places that had an effect on the situation; (*d*) appreciating the cultural expression of the conflict; (*e*) analyzing the situation to find truths which can be related to events in our lives.

Significant communicating and learning could take place in a group that designs a game. There are many biblical situations that would lend themselves to games. A dynamic game could be designed to recreate the conflict of forces among officials of the Roman government, members of the Sanhedrin, and Jesus' followers during his ministry.

Some games will create interpersonal conflict which can then be resolved through other interaction methods.

NONVERBAL COMMUNICATION

Within the past few hours what messages have you received nonverbally? Did you check the accuracy of your perception?

Helen Keller wrote that the eye is the most superficial of all the senses, the ear the most arrogant, smell the most voluptuous, taste the most superstitious or fickle, and touch the most profound. The components of our language without words are the human body, itself; psychological processes of human beings—trembling voice, shaking hands, nervous smile; and culturally approved gestures. The human face sends many messages, and persons with the greatest ability to interpret these expressions correctly are often older persons of high intelligence. We say much by posture and spacing. It has been noted that persons who tend to dislike one another choose to sit opposite each other, whereas friends sit beside one another. The culture dictates much about nonverbal language, such as Americans tend to keep an arm's length away from other persons, if it is possible, and they are uncomfortable in close quarters.

What nonverbal symbols may aid students? Which ones may hinder?

Silence speaks eloquently. It is frequently a part of the communication called, *"presencing,"* being there in support of another person. Although silence may also bespeak of hostility, power, or inwardness.

In what ways can you improve your use of silent times—your time alone?

Nonverbal communication most frequently stems from the unconscious. A person can learn to know himself better through silence—allowing his total environment to speak to him. The more one can know his inwardness, the greater skill he will have in self-assessment and in listening to others, while being unburdened of ego needs.

FEEDBACK IN INTERACTION

Methods used in interpersonal learning give the most direct and quickest communication feedback of all methods. In interaction, students are taught to find problems and state them. The problems are *their* problems: the discussions are *their* discussions: the responsibility for learning is *their* responsibility. This may be difficult for students for a while, but a teacher's attitude of careful listening and his willingness to initiate clarification and integration of ideas will soon begin to set a norm for participation. After a period of time, students will not only expect interaction, they will anticipate it with great pleasure.

Inherent in the discovery concept of teaching-learning is that student involvement in evaluation is, in itself, an important learning activity.

Prerequisites for interaction feedback are an atmosphere of mutual trust between students and teachers, an openness to change by teachers, an assurance that a support action will be taken in response to the feedback, and an agreement that learners will also change as the result of honest evaluation.

To use methods with the aim of improving interaction (developing communication skills) is at the outset not the easiest road for a teacher to take, nor does use of these methods guarantee immediate success (any more than the recitative methods). The student cannot depend on the teacher to tell him what he has read, pointing out the more subtle aspects, doing the job of analysis for him, and, finally, telling him the answer.

In a learning group which you attend, what percentage of time is being used by students to analyze their feedback?

SUMMARY

A student gains facts from many sources, but he tests them out in the context of his living. Usually, a person tries out concepts and values through interacting—thus communicating—with his fellow students and friends. In order to learn (to change) in a group, a person must have trusting relationships with persons in the group. Because of this, a teacher cannot rely on telling facts, explaining concepts, and recommending values and expect to have an effective teaching situation—where learning is taking place. Through methods of interaction, groups can create environments that can greatly increase their learning potential.

Exploring Communication in Enabling Learners

Helping persons in gaining the skills for seeking self-direction, self-selection, and discovery of meaning is teaching them lifelong habits of disciplined learning which benefit communication. If students are accustomed to being "told" what they should know, especially during their formative years, they cannot be expected to sound logical in their communications.

Discovery in learning is often the rearrangement or transformation of information already possessed by the student. It may not require any new information. Linking ideas together is creative and innovative; it accounts for many inventions—from Heloise's helpful household hints to the latest discoveries in aeronautical engineering. Dr. Jerome Bruner, developer of the discovery method in education, notes that discovery favors the well-prepared mind,

CHAPTER 24

Gifts Along the Way

one which is either expecting that there will be patterns of meanings to be found or which is expecting to devise ways of fruitful seeking.

The student's reward from the discovery method of teaching-learning comes from the learning experience itself and not from some "goody" that will be given after a certain amount of material is "covered,"—a "goody" such as going on a picnic could, in fact, be a part of teaching-learning for interaction.

When teaching-learning situations are inquiry-oriented—

In order for this statement to be applicable, would the learning experience need to fulfill the emotional needs of the students as well as their intellectual curiosities? Why? or Why not?

The teacher functions as:	The student functions as:
a stimulator	an inquirer
an environment planner	an explorer and discoverer
a diagnostician	an object manipulator
a prescriber	an idea organizer
a materials organizer	a generalizer, discusser, and a communicator of ideas and conclusions

How are these teacher and learner functions learner-oriented and suitable for modular programming.

A TEACHER AS STIMULATOR

When teaching results in students communicating new insights into a concept, it affirms individual differences. It recognizes each person's worth; it accepts each person; and it treats each person with respect. A teacher finds out where each student is in his learning process—what skills he has learned, what skills he needs. A teacher does not look for or desire assembly-line conformity. He helps each student according to his needs, interests, capabilities,

---

Guidance for Session 24
GIFTS ALONG THE WAY

Aim for the Session

To understand how the principles of communication (as they are described in this text) apply to teacher functions so that students in this course can make them operational.

Questions to Ponder

How can a teacher guide students in the learning process without telling them what is best to do? Do adults really know what is best for youth? Since "covering" Christian implications in all fields of knowledge is impossible, what will be the basis of our selectivity of content? Would you characterize your church's Christian education as future-oriented? What must the Christian teacher clearly teach as he carries out his teaching function in order to avoid future crises when changes are made in church authority, resolutions, or educational emphases? In what areas of your life as a Christian teacher do you feel the tension between freedom and authority? Is this tension creative or destructive? Should we try to make our teaching-learning groups be models of Christian community?

A Study Plan

Choose from the following suggestions and create your session plan.

I. If it is possible before this session to have each student practice teaching a group in the church's school —especially with one or two observers from this study group attending the practice teaching session and/or recording the session, then this session could consist of small groups evaluating the practice teaching sessions and helping each other to find ways of improving their communication.

II. Arrange ahead of time for a member of the group to lead a discussion. The teacher will do the following things:

A. Appoint an observer to note the teacher functions during the discussion.

B. Ask the group to choose a question they would most like to deal with from the questions in the marginal notes of chapter 22.

C. Encourage the members to state other questions than those in the marginal notes.

D. Get the discussion rolling. You may wish to have each member of the group give his **brief** answer to a question and to proceed without interruption.

E. Stimulate the discussion with questions.

F. Moderate differences of opinion by involving students other than those engaged in a dispute.

G. Check to see if the group has finished a problem, than ask one person to summarize the group's answer while another person records the summary on newsprint. Test the group's acceptance of the summary

and motivations. In doing this, a teacher establishes a natural base for the acquisition of meaningful learning.

On the first day, Bud Roberts and the ten youth in his section of a workshop told each other about their home churches and communities. The youth were quick to notice how different each person's situation was from all the rest. They were surprised, too. They talked freely about the problems they were facing, and they began to communicate their understanding that some problems were symptoms of more basic troubles.

Bud suggested that each person would have more time to work at the problem he was facing if the group worked in pairs. The group responded favorably to his suggestion. Using a problem-finder resource, which Bud made available to them, each person worked at finding and solving two problems—his own and his partner's. Bud joined each of the pairs at their request.

As a result of their communicating with each other, most of the youth were eager to try to lead the youth back home in finding and solving problems. They were aware that as leaders, they would need to give everyone a chance to communicate his understandings about problems and solutions.

Some blocks to communication are the assumptions we make as teachers:

Talking	assumes	hearing.
Reading	assumes	reacting.
Reading	assumes	listening.

and the record of newsprint. Change it until all are satisfied with it.

H. Move on to selecting and discussing another question.

About thirty minutes before the session is to close, stop the discussion. Ask the students to form small buzz groups for ten minutes to evaluate the leader's functions of stimulator, environment planner, diagnostician, prescriber, materials organizer. Come together for sharing the evaluations.

III. Observe a film depicting a teaching-learning group at work. The film may be professional or it may be an amateur film (perhaps of a group in your church). Before you show the film, divide the group into small groups and assign to each group the task of especially observing the teacher's communications as he/she carries out teaching functions—stimulator, environment planner, diagnostician, prescriber, materials organizer. After viewing the film, appoint a recorder for each small group and discuss the teacher's communications and functions observed in the film. Then ask the recorders to report to the total group. Discuss the reports—agreeing and disagreeing, adding and deleting, illustrating, clarifying, and summarizing.

Note for all groups, using suggestions I, II, or III: About ten minutes before the session closes, ask the group to evaluate the session, using the following guide, and to give these to the teacher.

Group Evaluation

Plan No. ———
Circle one number:

	Poor	Fair	Acceptable	Good	Excellent
1. My general reaction to the experience was	1	2	3	4	5
2. The efficiency of my group in doing the job was	1	2	3	4	5
3. The involvement of group members was	1	2	3	4	5
4. How effective was I?	1	2	3	4	5
5. How effective was the teacher?	1	2	3	4	5

Write in:
1. Problems in the group as I see them.
2. What I can do to help.
3. How could the teacher better meet the needs of myself and the class?

Illustrating assumes seeing.
Symbolizing assumes understanding.
Writing assumes reading.
Questioning assumes answering.
Demonstrating assumes imitating.
Gesturing assumes interpreting.

> Recall an experience in which assumptions blocked miscommunication.

When communication is blocked by assumptions, teaching-learning groups cannot interact. The resulting misunderstandings are inclined to become lodged in unhappy feelings and cloudy perception. Two of the basic principles for teachers using inquiry-oriented methods are, first, to be open and, second, to check assumptions as often as needed. This means to "walk in the other person's shoes," seeing the problem from his vantage point.

Teachers who see one of their tasks as stimulating inquiry will work at improving their skills in group roles that aid communication (see Chapter 16), as well as stimulating their students to assume responsibility for these roles.

A TEACHER AS ENVIRONMENT PLANNER

There are two kinds of learning behavior which Professor Bruner has emphasized. One can be characterized as meaningful, rational, purposeful, straightforward. The other is theoretical, tentative, playful, imaginative, and sometimes even wrong. Since we gain information through our senses and then clarify, classify, and appropriate it, we need to give attention to communicating Christian meaning when we are engaged in these. What makes a learning environment Christian or unchristian?

> Where does the person leave off and the environment begin?

A teacher has to "go" beyond adequate preparation and lesson planning and to "do" more than pleasantly smile or efficiently present concepts in order to communicate. He has to "dwell" in the situation—engrossed in its possibilities and possessed by its qualities.

That the young child needs to establish a good relationship with an adult in order to be able to learn is well documented in the literature of early childhood education. Students will respond to the image that they have of a teacher in markedly varied ways, ranging from fearing an authority figure to enjoying a friend. Most students respond in a way that is somewhere in between these two extremes.

A teacher may get objections from some students, and some of it will likely be directed at the amount of responsibility placed on the learner. At such times, it will be most helpful to all concerned if the teacher will listen closely and attentively, showing interest. Many objections can be converted to benefit the work of the group. Most objections come from two sources—ignorance and fear. A teacher may be able to allay fears and win confidences. There may be times when objections will clearly indicate that a teacher has "misread" the group and that the group has a communication problem they need to work through together.

A sixth-grade class had as its learning goal, "To understand how we feel about things that happen so we can think about what it means to be Christian when such things happen." Mrs. Lewis, their teacher, suggested that the group might role-play so that they could communicate strong feeling. She said that they might divide into groups of three persons and describe situations and act out varying responses. She gave an example: Pretend you are a mother waiting for your child to come home from school. He is two hours late. Act how you would feel waiting for him to arrive; act how you would feel when your child arrived late because he had been playing ball; act how you would feel if you discovered that in an emergency he had been helping a mother of his friend. The children's faces communicated their interest in the role-play suggestion, but no one was initiating any action to get started. Mrs. Lewis noticed the nonverbal communication of no action, and she inquired, "You look interested in role playing, but why are you hesitating?"

Ginny asked, "Are we just going to role-play here, or is someone else going to watch us?"

"Which would you like?" the teacher asked.

"Just us." There was immediate and total group consensus with Ginny's reply. Relieved of the fear that they might have to perform publicly, the children quickly moved into groups to describe roles that would communicate their feelings.

It is often assumed that teachers must choose between fostering their students' intellectual development and establishing good relationships with them. This is a false set of alternatives. There can be no worthwhile teaching-learning without good student-teacher relationships and communication. Why, then, should teachers assume they must sacrifice good relationships if they are to achieve intellectual progress? The either-or position probably rests on more subtle and implicit assumptions about teaching-learning such as (a) by the end of a certain period of time all students should achieve certain goals (this would be to ignore individual differences and to create considerable tension and difficulty), (b) students are not likely to become interested and involved in developing ideas and concepts (this would suggest strict disciplinary action), and (c) intellectual progress is achieved only through acquiring knowledge from books (this would imply that time used for learning skills in group roles, for setting goals and planning, and for communicating is a waste of time). As these assumptions are stated, it becomes apparent that none of them are valid.

A student needs the warmth and approval of a teacher as well as a road map or some hints to help him make an intuitive leap or

> What is your opinion about these subtle and implicit assumptions? Do you agree with the author? Discuss these three assumptions and parenthetical evaluations with a teacher.

recognize what he needs to look for. While each student must do his own learning, he needs the knowledgeable kind of teacher's guidance which not only spurs him on to search but also provides some needed tools and opportunities which can move him forward with satisfaction.

Offering students intellectual stimulation and expecting achievement and growth should enhance their self-imaging. A teacher may need frequently to encourage students by communicating an "of-course-you-can" philosophy. In due time, weak egos can be strengthened and students can establish a sense of personal worth and integrity. If a teacher inwardly embraces a "you-can't-get-along-without-me" or "you-really-need-to-have-me-tell-you" attitude, he will probably communicate his inner feeling, nonverbally, even when he is verbally encouraging.

The dynamics of communication are essential for students and teachers, guiding the learning process. A teacher reads the "pulse rate" of the group at all times and tries to keep it steady, asking pertinent questions of goal-setters, making suggestions to planners, helping students in individual study, and recommending methods of interaction to the group, assisting in reading feedback, and reminding students of ways to improve skills in group roles that aid communication.

A teacher needs to recognize his unique worth in encouraging and enabling learners, rather than telling them. A student's growing sense of mastery and ability to cope with and communicate some of the important ideas and issues of contemporary life should contribute to a growth of independence, responsibility, and love of learning.

A teacher creates an exciting learning environment in order to stimulate more meaningful activities that help people learn. Such an environment is free of destructive tension stemming from the anxiety of being accepted. It is out-going, dependable, encouraging, secure, full of friendship and goodwill, free, and concerned for all.

A TEACHER AS DIAGNOSTICIAN

A teacher can supply needed tools and materials because he plans with the group's learning needs in mind. Teachers contribute to the learning process with questions, materials, suggestions, and experiences that help learners progress toward clearly stated goals. A teacher can be highly selective in the content and form of the messages he offers, because the learning goals are held in common by teachers and students. Since not everyone perceives ideas and relationships the same way even when they are in the same teaching-learning situation, a teacher needs to find ways to communicate clearly ideas and relationships. Every experience has the potential of sparking interest and curiosity—spurring a person's desire to explore.

A girl in a good learning environment said, "The teachers are real people, not condescending. They exchange ideas with us on a more equal basis." What contributes to good communication?

Some good teaching questions are: Does anyone agree or disagree? How do you feel about that? Can you offer a possible answer to that question yourself? Add to this list.

Progress in classroom relationships usually will occur when students are interested. Discipline problems are frequently due to boredom. Eagerness for learning is enhanced by an intellectually stimulating environment where students are involved in manipulating things and exploring things of interest to them. When there is intellectual challenge, it is possible to have independent work, freeing the teacher for one-to-one communication which is warm, personal, and knowledgeable and which can grow into understanding, sympathy, and realistic appreciation.

Consider students who are challenged to explore their environment and who are supplied with appropriate tools and directions for their exploration. They are likely to mature considerably in their emotional and social growth, as well as advancing in their intellectual learnings. Teachers who use communication principles that are suggested in this book will find that their relationships with students will improve.

While curriculum innovations can originate from a variety of sources, it is the teacher who has the most control over the teaching-learning. The teacher can make innovations effective or he can guarantee that new practices will fail, depending on the degree of his conviction and excitement.

Counsel provided by a teacher should not seek its mirrored reflection in the student, influencing him to conform to what the teacher supposes is correct. Unimaginative teaching communicates the need for hints and signs of what is expected and tends to applaud mirrored behavior and passive understanding. A teacher may act as a guide for his students' "seeing" processes, intensifying their perceptions, enchancing feelings of empathy, sensitizing persons to media response. It is so much easier, of course, to tell a student what we wish him to know, rather than to wait for him to discover by himself. So an inexperienced or careless teacher can rarely resist the temptation "to tell." Having reached for meanings and experiences of the gospel and the significance of one's own action, a teacher often has a point of view and is faced with the responsibility of communicating about problems and issues and not simply telling his point of view!

A teacher giving direction to his students' curiosities may ask an occasional question, but he relies chiefly upon their powers for discovering concepts and some facts.

Lydia Roberts was confronted with finding a way to teach the meaning of "convert" to a class of fifth-graders. She chose to work first with the word "convince" because it was within the vocabulary of the group.

"How many of you like to ice-skate?" Lydia queried. Everyone responded positively, and so she asked John to pretend that he did not like to ice-skate and Tim to convince John that ice skating is enjoyable.

Would no theology be worse than boring theology?

As you reflect more deeply on the role of the teacher, what is your reflection telling you? Can you share these ideas and feelings with other teachers?

When differences of opinion arise, can you as a teacher state the differences clearly while remaining impartial and seeking a moderating opinion from the group?

Gifts Along the Way / 207

The boys moved into an open space in the room and began to work out their assignment. The conversation went like this, "Hey, John. Let's go ice skating this afternoon. It's a lot of fun."

"No, I don't want to go skating this afternoon. I'd rather play football."

"Oh, come on. Go skating with me. You don't have anything better to do," John pleaded.

"No, I might fall and get hurt. I really don't—I really don't like to skate."

The conversation continued along this line until John decided that using fists might be more successful. So the boys began to scuffle. About a minute later, Lydia called a halt and asked Tim if this procedure was going to work. He said, "No, it wouldn't."

The boys were puzzled about how they were going to complete the assignment when Roy went over to them, pointed to an area of the floor, and said, "Here is the ice." Then he said to John, "Let's skate." They pretended to skate around, and then they went over to Tim, each taking him by an arm. The three pretended to skate around. Soon Tim volunteered that he was beginning to be convinced.

Lydia Roberts asked the total group, "What methods were used to try to convince Tim?" After the group told about the three actions that were taken, they labeled them as follows: The first was "telling"; the second, "forcing"; and the third, "showing." The first two methods failed, but the method of showing succeeded.

The group was excited about their learning and was eagerly planning situations in which they could test it out. It would have been much easier, of course, for Lydia Roberts to tell the group that telling and forcing were not effective ways of convincing a person. Telling and forcing may neither communicate nor convince; but discovering, showing, and demonstrating are likely to do both.

When a group or individual wanders from an original plan, what do you think would be an appropriate and helpful teacher function?

As a general rule, it is better not to tell students that which they can discover for themselves. A teacher may bring his critical faculties to bear on testing premises or new ideas; he may keep an individual student or the total group from digressing; he may help a student in his efforts to put disorganized information into proper relationships; and he may help students clarify the meaning of words used in context to insure education rather than miseducation. A teacher may also help students to select media, to gain skill in manipulating it, and to interpret symbols.

A TEACHER AS PRESCRIBER

A kindly, unpressured attitude is needed by a teacher who wishes to help a student clarify his communication of an idea. Elements of compulsion, hostility, comparisons, punishment, or disapproval for lack of achievement create emotional blocks which need to be overcome before a student is free to communicate his ideas.

Planning for children usually requires some teacher's efforts, such as seeking authoritative information, coaching a song or play, preparing a map or chart or diagram, ordering supplies, evolving the details for some evaluative techniques, getting permission from a property committee for hanging a picture or bulletin board.

A teacher can suggest different ways of looking at things and thus enable each student in his building of a conceptual framework for dealing with the world. The teacher-leader is not an authority; he is a prescriber-suggester, keeping learning open, flexible, and tentative. Because the development of values is a life-long process, students need to be able to change as the world changes, as well as to strive to change the world. Each person who plans to find the most intelligent relationship between his life and the world around him will need to develop habits of examining his purposes, aspirations, attitudes, feelings, interests, beliefs, convictions, activities, anxieties. Then he will be able to identify his values—those things which he chooses from among alternatives to live by, to cherish, to affirm, and to use as criteria for decision-making—which become his hallmark.

If a group works well, do you agree that the group conclusions are usually better than those which the leader or any one member could formulate?

A teacher who is very familiar with curriculum resources can be a big help to a student who is trying to find in them the kind of content or process he needs for understanding, conceptualizing, or valuing. A teacher-prescriber will discover problems that students are having with skills of inquiry, such as listening, reading, logical thinking, perceiving, symbolizing, problem-solving, problem-finding; then the teacher will communicate with students in ways that will help them overcome these problems.

Removing the blocks that are causing miscommunication—misunderstandings, illogical conclusions, ill-founded assumptions, or any cloudy perception—is a great teacher-contribution. At every step of the communications model there are many possible filters or blocks which can distort the intent of the communication—

Does the religious content in teaching in the church make the question of freedom or coercion a serious one? How?

Someone	—understanding self-interest, motivation
perceives an event	—perceiving the significance
and reacts	—assessing self-abilities, skills
in a situation	—ascertaining relevance
to make available materials	—selecting communication method
in some form	—determining media
conveying content	—conceptualizing and symbolizing ideas
of some consequence	—relating, interpreting, integrating ideas

Gifts Along the Way / 209

Sometimes the response of a teacher (who is the receiver of a student-sender) is the feedback which directs a student's judgment of his communication—its effectiveness and clarity. As a result of his judgment, a student may revise his communication. Then the teacher's response (feedback) will probably be changed, also.

A TEACHER AS MATERIALS ORGANIZER

Discovery is a way of communicating. It is rearranging or transforming evidence in such a way that a person is enabled to go beyond the evidence to new insights. It is more than mere organizational manipulation. It involves a change in what the teachers do when they teach, what students do when they learn, and what they both do when they interact with one another. Critical thinking, inquiry, and self-directiveness are basic to rearranging or transforming evidence into insights.

Is an understanding of the Christian gospel a special dimension of any inquiry whatever into life? If so, what relationship should church teaching-learning situations have to public school curriculum?

The ability of learners to organize the religious understanding that they have arrived at from the raw materials of evidence is not acquired through memorizing many related or unrelated facts. Neither is it acquired through books that merely list basic concepts that the teacher is expected to convey at a specific grade level and that learners are supposed to assimilate by some magical means. The ingredients of learning include that which each person brings to the situation. One method of eliciting individual knowledge is stating a problem to which individual responses and solutions are desired. In responding to the problem, new questions will arise, leading to further explorations and experiences from which questions will be formed and new understandings derived.

The teaching-learning situation should not be considered merely a place where questions are answered, but rather as a place where, most of the time, questions are shaped. Conclusions, evaluations, or summaries should not always be thought of as the necessary final activity for all learning experiences. It is not necessary to summarize what has taken place or to be sure "the point is put across." Many teachers are reluctant to let students draw their own learnings from an experience. Instead, they feel that they should summarize at the end of a period of time together, telling what has happened and what they intended for persons to learn. This unfortunate tendency is so common among teachers that it has been given a name, *lysisphobia*—the fear of leaving "loose ends."

From this study, what answers can you give to those persons who object to methods which enable discovery as opposed to methods which indoctrinate?

Besides forcing on students conclusions that they are not capable of assimilating, or perhaps with which they disagree, this tying up things in a neat package cuts off the gradual growth and understanding which comes when persons try communicating their new ideas or insights. In fact, it is worthwhile occasionally to remind learners of the incompleteness of their understanding—of unanswered questions or ambiguous interpretations—so that their conclusions will not be crystalized and they will be stirred to do further learning.

Abstract thinking grows out of understandings derived from concrete experiences, and it is molded gradually to take increasingly general form. Students should be conscious of working toward generalizations, linking concrete experiences with abstract elements. Teachers should be helping their students to verbalize, to symbolize, and to communicate the ideas they are learning. Teachers can gradually introduce unfamiliar elements that their students can use in building bridges between the world of concrete experiences and the abstract ways of representing it. The teacher is a mediator between a person's present stage of development and the organized body of knowledge which he can attain.

How can you put this statement into practice?

Practically no aspect of our daily existence takes place without involving some Christian implication. Consequently, confining Christian experiences and Christian thinking to special times is unrealistic. Preparing to teach becomes richer when it is not relegated to a short period of time (particularly not Saturday night), but is a conscious part of daily existence.

Relating the Gospel to Day-to-Day Concerns

Jesus drew near and said to them: "I have been given all authority in heaven and on earth. Go, then, to all peoples everywhere and make them my disciples: baptize them in the name of the Father and of the Son and of the Holy Spirit, and teach them to obey everything I have commanded you. And remember! I will be with you always, to the end of the age."

—Matthew 28:18-20, TEV

So it is that Jesus Christ faces us with the problem of how to communicate what the kingdom of God is so that it might be extended throughout the world. If our task is to learn how to communicate the kingdom of God, we might look to an example of how it is best done. Most of us would agree that Jesus most fully revealed God. It is interesting to note that Jesus did not use intellectual persuasion or telling. He did not imitate the logic of the Greek philosophers. Neither did he suggest force, law, or organization, though the Code of Hammurabi was exceedingly sophisticated and preceded him in time. In fact, he only briefly referred to the Old Testament tradition which was closest to their understanding. Even when he did refer to the former ways, it was often with a negative connotation—"You have heard it said, but I say. . . ."

Jesus communicated what the kingdom of God was like most eloquently by his style of living and dealing with persons.

CHAPTER 25

"I Am the Way"

Do you agree that it is our task to communicate what the kingdom of God is? Is all of life the content of Christian teaching?

Search the Gospels for illustrations of this.

When he did use words he used "word pictures." He referred to God not in definitions like

> the ground of all being,
> the transcendent one, or
> omniscient originator and
> ruler of the universe.

Instead, he spoke of religious truth with terms like

> a sower,
> a mustard seed,
> a pearl of great price,
> a father who received his son who had deliberately left his house,
> a woman who had lost a coin,
> a shepherd who sought a lost sheep,
> a fisherman casting his net into the sea,
> yeast,
> good seed,
> hidden treasure.

He used words like

> Spirit,
> Bread of Life,
> Light of the World,
> Door for the Sheep.

These descriptive words force us back to understanding the attributes and elements of the realities behind the word pictures, and thus God is surrounded once again with mystery.

What do Jesus' acts of forgiveness communicate?

The life-style of Jesus was shocking to persons, although not mysterious. They were surprised at the way in which he forgave,

Guidance for Session 25
"I AM THE WAY"

Aim for the Session
To maintain dialogical relationships as the group engages in problem-finding and problem-solving related to communications gaps in the educational program of the church.

Questions to Ponder
Do the teachers and leaders of the educational program expect to achieve the same goals as the rest of the church people expect? Do parents expect that the church's educational programs will change their children in any fundamental ways? If the premises of this book were carried out in your church, would it mean a minor revolution in teacher training? or in budgeting? How can you initiate these changes? What happens in a teaching-learning situation when a teacher defines (and lives according to) faith as an intellectual assent while the students define (and live according to) faith as engaging oneself? Does knowing that in our technetronic society no person can learn all there is to know affect the content of Christian teaching-learning? What are the deep, underlying ideas of Christianity that can be related to every decade, century, or age of man? How can teachers be encouraged to allow learning groups to engage in problem-finding as well as problem-solving? How does your Christian community practice nonviolence? What dilemmas are facing the church at the present time? Are dimensions of creativity and freedom characteristic of your church? Is your educational program closer to the educational models of the future or to models of the past? If man is the responder and cocreator, where will he find the ideals in which service he can enlist his creative efforts?

A Study Plan
(to be continued in Session 26)

Search out communication gaps/problems in the educational program of the church and propose possible solutions for some of them. Students may choose to be in the following communication groups (modular programming).

A. Reading. The learners may review this text and related materials as it applies to their church and record problems which contribute to a communication gap. Write a brief report to present during session 26.

B. Research. The learners may

212 / Basics for Communication in the Church

and much of his teaching had to do with God's forgiveness. Jesus recognized the weakness of men. This is obvious to a reader of the Gospels. He knew a person's weaknesses would show themselves. Think of the blind persons to whom Jesus restored sight. He knew they were going to spread the word, and so he spoke harshly to them, "Don't tell this to anyone!" But they did. Later, Jesus announced the coming betrayal of Judas and the denial of Peter, yet in his actions he forgave them—even before the event and again after the event while he was on the cross.

Despite his understanding of human weaknesses, Jesus commissioned us to extend the kingdom of Love. A special temptation that we face—those of us who teach or lead in the church—is in so identifying ourselves with our teaching and its ministries that we forget the responsibility that we bear in our daily relationships with persons. Daily we have encounters with persons who are not a part of the church. These persons may serve us—clerks, waiters, waitresses, maids, salesmen, repairmen. They may know that we teach in a particular church, and for them it may be a symbol of Christianity. A young, airline reservationist left her desk after receiving an offending call from an executive of a Christian institution. She called a friend from a pay phone, and tearfully she told him how hurt she was by the conversation. Was she to doubt this man's love for God? Or was she to recognize human failing and to extend forgiveness? Jesus did not doubt Peter's love though he knew Peter would deny him. He took Peter to the Garden of Gethsemane, and after his resurrection he gave Peter a way to prove his love to himself and to the world when he said, "Feed my sheep."

> How can we communicate the gospel so as to extend the kingdom of God?

---

select some aspect of the "Aim for the Session" and gather related materials from books, magazines, journals, films, interviews, surveys, or field trips and write a research paper to read at session 26. Some of the topics might be "Maintaining Dialogical Relationship in the Teaching-Learning Session," "Enlisting Persons in a Course of Study, Using the Text, **Basics for Communication in the Church**," "Ways of Involving Parents in the Educational Program of the Church," "Testing and Financing Communications Equipment for the Church," "Church Schools of Tomorrow," "Shared Time Program of Christian Education in Our Community," "Communications Gap As It Relates to the Generation Gap."

C. Discussing. 1. Brainstorming to list problems or gaps in communication in the educational program of the church. 2. Role-play a situation in which there is a known problem in order to get a new understanding of the situation and insight into how to solve it. 3. Role-play possible solutions. 4. Write an Agree-Disagree Sheet about a problem to present to the entire group at session 26. 5. Decide on one of the activities above (1 through 4) to lead the whole group in during session 26.

D. Creative Activity. Students may write a service of worship related to the communications gap in the church, compose poetry, draw cartoons, construct mobiles, make posters or a collage, decorate a bulletin board, make a film depicting problems/solutions and write/tape record a script to go with it. Plan to present creations at session 26 or some other specified time.

E. Listening. Listen to tapes illustrating communication problems in classes, age level meetings, retreats, or leadership training event. Tape record your group's discussion about the communication problems pointed out in listening to the tapes and record on newsprint or the blackboard a few words to identify each problem. Listen to the tape of your group discussion and list communication problems that you find in it.

F. Seeing. View films which might give you insights into possible communication gaps which may occur in your educational program. Observe some teaching learning groups between this session and the next. Create an observation sheet to use answering the question, What shall I look for? You may choose to divide and become observers of learning groups A through E. Decide on the nature of your report to the whole group at session 26.

"I Am the Way"

Our teaching should *reveal the kingdom* of God, interpreting the gospel for our world; however, *extending the kingdom* depends most vitally on the contacts that we have with non-Christians. Extending the kingdom of God really depends upon how we communicate our understanding of his kingdom in our living.

Each of us needs to reexamine the way God, in Jesus, communicated love to the world and then to evaluate how we are fulfilling his commission. Are we depending upon materials and philosophies? Are we depending upon institutions and laws? Are we extending the kingdom of Love through interpersonal relationships? Can we forego judging, which builds barriers, and allow forgiving to be our natural, normal expression of love? Can we keep the lines of communication open?

Are all of your communication lines open?

ENGAGEMENTS IN COMMUNICATING THE CHRISTIAN FAITH

Communication means life; lack of communication means death. In a time characterized by a revolution in mass media and communication, and the extreme acceleration of change, our churches are finding it increasingly difficult to adapt and to renew themselves—to keep in touch with each other and with God. Educators in the church are in the envious position of influencing persons to examine life's issues, as they are facing them, and to bring into a single focus the personal and social relevance of the gospel.

DIALOGUE

Meeting one's self and another in the mutual give-and-take of dialogue is a source of basic meanings; it stimulates the search for truth; it heals alienation, insecurity, and ill feeling toward one's self and toward another; and it brings into being the relationship of love. In order to love a person in another part of the world, it is necessary to experience loving and being loved by someone near. Love, communicated nonverbally and verbally, is a greater teacher of faith than all of the stockpiles of words, phrases, sentences, and books *about* love—although words describing love's qualities may motivate us to risk dialogical love.

Dialogue differs from discussion or simple conversation in its depth of relationships.

Barriers to communication may arise from such things as language, culture, emotions, misunderstandings, lack of experience. A barrier may also be erected by two or more persons holding contrary purposes. Through dialogue, these barriers can be overcome, because all of them are rooted in our deepest (though perhaps unconscious) concern—our concern for our being. Dialogue is encounter (communication) between persons aimed at producing understanding, friendship, trust, challenge, and action. Dialogue implies that two persons or a group of persons are both speaking and listening (though not, for best results, simultaneously). Dialogue is address and response. It is that interaction between persons in which they give to each other that which they truly are.

Dialogue is not a method, but a relationship.

The engagement of dialogue implies empathy, through which we know another and we are known by another person. Any method of communication can be the midwife of dialogue, and educators in the church would be greatly assisted in their tasks if they would carefully study the feedback they get from every method to see if dialogical communication has taken place.

Through the church, a person may become aware of his place in the family of God. Dr. Reuel Howe writes, "We are born into our own families that in many ways are competent to take care of us, but we are also born into God's family who watches over our human family, saves us from the sins and failures of our human parents, and completes the love that we have from them."[1]

Dr. Howe further states that the purposes of dialogue are (a) to communicate information and meaning between individuals and groups, (b) to help persons make a responsible decision in relation to the truth that is being presented, (c) to restore the vitality of relationships which have diminished, and (d) to bring persons into being. Man cannot really know himself except in relationship, which is dialogue (address and response between person and person). Dr. Howe warns that dialogue is not for the purpose of one person giving his answers to another person's questions nor is it to secure a consensus with the point of view of the communicator.

Dialogue does not manipulate.

Dialogue serves us when we wish to concentrate on the unknown and speculative, using the known and established as a basis for our educated guesses. When we concentrate on the unknown in dialogue everyone is equal in the quest for truth; there is no one "who knows" and others "who do not know." "Seekers" will have difficulty in coming into dialogue with "knowers," for the seekers will hit head on with the authority of the knowers. Knowers are not learners, except as they blindly accept the authority of a respected other. A person desiring to learn is one who has become unsatisfied with what he knows and is committed to knowing something more or different.

To learn one must be dissatisfied with not knowing.

The existence of man on earth is becoming more and more dependent upon his ability to keep in communication. Dialogue will become perfected as an instrument of civilization whenever man and his societies adopt the primary requirement for civilization: nonviolence. Nonviolence means more than not killing; it means respect, even reverence. It means caring enough about each person in every society to renounce any action that will violate him in any way—physically, psychologically, or spiritually. A civil society is one that believes that dialogue is the effective way of achieving good and relies on it. A civil society will be ruled by dialogical love, and it shall know The Way which Jesus pointed to and was. Dialogue is one of our engagements in communicating the faith.

*Do you think every teacher **should** communicate in depth?*

What methods will help one to communicate deeply felt experience so that he will be open to the reality of living with other men in the world and be perfected unto God?

---

[1] Reuel L. Howe, *The Miracle of Dialogue* (Greenwich, Connecticut: The Seabury Press, 1963), p. 44.

PROBLEM-SOLVING

Many times we can merit by letting our imaginations run wild; from this will come new discoveries if we are motivated to find them there. If all knowledge could be written in books and placed in a library, perhaps nothing would come of it. But, if it were placed in the minds of persons who would use it imaginatively, it would bring new understanding and new discoveries for the progress of the human race. A complete new thought must come from an individual. It may be added to by a second person, but one cannot have half an idea; although it seems at times we have a fleeting glimpse of an idea that we can't quite get hold of.

Problem-solving can be a meaningful engagement in communicating the faith. Christianity is active; it is neither static nor passive. When a learner is placed in a situation that requires him to make decisions, he must depend on his ability to organize meaning out of raw experience and react to his present situation. Students will improve their abilities to think, to relate, and to observe only if they are given time to practice thinking, relating, and observing.

Do you feel at home with this conclusion or would you wish to dispute it? Why?

To gain practice in decision-making, groups of learners can face dilemmas as they are presented in unfinished stories found in films, newspaper clippings, case studies, novels, biographies, or plays. Through the presentation of an unfinished story, students may learn the details of that problem situation and something about the persons involved in them. Then the learners are presented with questions such as, How will Kathy vote? Will Ted tell the truth or continue to bluff his way through? Will Christy cover her brother's guilt or will she tattle on him? What will Pete do with the rumor he has started? Will Ramona own up to her liability? How can Kevin allow Leo to save face and remove the imminent danger he is in because Kevin called his bluff? Will Carlo inform the authorities and endanger his acceptance by the gang?

The dilemmas faced in these situations can be resolved by the group through role play, through writing an agree-disagree sheet and working through reformulations of it, through buzz groups, or through brainstorming. After using any one or more of these methods, the group would benefit by engaging in dialogue.

The skills of communicating through problem-solving need to be given a chance to develop on problems that have an inherent passion—whether racism, crime, injustice in law enforcement, pollution, war and aggression, abortion, women's rights, marriage, family, communism, nationalism, patriotism, or space programs. The Christian faith does not uphold a position of neutrality and objectivity. It demands conviction and commitment—engagement in communicating the faith.

Is our Christian teaching relevant to the personal faith of our students? Does it communicate?

VALUING

Students, as well as teachers, should know that the kind of living and thinking they are doing, if carefully done, is just as good as that of persons who are designated as specialists. Christianity is carried forward by those persons who are committed to Christ, regardless of how intelligent or clever they are.

A person who knows the richness of an integrated life is one who relates to the world in the fullest dimensions. Teachers may need to live more intensely, otherwise they may be serving as channels for someone else's experience (such as an author) either wittingly or unwittingly. If a teacher allows himself to be a channel for the experience of others, rather than experiencing life for himself and interpreting it in light of the gospel, he will probably be inconsistent (representing many persons and authors, even those at variance with each other), inauthentic, unrealistic, unconvincing, and probably uninteresting.

Perceiving value—valuing—at its best is actively seeking an unmoving standard, but never quite experiencing it. This is a vital process of establishing meaning in one's life. If communicating the faith is our intention and we are goal-directed in our learning, we will achieve skills and goals of personal significance. And, if enough of us can do this, perhaps we will assure a society in which personal significance can still be possible.

A good program of Christian teaching-learning will do more than acquaint students with facts and concepts (see chapter 17, "Levels of Teaching"). It should resist turning students into walking biblical encyclopedias or concordances of supposedly important religious information. Instead the greatest concern should be helping students to learn how to use the Bible and other Christian literature as tools for understanding. Learners should be freed to explore skills in investigative know-how and to apply their learnings in the laboratory of life—to create and relate. Any experience can be informed by Christianity, which means it can point to valuing the underlying unity of men in the world, under God.

BEAUTY SERVES THE COMMUNICATOR OF THE FAITH

When fine arts fulfills its function it is essentially religious and when it is used by Christians it communicates faith. Art provides insights; it informs man in the deepest, most powerful way of the human condition of estrangement and the possibility of reunification. Artists look at real conflicts and polarities in our culture and bring them together in a creative unity. The fine arts recognize the basic aspects of life—the interpenetrating systems of mutual support, mutual ratification, and mutual control.

Love is essentially a category of beauty. Our idea of beautiful and good shapes our idea of what is valuable, appreciated, and just. Love is nothing without the beauty of sensitivities and feelings. Sensitive love informs judicious love. We don't know what to distribute with justice unless we have something to hold as beautiful, good, and meaningful.

In the teaching-learning situation do we hold out for freedom in valuing? Do we sometimes communicate that we are God-appointed authorities sent to tell children, youth, and adults what they must believe under threat of being read out of the "Christian Club"? Explain.

Communication is as much involved with the factors of feelings and values as it is with facts and concepts. Through the awakening and growth of appreciation or meaning, a person decides what are generally worthwhile or specifically rewarding values.

SUMMARY

Every man is an artist called to shape the stuff of his daily life into something which communicates his own person and the One who called him into being.

Our engagements—
    in dialogue (address and response between persons)
    in problem-solving (conviction and commitment)
    in valuing (unity of expressive and rational powers)
communicate the Christian faith—
    God's redeeming love and
    man's response, restored in grace.

Corita Kent writes, "To create is to relate." Is art a form of communication? Is faith communicated through art? Would the meaning of the quotation be changed if it said, "To create is to communicate"?

CHAPTER 26

Bridges to Other Persons

In the past twenty years, what other cultural and social relationships have changed?

Exploring Communication in Accepting and Transforming Culture

Each person is in continual communication with whatever surrounds him. We are linked into the highly complex and intricate network of human interaction (communication). Consciousness presupposes communication. We send messages, receive messages, and constantly interpret the messages we send and receive within the framework of our own meanings. Even a person who chooses to drop out of society is discernible in his modes of reaction, which also communicate. We cannot be human alone.

Built into communication is miscommunication. Communication is still taking place, but the message perceived is not the message intended, and networks deteriorate due to blocked interaction. When communication is blocked interminably, we speak of gaps—generational, cultural, economical, racial, ideological, social.

Systems and techniques of communicating become outmoded and new systems are created. There is nothing unchangeable about cultural and social relationships; for instance, the way we were able to deal with children twenty years ago doesn't seem to work today.

CULTURE AND CHURCH IN COMMUNICATION

Throughout the history of the church there has been a tension between the claims of God on men and the claims of the culture. The followers of Christ have taken two basic positions in response to this tension—(1) Christ against culture; (2) Christ transforming culture.

In the past many communicators of the faith renounced the culture, and they and their followers formed communes in which members held all their resources in common and an individual's behavior was prescribed by the group. This option of resolving the tensions of political power, economic problems, and social morals is becoming more and more unachievable in our complex societies, though we see some movements back to this life-style.

In communicating the faith in the context of our present culture, we are challenged by

—contaminating and corrupting influences of a depersonalized and technical society
—the crass material values that sustain it
—the moral quandary that often results
—dislike of most workers for what they do
—frantic use of "leisure" time to seek relief from boredom and escape from effort
—an atmosphere of consistent and largely accepted conformity
—momentary diversions and the neglect of creative engagement

To meet these challenges—and many others—we bring our
—belief in the infinite potential of man
—trust in education for change

What would you add to these lists?

Guidance for Session 26
BRIDGES TO OTHER PERSONS

Aim for the Session
To maintain dialogical relationships as the group engages in problem-finding and problem-solving relating to communication gaps in the educational program of the church and to evaluate the learning experiences of Sessions 25 and 26.

Questions to Ponder
Are all national problems Christian problems as well as world problems? Can Christian leaders help an individual to discover and use his powers? What is to stop teachers from working out their own needs rather than those which students need help in working out? Should teachers who are trusted with important confidences have the legal privilege which a lawyer or minister has? What causes a person not to misinterpret our intent even when our language is clumsy? How can a teacher relieve the from-child-to-teacher communication pattern and allow children to freely discuss among themselves? How is intellectual development assisted by instruction? How can we find out more about the dynamics of our student's experiences? What are church school dropouts communicating to us? Do the "house churches" which are springing up in the United States communicate something about us? How is our culture shaping us? How can Christianity help to shape the culture? How much have I changed recently as a result of my learning from the group that I lead or teach?

A Study Plan
(Continued from session 25)

If your learning group is larger than twelve, divide into two groups to carry out the session plan.

I. Receive the work done by groups in session 25.

A. Listen to speakers giving reports of their learning from the activity of "Reading." Listeners should be prepared to summarize what the speaker said and respond to it. A First Responder will summarize the report, adjusting it until the speaker agrees that he was understood. Then, the First Responder may comment on the report. A Second Responder will summarize the First Responder's comment, changing it if necessary until the First Responder is satisfied that he was understood. Then, the Second Responder comments on the report. A Third Responder will follow through the same procedure of the First and Second Responder.

B. Listen to the research papers read by those who chose the learning activity, "Research," in session 25. Assign persons the task of listening in order to (1) ask questions for clarification, (2) disagree with content, (3) add to content, (4) give illustrations of the ideas, values, or skills presented in the research.

C. Participate in the learning activity to be directed by the group that chose "Discussion" in session 25.

D. Discuss the communication of the various creations made by persons who participated in "Creative Activities" during session 25.

E. Listen to the report of the group who chose the learning activity, "Listening," in session 25, and write on newsprint or chalkboard whatever you learned from this report.

—openness in interpersonal relationships
—search for beauty
—communion with God and man
—celebration of life

Through dialogical teaching we stimulate fresh thinking patterns, motivate for greater self-expression, and develop understandings to be communicated.

Any communication which intends to transform the culture and which is confined to the educational settings of the church and not heard by society at large is doomed to eventual triviality.

COMMUNICATIONS CONTROL

In the public sectors of communications, we are occasionally reminded of communications control and/or censorship. We have become increasingly aware of "managed news" and the difficulty, if not impossibility, of presenting an objective newscast. When we move into the area of church communications, we tend to neglect our critical faculties, perhaps because we think that somehow we have successfully separated church and state. An examination of the following chart of comparison will show how much the church is actually influenced by culture.

Do you feel at home with this conclusion or would you wish to dispute it? Why?

F. Receive the report of the group who worked with "Seeing" during session 25. Decide how this report can best be utilized by the church.

II. Evaluate the participation of groups during sessions 25 and 26, using the following Evaluation Sheet:

Evaluation Sheet
(Sessions 25 and 26)

1. The learning group I participated in was
   ___ A. Reading.
   ___ B. Research.
   ___ C. Discussing.
   ___ D. Creative Activity.
   ___ E. Listening.
   ___ E. Seeing.

2. Group members concentrated on the tasks
   ___ most of the time.
   ___ some of the time, but were distracted by other things.
   ___ very little, used time doing other things.

3. When the group was distracted, the cause was
   ___ arguing over irrelevant matters.
   ___ being sociable, joking, etc.
   ___ one or more persons who blocked group work.
   ___ frustration with the task.

4. Talking was
   ___ shared by members of the group.
   ___ dominated by a few persons.
   ___ controlled by the leader.

5. Differing points of view were
   ___ acknowledged and considered objectively.
   ___ acknowledged, but not dealt with.
   ___ ignored.

6. Members engaged in the following group rules which aided the communication
   ___ initiated activity.
   ___ contributed information or skill.
   ___ looked up some information.
   ___ elaborated on an idea.
   ___ clarified a statement.
   ___ coordinated the activity.
   ___ took consensus of group's opinions.
   ___ evaluated what we were doing.
   ___ provided enthusiasm for the task.
   ___ tested our outcomes.
   ___ recorded our work.
   ___ encouraged us.
   ___ helped the group to be harmonious.
   ___ served as observer.
   ___ worked to follow through on plans.

7. Members listened to each other
   ___ all of the time
   ___ most of the time
   ___ occasionally
   ___ never

8. Members understood each other
   ___ very well
   ___ fairly well
   ___ very little
   ___ not at all

9. Attempts were made to uncover assumptions made by members
   ___ always
   ___ frequently
   ___ sometimes
   ___ rarely
   ___ never
   ___ by members
   ___ by leader

10. Aim was achieved by
    ___ everyone
    ___ most persons
    ___ a few persons
    ___ none

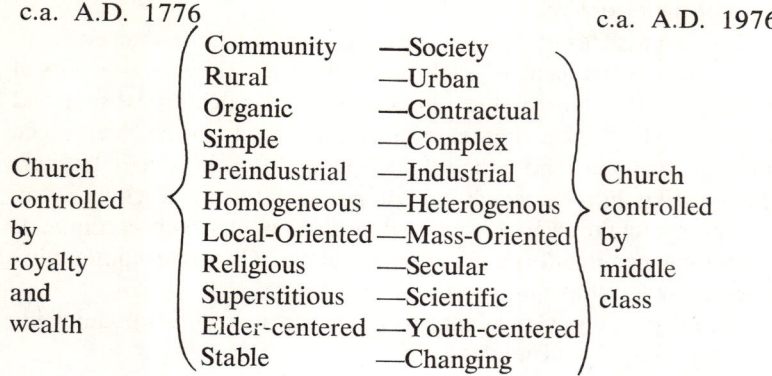

Cultural Contrasts

A mass culture usually caters to the lowest common denominators of taste and commercial interests. Communication becomes standard and stultified, while communion is almost completely neglected. Are we trapped within a set of inventions we call, "civilization," that is now so well supported by technology and population explosion that we must follow what seems to be an inevitable path to destruction? Each of us communicators—students, teachers, leaders—will participate in the answer to that question. It will be determined by the kind of group and social roles we choose, by the values we pick, by the goals we set, by the planning we authorize, by the curriculum resources we select, by the learning habits we form, by the thinking skills we master, by the media we use, by the feelings we express, by the responsibility we assume, by the commission we accept, by the dialogue we enter, by the problem-solving we do, and by the faith we communicate.

In the final anlaysis, communications control resides in the selectivity of the receiver-learner. The learner, as well as the teacher, is greatly influenced by culture, and he may influence culture to some degree in his lifetime. What the learner hears, he selects from what is presented. It is at the point of determining, to some degree, what is presented to the learner that the teacher controls communication. Bayard Hooper said in *Life:* "To be relevant demands trust; to be trusted demands openness; to be open demands a sense of security and self-esteem on the part of the teacher. To be any of these things demands skill, and beyond that the support and confidence of the community. . . ."¹

SIGNIFICANCE OF CHRISTIAN COMMUNICATION

The end result of a system of communication in faith and action is a Christian life-style. In a meaningful teaching-learning experience, the specific needs of individuals and the affirmations of the Christian faith are interrelated. Teachers who engage themselves

---

¹Bayard Hooper, The task is to learn what learning is for," *Life,* Vol. 66, No. 19 (May 16, 1969), p. 39.

and their students in communicating the faith will be changed, and so will their students.

Every possible effort should be made to seek the interest, support, and involvement of each member of a family in educational settings of the church. Ideas, concepts, and values presented and discussed in a teaching-learning group need to be reenforced through dialogue and practice at home. If teachers and learners fully engage in roles which aid communication in a teaching-learning group, children and youth, as well as adults, will continue to communicate in informal gatherings of the Christian community, such as fellowship dinners and coffee hours.

Those persons who advance on the journey of communicating and learning should move:

> Rate a teaching-learning situation of which you are a part, using a scale of 0 to 10. Score "from this" as 0 and "to this" as 10.

from this	to this
Assume that a student acquires (accepts) knowledge, which has existed for a long time and is handed down on authority.	Assume that learning is rearranging messages, both their form and content, and transforming them in such a way that a person can go on to new insights.
Assume that subject matter taken on authority and acquired by a student automatically educates him.	Assume that in learning a person continuously examines life's issues, as he faces them, and brings to them a single focus of the gospel's personal and social relevance.
Assume that subject matter (content) can best be learned apart from complex forms—separate each concept and teach it by itself.	Assume that the content of Christ's message deals more with attitudes, values, life-styles, and human relationships than dogmas, definitions, or formulas.
Assume that a student sees the same significance in facts as teachers do.	Assume individual differences in students; help each student according to his needs, interests, capabilities, and motivations; the aim of leadership is not carbon copies.
Assume that education is supplementary to and preparatory to life, not life itself.	Assume that students are learning skills for analyzing their habitual forms of dealing with life and for developing new responses.
Assume that when a student is acquiring abstractions, he ignores all social aspects of the situation.	Assume teaching-learning setting is packed with human relations needs which have to be met before persons can master a subject.

Assume teacher can and should furnish purposes needed for acquiring knowledge and shall decide what is taught.	Assume that students sharing their knowledge, understandings, and insights help each other in setting realistic group goals.
Assume that working on tasks devoid of purpose or interest is good discipline.	Assume a student who is excited about increasing his skill in achieving goals of personal significance will be involved in purposeful listening.
Assume that the answer to a problem(s) is more important than the process.	Assume that greater importance is attached to methods of acquiring and utilizing content than upon learning the content. If we stress content learning, we must prepare our students for unlearning.
Assume that it is more important to measure what has been learned than it is to learn.	Assume that the more open a group is — knowing, trusting, and feeling for each other, the more each student will be motivated to work up to his individual level of competence.

Communicating may stimulate fresh thinking patterns, motivate greater self-expression, and develop understanding and acceptance of persons which ultimately contributes to the fullest development of a human being. We know that a person's feelings are a crucial determinant of his public behavior and private well-being, but educational settings that explicitly educate both the feelings and the intellect are not only significant but novel. Does a society expect that through communication in the educational settings of the church students will change in any fundamental way? Have we, as learners, made any significant adjustments in our thinking and behavior as a result of communicating with other persons in the church? Teaching-learning situations that educate both feelings and intellect raise questions about purpose and meaning—tough questions which are not easy to answer. But, they offer a possibility for building a saner world—a world where people are more open about their feelings, careful in their thinking, and responsible in their actions.

> Lives of great men all remind us,
> We can make our lives sublime,
> And, departing, leave behind us
> Footprints on the sands of time.
> —Henry Wadsworth Longfellow

What might some of these questions be?

SUMMARY

I.	II.	III.
Chapter Titles	Chapter Subtitles	Communication Model
		Relationship to Model
A Starting Place for the Journey	Exploring Communication —in Teaching-Learning	
Reach Out for Someone	—in group development	Someone
New World, New Wineskins	—in new situations	in a situation
A Vision of Tomorrow	—in setting goals	perceives an event
Bridges to Tomorrow	—in planning	and reacts
Inner Resources for the Journey	—in individual study	to make
Media Resources for the Journey	—in using media	available
Awareness of Fellow Travelers	—through sensitivity to self and others	materials
Interaction with Fellow Travelers	—through interaction	in some
Gifts Along the Way	—in enabling learners	form
"I Am the Way"	—in relating the gospel to day-to-day-concerns	conveying content
Bridges to Other Persons	—in accepting and transforming culture	of some significance